OXFORD MONOGRAPHS IN INTERNATIONAL LAW

GENERAL EDITOR: PROFESSOR IAN BROWNLIE CBE, QC, FBA
Chichele Professor of Public International Law in the University of
Oxford and Fellow of All Souls College, Oxford.

THE TERMINATION AND REVISION OF
TREATIES IN THE LIGHT OF NEW
CUSTOMARY INTERNATIONAL LAW

OXFORD MONOGRAPHS IN
INTERNATIONAL LAW

The aim of this series of monographs is to publish important
and original pieces of research on all aspects of public international law. Topics which are given particular prominence are
those which, while of interest to the academic lawyer, also have
important bearing on issues which touch the actual conduct of
international relations. None the less the series is wide in scope
and includes monographs on the history and philosophical
foundations of international law.

RECENT TITLES IN THIS SERIES

Land-Locked and Geographically Disadvantaged
States in the International Law of the Sea

S. C. VASCIANNIE

Surrender, Occupation, and Private
Property in International Law

NISUKE ANDO

The Human Rights Committee: Its Role in
the Development of the International Covenant
on Civil and Political Rights

DOMINIC McGOLDRICK

Human Rights in States of Emergency
in International Law

JAIME ORAÁ

China's Practice in the Law
of the Sea

JEANETTE GREENFIELD

The International Law of
Maritime Boundaries and the
Practice of States in the
Mediterranean Sea

FARAJ ABDULLAH AHNISH

Human Rights in the Private Sphere

ANDREW CLAPHAM

The Termination and Revision of Treaties in the Light of New Customary International Law

NANCY KONTOU

CLARENDON PRESS · OXFORD
1994

Oxford University Press, Walton Street, Oxford OX2 6DP
Oxford New York
Athens Auckland Bangkok Bombay
Calcutta Cape Town Dar es Salaam Delhi
Florence Hong Kong Istanbul Karachi
Kuala Lumpur Madras Madrid Melbourne
Mexico City Nairobi Paris Singapore
Taipei Tokyo Toronto
and associated companies in
Berlin Ibadan

Oxford is a trade mark of Oxford University Press

Published in the United States
by Oxford University Press Inc., New York

British Library Cataloguing in Publication Data
Data available

Library of Congress Cataloging in Publication Data
Data available

ISBN 0–19–825842–9

1 3 5 7 9 10 8 6 4 2

Typeset by Graphicraft Typesetters Ltd., Hong Kong
Printed in Great Britain
on acid-free paper by
Bookcraft Ltd., Midsomer Norton, Avon

Editor's Preface

THE work of Dr. Kontou originated as a doctoral thesis prepared at Cambridge under the supervision of Professor D.W. Bowett, C.B.E., Q.C., then the Whewell Professor of International Law. The result is a lucid account of certain classical problems which are of considerable practical significance.

The essential question addressed is in what conditions supervening custom can terminate or modify prior incompatible treaties as a result of the exercise by one party of a right to that effect. This issue was left aside in the final text of the Vienna Convention on the Law of Treaties, and has been neglected by writers. The study necessarily involves the exploration of a family of interrelated issues involving the relations of treaties and custom, and the relevance of fundamental circumstances and desuetude.

The study invokes a substantial amount of State practice and the relevant jurisprudence, which is considerable. The examination of State practice includes a substantial exploration of the impact of developments in the law of the sea upon prior fisheries agreements, which provides an added attraction to a most helpful work.

All Souls College,   IAN BROWNLIE
OXFORD.

14th September 1994

Preface

THIS book is an amended version of a doctoral thesis submitted at the University of Cambridge, England, in 1990.

This work is aimed at readers interested in fundamental questions concerning the sources of international law. It examines in particular the effect of new customary law on prior incompatible treaties, a topic that is not satisfactorily covered in the literature. State practice in the law of the sea and other areas of international law contains a number of examples of treaties that have been terminated or revised on account of the emergence of subsequent conflicting custom. Decisions of international tribunals have also dealt with this issue. This book attempts to develop a theory that adequately explains the state of international law on the matter.

I would like to thank the members of the Law Faculty of the University of Cambridge as well as my fellow Ph.D. students and other researchers in Cambridge from whose comments and discussion I benefited greatly. I am also grateful to the staff of the Squire Law Library for their assistance. Above all I would like to thank my supervisor, D. W. Bowett, Member of the International Law Commission and former Professor of International Law at the University of Cambridge, for his guidance and encouragement. A special mention should be made of the 'Onassis Foundation', Athens, Greece, for its financial support, without which this work could not have been completed. Finally, I am grateful to my family and friends for their support during the period of my research.

Brussels   NANCY KONTOU
August 1993

Contents

Abbreviations

AIDI	*Annuaire de l'Institut de droit international*
AFDI	*Annuaire français de droit international*
AJIL	*American Journal of International Law*
Br. & For. State Papers	*British and Foreign State Papers*
BYIL	*British Yearbook of International Law*
CYIL	*Canadian Yearbook of International Law*
EC	European Community
ECHR	European Court of Human Rights
ECOSOC	UN Economic and Social Council
EEC	European Economic Community
FAO	Food and Agriculture Organization
GAOR	General Assembly of the United Nations, Official Records
GYIL	*German Yearbook of International Law*
HC Deb.	*Hansard, House of Commons Debates*
HL Deb.	*Hansard, House of Lords Debates*
IATTC	Inter-American Tropical Tuna Commission
ICCAT	International Commission for the Conservation of Atlantic Tuna; International Convention on the Conservation of Atlantic Tunas
ICJ	International Court of Justice
ICJ Reports	Reports of Judgments, Advisory Opinions and Orders of the International Court of Justice
ICLQ	*International and Comparative Law Quarterly*
ICNAF	International Commission for the North-West Atlantic Fisheries; International Convention for North-West Atlantic Fisheries
ILC	International Law Commission
ILM	*International Legal Materials*
ILR	International Law Reports
INPFC	International North Pacific Fisheries Commission
Iran–US CTR	Iran–US Claims Tribunal Reports
Keesing's	*Keesing's Contemporary Archives* (continued as *Keesing's Record of World Events*)
LNTS	*League of Nations Treaty Series*
NAFO	North-West Atlantic Fisheries Organization

NILR	*Netherlands International Law Review*
NIOC	National Iranian Oil Company
ODILJ	*Ocean Development International Law Journal*
OJ	*Official Journal of the European Communities*
ÖZöR	*Österreichische Zeitung für öffentliches Recht*
PCIJ	*Publications of the Permanent Court of International Justice*
PRC	People's Republic of China
PYIL	*Polish Yearbook of International Law*
RC	*Recueil des cours de l'Académie de droit international*
RGDIP	*Revue générale de droit international public*
UKTS	*United Kingdom Treaty Series*
UN	United Nations
UNCLOS	United Nations Conference on the Law of the Sea
UNTS	*United Nations Treaty Series*
YBWA	*Yearbook of World Affairs*
YILC	*Yearbook of the International Law Commission*
ZaöRV	*Zeitschrift für ausländisches öffentliches Recht und Völkerrecht*

Table of Cases

Table of Treaties

1

Introduction

Treaties and Customary Law

The consent of States to be legally bound internationally may be expressed in different forms. States may create legal rights and obligations *inter se* by concluding a treaty, or their consistent practice in a certain area may be the basis for the creation of customary law, if it is also accompanied by an *opinio juris*.

Treaties are concluded in the context of general international law in force at the time of the parties' agreement. They can repeat the general norm, refine and complete it, or apply special rules in the relations between the contracting parties.

A treaty codifying State practice in a certain area repeats the general customary norm in the interest of clarity, legal certainty, and ease of proof. A treaty can refine or complete a general principle by specifying the details of its application. Consider, for instance, the Capitulatory treaties based on the general principle of the personality of laws providing that the laws of the home State applied to merchants wherever in the world they may be. The treaties implemented this principle by creating the institution of consuls who were empowered to apply to foreign residents the laws of their country of origin.

A treaty may apply special rules in the relations between the parties in derogation from ordinary customary law. If, for instance, under general customary law coastal States have sovereign rights over fisheries adjacent to their coasts, a treaty may give third States access to these resources, from which they would otherwise be excluded. Or, if States are free under general customary law to decide whether or not to extradite each other's nationals, a treaty may impose on them the duty to do so.

Conflict of a Treaty with Supervening Custom

Customary law may continue to evolve outside the treaty leading to the establishment of new rules conflicting with the treaty text. In cases where supervening custom is incompatible with a prior treaty, the attitude of the contracting parties may vary. The parties may decide to continue applying the treaty rule in their *inter se* relations as an exception from the general norm. Or the treaty may be revised or even terminated in the light of the new custom.

There are different ways in which supervening custom may bring the treaty to an end or cause its revision. All contracting parties may decide to terminate or revise the treaty by express or implied agreement (*des-uetude*) in order to take account of the new general rules. Or one of the contracting parties may claim that the treaty should be revised or terminated on account of supervening custom. In this case it is important to specify in what circumstances a party has the right to do so and what legal means can be used, if necessary, to enforce this claim against the will of the other parties.

The Vienna Convention on the Law of the Treaties provides that new custom is a ground of treaty termination if it has the character of the *jus cogens*. This book examines whether and under what conditions the emergence of new custom other than *jus cogens* may also be a ground of termination or revision of prior incompatible treaties. By way of introduction, the remainder of this chapter defines certain basic concepts relating to this issue—that is, the notions of customary law and treaty termination or revision—and explains its importance.

As a starting-point for the examination of the effect of supervening custom on prior treaties, Chapter 2 offers a brief overview of the relevant literature. We shall see that the analysis of the literature reveals general agreement on the principle of treaty termination on account of supervening custom, but divergence as to the details of its operation.

The following chapters (Chapters 3 and 4) review a number of incidents from the law of the sea and other fields of international law where treaties became incompatible with supervening customary law. In our view, the manner in which they were resolved supports the proposition that one party has the right to call for the termination or revision of a treaty on account of the development of new custom. Chapter 5 examines a number of judgments of international tribunals dealing with the effect of supervening custom on prior incompatible treaties.

In Chapter 6 we anticipate and answer some objections to the notion of supervening custom as a ground of termination or revision of prior incompatible treaties. The final chapter draws on State practice and international case law to argue that supervening custom may, under certain conditions, be a ground of termination or revision of prior incompatible treaties in the sense that it gives one party the right to call for the necessary adjustments to be made to the treaty relationship.

1.2. DEFINITIONS

1.2.1. Customary Law

Customary law is unwritten international law based on a general and consistent practice of States accepted by them as legally binding. Customary law is based on the consent of States in general, but not necessarily of each and every State. Unlike treaties, customary law is the product of general consensus and not of the meeting of wills of individual States.[1]

Customary law has general application, because it binds all States with the exception of persistent objectors. General customary law admits derogations in the form of special customary rules that bind only a limited number of States. When special customary rules are formed, they apply to the relations of the groups of States bound by them *inter se*. The relations between the members of the different groups, as well as the relations between each of them and the rest of the international community, are governed by general customary law. In this sense it can be said that general customary law provides the unitary element of the component parts of the international legal system, and forms the legal background against which special customary rules are created and treaties are concluded.

(a) The Formation of Customary Law

Article 38, para. *c*, of the ICJ Statute provides that 'the Court whose function is to decide in accordance with international law such disputes as are submitted to it shall apply . . . international custom as evidence of a general practice accepted as law'. According to this Article, which is generally considered to be a more-or-less authoritative statement of the law,[2] there are two requirements for the formation of custom, State practice and *opinio juris*.

State practice

It is generally agreed that state practice establishes customary law only if it is general and consistent.

State practice is general if it is extensive and representative and includes the practice of States whose interests are specially affected.[3] State practice need not be universal; a few dissenters cannot prevent the creation of

---

[1] See e.g. H. Lauterpacht, *International Law: Collected Papers*, ed. E. Lauterpacht, i (Cambridge, 1970), at 66; J. L. Brierly, *The Law of Nations*, ed. H. Waldock (6th edn., Oxford, 1963), at 61; R. Y. Jennings, 'General Course on Principles of International Law', 121 *RC* (1967-II), 323, at 335–6; E. Jiménez de Aréchaga, 'General Course in Public International Law', 159 *RC* (1978-I), 1, at 28–9; M. R. Villiger, *Customary International Law and Treaties* (Dordrecht, 1985), at 27. Cf. A. A. D'Amato, 'The Authoritativeness of Custom in International Law', *Rivista di diritto internazionale* (1970), at 491; A. V. Lowe, 'Do General Rules of International Law Exist?', 9/3 *Review of International Studies* (1983), at 207. For a voluntarist perception of customary law, see e.g. G. I. Tunkin, 'Co-existence and International Law', 95 *RC* (1958-III), 1, at 13–14; *Theory of International Law* (London, 1974), at 118 *et seq*.

[2] See e.g. the latest Restatement of the Law of the Foreign Relations of the United States (1986), §102 (2): 'Customary international law results from a general and consistent practice of States followed by them from a sense of legal obligation.'

[3] See *North Sea Continental Shelf Cases*, ICJ Reports (1969), at 43; Villiger, *Customary International Law*, at 14–15; M. Akehurst, 'Custom as a Source of International Law', 47 *BYIL* (1974–5), 1, at 16, 23.

customary law.[4] Failure to protest to an emerging practice in circumstances where a reaction would be expected contributes to the formation of new custom.[5]

Since general customary rules are the product of general consensus and not of the will of every single State, once they are formed, they are binding *erga omnes*.[6] It is, however, generally accepted that a State may opt out of an *evolving* rule of general customary law by expressing its opposition to it in a timely and consistent manner (persistent objector).[7]

State practice is consistent if the various manifestations of a State's conduct support one and the same rule. While few uncertainties and con- tradictions may not prevent the transformation of a certain practice into a rule of law,[8] discontinuity[9] or substantial inconsistencies undermine the establishment of custom.[10]

Although time may be necessary for a practice to gain general accept- ance and for any inconsistencies to sort themselves out, it is generally accepted that 'the passage of only a short period of time is not necessarily, or of itself, a bar to the formation of a new rule of customary international law'.[11] On the other hand, opinions differ as to whether repetition of a certain practice is required for the formation of customary law.[12] In our view, it is conceivable that a single act involving a large number of States and revealing a clear *opinio juris* may at least constitute prima-facie evidence of customary law.[13]

According to the prevailing view in the literature, statements or non- physical acts in general are included in the definition of State practice, at

---

[4] Judge Tanaka in *South West Africa Cases* (Second Phase), ICJ Reports (1966), at 291.

[5] See *Anglo-Norwegian Fisheries Case*, ICJ Reports (1951), at 138; *Right of Passage Case*, ICJ Reports (1960), at 40; M. Sørensen, 'Principes de droit international public', 101 *RC* (1960-III), 1, at 41; Tunkin, *Theory of International Law*, at 129; Villiger, *Customary Inter- national Law*, at 18–20; M. Virally, 'The Sources of International Law', in Sørensen (ed.), *Manual of Public International Law* (London, 1968), 116, at 130–1; H. Waldock, 'General Course on Public International Law', 106 *RC* (1962-II), 1, at 50–1.

[6] *North Sea Continental Shelf Cases*, at 38.

[7] See *Anglo-Norwegian Fisheries Case*, ICJ Reports (1951), at 131; Akehurst, 'Custom', at 23 *et seq.*; I. Brownlie, *Principles of Public International Law* (4th edn., Oxford, 1990), at 10; Villiger, *Customary International Law* at 15 *et seq. Contra* A. A. D'Amato, *The Concept of Custom in International Law* (Ithaca, NY, 1971), at 261; J. I. Charney, 'The Persistent Ob- jector Rule and the Development of Customary International Law', 56 *BYIL* (1985), at 1; T. L. Stein, 'The Approach of the Different Drummer: The Principle of the Persistent Objector in International Law', 26 *Harvard Journal of International Law* (1985), 457, at 459 *et seq.*

[8] See *North Sea Continental Shelf Cases*, at 43; *Anglo-Norwegian Fisheries Case*, at 137–8.

[9] See Virally, 'Sources', at 132; hesitantly, Tunkin, 'Co-existence', at 10–11; Akehurst, 'Custom', at 20–1.   [10] *Asylum Case*, ICJ Reports (1950), at 276.

[11] *North Sea Continental Shelf Cases*, at 43; *Fisheries Jurisdiction Case (UK–Iceland)*, ICJ Reports (1974), at 23; R. R. Baxter, 'Treaties and Custom', 129 *RC* (1970-I), 25, at 67; Akehurst, 'Custom', at 15–16; G. I. Tunkin, 'Remarks on the Juridical Nature of Customary Norms of International Law', 49 *Californian Law Review* (1961), 419, at 420; Villiger, 'Sources', at 24–5.

[12] Akehurst, 'Custom', at 12 *et seq*. See also D'Amato, *The Concept of Custom*, at 91–8.

[13] See Akehurst, 'Custom', at 14; Tunkin, 'Remarks', at 419.

least as evidence of a presumptive nature.[14] If there are, however, discrepancies between what States say and what they actually do,[15] State practice is not consistent enough to support the establishment of custom.

Opinio juris

State practice establishes custom only if it is accompanied by an *opinio juris*: 'not only must the acts concerned amount to a settled practice, but they must also be such, or be carried out in such a way, as to be evidence of a belief that this practice is rendered obligatory by the existence of a rule of law requiring it . . . The States concerned must therefore feel that they are conforming to what amounts to a legal obligation. The frequency, or even the habitual character of the acts is not in itself enough.'[16] *Opinio juris* allows us to distinguish between conduct with legal implications and acts motivated by considerations of morality or courtesy that are not intended to be legally binding.

Explicit evidence of a sense of legal obligation, such as official statements, is not necessary. *Opinio juris* may be inferred from the circumstances surrounding particular acts or omissions.[17] In any event, what is required is *opinio juris communis*. The *opinio juris* of one State only is not sufficient, but other States must also follow the rule or fail to protest in the belief that their conduct is legally obligatory.

(b) Special Customary Law

We have so far discussed customary law of general application—that is, rules binding *erga omnes* with the exception of persistent objectors. However, customary rules may also be special if they bind only a limited number of States.[18]

Special customary rules may be created in the first stages of the development of new general custom, or if State practice supporting the new rule

---

[14] See e.g. Akehurst, 'Custom', at 1 *et seq.*; Villiger, 'Sources', at 6 *et seq.*; US Restatement (1986), §102, comment (*b*), reporter's note no. 2; *US Nationals in Morocco Case* (diplomatic correspondence), ICJ Reports (1952), 200; Anglo-Norwegian *Fisheries Case* (national laws), at 131; *Asylum Case* (official views as to diplomatic asylum), at 277; *YILC* (1950-II), at 370–1; Brownlie, *Principles*, at 5. *Contra*, dissenting opinion of Judge Read in the *Anglo-Norwegian Fisheries Case*, at 191; A. A. D'Amato, *The Concept of Custom in International Law* (Ithaca, NY, 1971), at 88. Hesitantly, H. W. A. Thirlway, *International Customary Law and Codification* (Leiden, 1972), at 58.

[15] In this sense Judge Read, *Anglo-Norwegian Fisheries Case*, 191.

[16] ICJ Reports (1969), at 44; *Lotus Case* (1927), *PCIJ* Ser. A, No. 10, at 28; Judge Hudson, *YILC* (1950-II), at 26.   [17] US Restatement (1986), §102; comment (*c*).

[18] See Akehurst, 'Custom', at 28; D'Amato, 'The Concept of Special Custom', at 211; J. G. Cohen, 'La Coutume locale', 7 *AFDI* (1961), at 119; G. Fitzmaurice, 'The Law and Procedure of the International Court of Justice, 1951–1954: General Principles and Sources of Law', 30 *BYIL* (1953), 1, at 68; P. Guggenheim, 'Locales Gewohnheitsrecht', 11 *ÖZöR* (1961), at 327; I. C. MacGibbon, 'Customary International Law and Acquiescence', 33 *BYIL* (1957), at 115; Thirlway, *International Customary Law*, at 135.

is not extensive enough. If the new rule eventually becomes general custom, the old rule may still apply as special custom *vis-à-vis* persistent objectors. Special customary rules may also be established with a view to creating an exception to the prevailing general rules because of special circumstances peculiar to certain States only.

In all cases, special customary law governs only the relations of the States bound by it *inter se*. By contrast, general customary law governs the relations between States bound by a special customary rule and States bound by the general rule, as well as the relations between States bound by different special customary rules.

Special customary rules can be regional or localized,[19] or they may bind as few as two States[20] with no other links between them 'apart from the fact that they follow a particular custom'.[21] The term special customary law is also used to describe special historic rights 'built up by a particular State or States, through a process of prescription' and 'acquired as against the world in general'.[22]

Special customary rules are by definition a derogation from existing general law. As a result, 'a party which relies on a custom *of this kind* must prove that this custom is established in such a manner that it has become binding on the other party'.[23] While general customary law requires proof only of general acceptance, a State relying on a special customary rule must therefore prove that the party against which the rule is invoked has expressly or implicitly consented to it or recognized it.[24]

(c) *Two Examples of State Practice Establishing Customary Law*

General Assembly Resolutions

In exercising its powers to make recommendations,[25] the General Assembly of the United Nations adopted resolutions laying down general and abstract rules of conduct for States.[26]

---

[19] *Asylum Case*, at 266.   [20] *Right of Passage Case*, at 39–40.

[21] Akehurst, 'Custom', at 31.

[22] Fitzmaurice, 'Law and Procedure', at 68–9; K. Wolfke, *Custom in Present International Law* (Wroktaw, 1964), at 90–1; MacGibbon, 'Customary International Law', at 122–3; the *Anglo-Norwegian Fisheries Case*, at 130.

[23] *Asylum Case*, at 276–8. See also *US Nationals in Morocco Case*, at 200.

[24] See Akehurst, 'Custom', at 29; D'Amato, 'The Concept of Special Custom', at 211; Jennings, 'General Course' at 336; Villiger, *Customary International Law*, at 33.

[25] See e.g. Articles 11 and 13 of the UN Charter.

[26] See e.g. Report of the Institute of International Law, 'Resolutions of the General Assembly of the United Nations', 61 *AIDI* (1985-I), at 29 *et seq.*; G. Aranzio-Ruiz, 'The Normative Role of the General Assembly and the Declaration of Principles of Friendly Relations', 137 *RC* (1972-III), at 419; J. Castañeda, *Legal Effects of United Nations Resolutions* (New York, 1969); B. Cheng, 'United Nations Resolutions on Outer Space: Instant International Customary Law?', in Cheng (ed.), *International Law: Teaching and Practice* (London, 1982), at 237; R. A. Falk, 'On the Quasi-Legislative Competence of the General Assembly', 60 *AJIL* (1966), at 782; R. Higgins, *The Development of International Law through the Political Organs of the*

The term UN resolution or declaration covers a wide variety of instruments, whose legal effects may differ. Some resolutions may, for instance, purport to state the law, while others may intend to create new rules.[27] It is thus suggested that the value of resolutions as a source of customary law must be assessed in the light of the particular circumstances of each case, including the wording of the resolution, the conditions of its adoption, such as voting patterns and statements made by States with regard to its legal character, and its relationship to pre-existing law and/or subsequent State conduct in the same field: 'What is required is an examination of whether resolutions with similar content, repeated through time, voted by overwhelming majorities, giving rise to a general *opinio juris*, have created the norm in question.'[28] Consistency with subsequent State practice will also be required in order to establish that a rule generated by a resolution still remains in force.

Although opinions differ on the subject, it is generally accepted that law-declaring resolutions, if not a source of law, at least constitute prima facie evidence of existing customary law, while resolutions purporting to create new rules may provide the basis for the generation of customary law by initiating or influencing State practice leading to its formation.[29]

In the *Nicaragua Case* the Court examined the existence of an *opinio juris* with regard to the principles enunciated by a number of UN resolutions, such as the Resolution 2625 on the the Principles of Friendly Relations and Resolution 3314 on the Definition of Aggression. The Court took the view that 'the effect of consent to the text of such resolutions . . . may be understood as an acceptance of the validity of the rule or set of rules declared by the resolution by themselves'.[30] Having inferred the existence of a customary rule from the relevant UN resolutions, the Court examined

United Nations (Oxford, 1963); 'The Development of International Law by the Political Organs of the United Nations', *Proc. Am. Soc. Int. Law* (1965), at 116; 'The United Nations and Law-Making: The Political Organs', ibid. (1970), at 37; Jiménez de Aréchaga, 'General Course', at 30; D. H. N. Johnson, 'The Effect of Resolutions of the General Assembly of the United Nations', 32 *BYIL* (1955), at 97; B. Sloan, 'General Assembly Resolutions Revisited', *BYIL* (1987), at 39; O. Schachter, 'The Relation of Law, Politics and Action in the United Nations', 109 *RC* (1963-II), at 169; M. Virally, 'La Valeur juridique des recommendations des organisations internationales', 2 *AFDI* (1956), at 66; P. Weil, 'Towards Relative Normativity in International Law', 77 *AJIL* (1983), at 413.

[27] See e.g. Report of the Institute of International Law, 81 *AIDI* (1985-I), at 314–5.

[28] Higgins, 'The United Nations and Law-Making', at 43; see also Jiménez de Aréchaga, 'General Course', at 31; Report of the Institute of International Law, 61 *AIDI* (1985-I), at 315 *et seq.*; the *Texaco Case*, 53 *ILR* (1979), at 486 *et seq.*; C. Greenwood, 'State Contracts in International Law: The Libyan Oil Arbitrations', 53 *BYIL* (1982), 27, esp. at 55 *et seq.*

[29] Report of the Institute of International Law, 61 *AIDI* (1985-I), at 330; Weil, 'Towards Relative Normativity', at 16–17.

[30] ICJ Reports (1986), para. 188 at 99–100; see also paras. 193, 202; less emphatically, ibid., para. 191: 'the adoption by States of this text affords an *indication* of their *opinio juris* as to customary international law on the question' (emphasis added). For a presumption in favour of the existence of *opinio juris*, para. 203.

state practice in order to establish whether a modification of the rule had taken place.[31]

Treaties

The possibility of interaction between treaties and customary law is recognized by Article 38 of the Vienna Convention on the Law of Treaties providing that a rule set forth in a treaty can become binding upon a third State as a customary rule of international law, recognized as such. In the *Nicaragua Case* the International Court of Justice held that the incorporation of a rule in a treaty does not exclude its parallel existence and application *qua* customary law.[32]

It is thus generally accepted that treaties may be declaratory of customary law in force at the time of their conclusion.[33] Rules originating in treaties may pass 'into the general corpus of international law', and become 'accepted as such by the *opinio juris*, so as to have become binding even for countries which have never, and do not, become parties to the Convention'.[34]

In order to conclude that a treaty has since its adoption generated customary law, courts must be satisfied that 'there exists in customary international law an *opinio juris* as to the binding character' of the relevant treaty provisions.[35] In the *Continental Shelf (Libya* v. *Malta) Case* the Court thus stated that, although 'the 1982 Convention is of major importance, having been adopted by an overwhelming majority of states', it was its duty 'to consider in what degree any of its relevant provisions *are binding upon the parties as a rule of customary international law*'.[36]

1.2.2. Treaty Termination and Treaty Revision

Termination is the ending of a treaty and of the binding force of the rights and obligations it has created.[37] When a treaty is terminated the parties are

---

[31] Paras. 206 *et seq.* For criticisms of the judgment, see A. A. D'Amato, 'Trashing Customary International Law', 81 *AJIL* (1987), at 101; F. L. Morrison, 'Legal Issues in the Nicaragua Opinion', 81 *AJIL* (1987), at 160–2.   [32] Paras. 175, 177, *et seq.*

[33] See e.g. with regard to the Vienna Convention on the Law of Treaties, the *Fisheries Jurisdiction Case*, ICJ Reports (1973), at 18, Article 62 (fundamental change of circumstances)'; Namibia Advisory Opinion, ICJ Reports (1971), at 47, *Jurisdiction of the ICAO Council*, ICJ Reports (1972), at 67, Article 60 (treaty termination on account of material breach). See also *Nicaragua Case, ICJ Reports* (1986), para. 212 (principle of State sovereignty in Art. 2, para. 1, of the UN Charter).

[34] *North Sea Continental Shelf Cases*, para. 71. See also *Libya* v. *Malta (Continental Shelf) Case*, ICJ Reports (1985), at 29.

[35] The *Nicaragua Case*, para. 188; see also para. 185.

[36] ICJ Reports (1985), at 30 para. 27; the *North Sea Continental Shelf Cases*, para. 70; *US Nationals in Morocco Case*, at 200.

[37] See e.g. S. Bastid, *Les Traités dans la vie internationale* (Paris, 1985), at 169 *et seq.*; F. Capotorti, 'L'Extinction et la Suspension des traités', 134 *RC* (1971-III), 427, esp. at 464–5; R. K. Dixit, 'Amendment or Modification of Treaties', 10 *Indian JIL* (1970), at 37; T. O. Elias, *The Modern Law of Treaties* (Leiden, 1974), at 89–100.; A. D. McNair, *The Law of Treaties* (Oxford, 1961), at 534–5; M. Morelli, 52 *AIDI* (1967-I), at 290; W. Karl, *Vertrag und*

discharged from any obligation further to perform it; any right, obligation, or legal situation of the parties created through the execution of the treaty prior to its termination is not affected.[38] The concept of termination differs from that of invalidity, because an invalid treaty is considered never to have had any legal force.[39]

In the case of a multilateral treaty, the situation may arise where only one or some of the parties withdraw from it or denounce it, with the result that they are discharged from their treaty obligations in their *inter se* relations.[40] The treaty, however, continues to apply between them and the remaining parties as well as between the remaining parties *inter se*. The expression 'treaty termination' will be used in this book to cover also this type of situation.

The process of treaty termination is distinct from that of amendment, which entails the alteration of the provisions of a treaty that remains in force subject to whatever modifications are introduced into it, and continues to be the legal basis of the relations between the parties.

The terms 'revision'[41] and 'modification' are also used in State practice and writings to denote the alteration of the provisions of a treaty by agreement of the parties. The term 'revision' is sometimes used to describe in particular the review of the treaty as a whole, as opposed to the amendment of certain treaty provisions, and 'modification' sometimes denotes an agreement between some of the parties to a multilateral treaty that is intended to apply *inter se*, as opposed to a formal amendment intended to alter the treaty provisions with respect to all the parties.[42] However, these distinctions are not always made in writings or State practice.[43] Hereinafter the terms 'revision', 'amendment', or 'modification' will be used interchangeably in respect of bilateral and multilateral treaties to cover both the alteration of certain treaty provisions and the review of the treaty as a whole.

Legal Basis and Methods of Treaty Termination

A treaty can be terminated:

(i) on the basis of the consent of all parties, express or implied; or
(ii) on the basis of a rule of general international law.[44]

Spätere Praxis im Völkerrecht (Berlin, 1983), 2.1.3., at 11; C. Parry, 'The Law of Treaties', in M. Sørensen (ed.), *Manual of Public International Law* (London 1968), 175, at 222; C. Rousseau, *Droit international public*, i (Paris, 1970), at 230 *et seq.*

[38] See Article 70 of the Vienna Convention on the Law of Treaties.
[39] See Article 69 of the Vienna Convention on the Law of Treaties; *YILC* (1966-II), at 265.
[40] See Article 70, para. 2, of the Vienna Convention.
[41] Sometimes with negative connotations, see *YILC* (1966-II), at 232.
[42] See Articles 40–1 of the Vienna Convention; *YILC* (1966-II), at 232.
[43] See *YILC* (1966-II), at 232; Brownlie, *Principles*, at 625.
[44] Fitzmaurice's Second Report on the Law of Treaties, *YILC* (1957-II), at 23 *et seq.*; same, 52 *AIDI* (1967-I), at 267; Capotorti, 'L'Extinction', at 471–2; Morelli, 52 *AIDI* (1967-II), at

The parties' consent to the termination of a treaty can be expressed:

(i) in the treaty itself in the form of expiry, denunciation, or other termination clauses; or
(ii) in a separate subsequent agreement between all the parties, either express or implied (*desuetude*).

As to the methods of treaty termination, a treaty can be brought to an end:

(i) automatically, by virtue of general international law, or as a result of expiry clauses; or
(ii) by specific acts of the contracting parties.

In cases where termination requires a specific act, this may be:

(i) an act of one of the parties, in exercise of a legal power conferred upon it by general international law or by the treaty itself (denunciation provision); or
(ii) a joint act, such as an agreed decision of all parties to terminate the treaty or the conclusion of a new treaty.

In cases where customary law becomes incompatible with a prior treaty, the treaty can be brought to an end by a joint agreed decision of all contracting parties, that is on the basis of their consent. Or one of the parties may denounce or withdraw from the treaty in accordance with its terms. By contrast, when we ask whether supervening custom is a *ground* of termination of a prior incompatible treaty, we attempt to answer the question whether one of the contracting parties has the right to call for the termination of the treaty in exercise of a legal power conferred by general international law.[45]

1.3. IMPORTANCE OF THE ISSUE

1.3.1. Occurrence in Practice

A convention, however wide its membership and general its acceptance, cannot freeze the development of the law. State practice may continue evolving outside the convention in response to changing conditions or perceptions of interests, and new conflicting custom may emerge as a result. The likelihood of this situation arising in practice will depend on the

---

325; *AIDI* (1967-I), at 292; S. Rosenne, 'The Settlement of Treaty Disputes under the Vienna Convention of 1969', 31 *ZaöRV* (1971), 1, at 52; I. Sinclair, *The Vienna Convention on the Law of Treaties* (Manchester, 1984), at 181.

[45] For the effects of the grounds of treaty termination provided by the Vienna Convention, see Articles 65–8 of the Convention.

duration of particular treaties and the pace of legal developments outside the treaty.

In practice the speed of customary law developments varies. We have seen that customary law can be formed even after the passage of only a short period of time. The law of the sea is an example of a field that underwent rapid transformation in the course of the twentieth century. State practice in this area moved away from the concept of a three-mile territorial sea prevailing at the beginning of this century towards wider jurisdictional zones, first of twelve miles, and subsequently of 200 miles from the shore.[46] In other areas customary principles remained unchanged for long periods of time until they were transformed or replaced by new concepts through a process of varying length. For instance, some of the fundamental principles of the post-Second World War legal order laid down by the UN Charter, such as the concept of universal protection of human rights, did not exist under traditional international law, while others, such as the principle of intervention in another State's internal affairs or the prohibition of the threat or use of force, existed, but were different in content.[47]

Treaties concluded in perpetuity or for a very long term are likely to become obsolete at some point as a result of supervening developments in customary law. Consider, for instance, the Capitulatory treaties concluded between the sixteenth and nineteenth centuries whose validity was challenged in the twentieth century on account of developments in the general rules on State jurisdiction; or the Treaty on the Panama Canal concluded in perpetuity at the beginning of the twentieth century and containing jurisdictional restrictions which were considered to be incompatible with post-Second World War perceptions of the duty of non-intervention in another State's affairs.

In areas where customary law changes rapidly, even treaties concluded for a shorter period of time may become incompatible with new general norms. Some of the fisheries agreements examined below in Chapter 3 fall within this category. Similarly, treaties concluded towards the end of the period of validity of long-standing concepts may become incompatible with new custom within a short period from their entry into force. Consider the case of the minorities treaties that were concluded under the League of Nations system and were regarded as having been superseded by the concept of human rights when the UN Charter was adopted; or the Antarctica Treaty regime which was alleged to have become incompatible with legal developments taking place in the course of the two decades following its adoption.

---

[46] See Ch. 3.
[47] See A. Cassese, *International Law in a Divided World* (Oxford, 1986), esp. at paras. 76 *et seq.*

1.3.2. The Problem of Peaceful Change

The problem of peaceful change, that is the alteration of the *status quo* without the use of force, also arises in cases where a treaty is overtaken by customary developments. It is important to examine the methods of peaceful adaptation of treaties to changes in the law, because at present there is no effective international legislation that can repeal or revise obsolete agreements.[48]

The term international legislation is used in this context to denote a procedure for introducing changes in the *status quo* that go beyond the agreement of the parties. Claims for the revision of the law are considered by a central authority in the light of the general interest of the international community that overrides any conflicting individual interest.

Article 19 of the Covenant of the League of Nations is often cited as 'the first deliberate attempt to create an institution of peaceful change within the framework of a comprehensive system of legal organisation'.[49] Under this Article the Assembly of the League had the power to advise from time to time 'the reconsideration by the members of the League of treaties which have become inapplicable and the consideration of international conditions whose continuance might endanger the peace of the world'. This formulation was wide enough to embrace all claims for revision, including the reconsideration of treaties that had become incompatible with supervening customary law.

However, the effectiveness of Article 19 was limited by its own terms, because it did not empower the Assembly to alter obsolete treaties without the consent of the contracting parties. Its authors only contemplated the situation where the Assembly would investigate claims for revision and make non-binding recommendations to all interested. These recommendations could be of value as authoritative findings to the effect that a change of the *status quo* was required, but did not change the fact that the existing procedures were primarily based on persuasion. Consequently, they were 'definitely limited in the face of established attitudes and conceptions of vital interests'.[50] Article 19 was never applied by the Assembly and was rarely invoked by States.

If Article 19 fell short of being an instrument of international legislation, the procedures available under contemporary international law are equally limited. Article 19 was not repeated in the UN Charter, and its nearest equivalent is Article 14 empowering the General Assembly to recommend

---

[48] See ibid., esp. at 13–14; F. S. Dunn, *Peaceful Change* (New York, 1937); H. Lauterpacht, 'Peaceful Change: The Legal Aspect', in C. A. W. Manning (ed.), *Peaceful Change: An International Problem* (London, 1937), 133, at 153; Q. Wright, 'Article 19 of the League Covenant and the Doctrine *rebus sic stantibus*', *Proc. of the American Society of International Law* (1936), 55, at 65 *et seq.*

[49] Lauterpacht, 'Peaceful Change', at 156.   [50] See Dunn, *Peaceful Change*, at 107.

measures for the peaceful adjustment of 'any situation, regardless of origin, which it deems likely to impair the general welfare or friendly relations among nations'. The General Assembly's recommendations may contain proposals for the revision of existing treaties but it is up to the contracting parties to accept or reject them.

The Security Council may intervene at the request of any Member of the United Nations in cases where the continuance of the dispute 'is likely to endanger the maintenance of international peace and security' and attempts to settle by other peaceful means under Article 33 of the Charter have failed. It may also intervene in any other dispute, provided that all parties have so requested (Article 38 of the UN Charter).

The Security Council may recommend appropriate procedures or methods of adjustment (Article 36) or even the actual terms of settlement it may consider appropriate. In all cases it is up to the parties to the dispute to consider the substance of these recommendations and decide on the course of action to be followed.

It follows that the international system lacks a legislative process for the revision of treaties. In the absence of a central authority charged with creating and changing international law, these functions are entrusted to individual States.

1.3.3. Lack of Codification

The 1969 Vienna Convention on the Law of Treaties[51] is one of the major instruments of codification and progressive development of international law. It is generally regarded as an authoritative guide to treaty law for members and non-members alike and several of its provisions are considered to be declaratory of existing customary law on the subject.[52]

The Vienna Convention covers a wide range of treaty topics, including treaty amendment and modification (part IV), invalidity, termination, and suspension (part V). The Convention does not deal with the effect of

---

[51] Opened for signature on 23 May 1969; entered into force on 27 Jan. 1980; 1155 *UNTS* 331; 8 *ILM* (1969), 679. See R. Ago, 'Droit des traités à la lumière de la Convention de Vienne', 134 *RC* (1971-III), at 297; P. Reuter, *La Convention de Vienne du 23 mai 1969 sur le droit des traités* (Paris, 1970); S. Rosenne, *The Law of Treaties: A Guide to the Legislative History of the Vienna Convention* (Leiden, 1970); *Developments in the Law of Treaties: 1945–1986* (Cambridge, 1989); Sinclair, *The Vienna Convention*. For the history of the Convention, see Yearbooks of the ILC and *UN Conference on the Law of Treaties*, Off. Records, First and Second Sessions (1968 and 1969), UN Docs. A/CONF. 39/11 and Add. 1.

[52] See, *inter alia*, the cases cited above, n. 33, and the Beagle Channel Arbitration (*Argentina* v. *Chile*) 52 ILR (1977), at 93, the *Young Loan Case*, 59 ILR (1984), at 529 (rules of treaty interpretation), United Kingdom v. France Continental Shelf Arbitration (First Decision), 54 ILR (1979), paras. 38, 58, 61 (Articles 19–23 of the Convention). See also Transmittal of the Vienna Convention to the US Senate, Message from President of the United States, Senate Executive L (92nd Congress, 1st Session) of 22 Nov. 1971, reproduced in *ILM* (1972), at 234.

supervening custom other than *jus cogens* on a prior incompatible treaty. In view of this omission, the state of the law on this subject can be determined only by reference to existing State practice and the relevant case law of international tribunals.

1.3.4. Intertemporal Law

It may be asked whether the doctrine of intertemporal law[53] can provide an easy answer to the problem of conflict between custom and prior treaty. In our view, it cannot, for the reasons stated below.

The theory of intertemporal law was developed by Judge Huber in the Island of Palmas Arbitration. The issue in that case was whether the United States, as the legal successor to certain Spanish territories, had title to the Island of Palmas originally discovered by Spain but effectively occupied and controlled by the Netherlands East India Company at least since 1677. According to Judge Huber, although discovery alone had conferred a full and perfect title to Spain under the law of the seventeenth century, it had to be shown that Spain's sovereignty had been maintained in accordance with the requirements of the modern law of effective occupation:

as regards the question which of different legal systems prevailing at successive periods is to be applied in a particular case (the so-called intertemporal law), a distinction must be made between the creation of rights and the existence of rights. The same principle which subjects the act creative of a right to the law in force at the time the right arises, demands that the existence of the right, in other words its continued manifestation, shall follow the conditions required by the evolution of the law.[54]

This theory is cited with approval by some authors but criticized by others on the ground that it requires the constant re-examination of acquired rights in the light of subsequent developments of the law.

There have been attempts to extend the theory of intertemporal law to the law of treaties. According to Article 56 of Sir Humphrey Waldock's Third Report on the Law of Treaties, although a treaty must be interpreted in the light of the law in force at the time when the treaty was drawn up, its application shall be governed by the rules of international law in force at the time when the treaty is applied.[55]

---

[53] See 55 *AIDI* (1973), 56 *AIDI* (1975); *YILC* (1964-II), at 8 *et seq.*, 33 *et seq.*; T. O. Elias, 'The Doctrine of Intertemporal Law', 74 *AJIL* (1980), at 285; W. Friedman, *The Changing Structure of International Law* (London, 1964), at 130–1; G. Schwarzenberger, *International Law as Applied by International Courts and Tribunals I* (3rd edn., London, 1957), at 21–4; E. McWhinney, 'The Time Dimension in International Law', in J. Makarczyk (ed.), *Essays in International Law in Honour of Judge Manfred Lachs* (Dordrecht, 1984), at 181.
[54] Award of 4 Apr. 1928, *Rep. Int. Arb. Awards* (1928-II), 829, at 845.
[55] *YILC* (1964-II), at 8–9.

This solution is not free from difficulty. The distinction between interpretation and application of the treaty does not provide a clear criterion for the application of the earlier or the later law. Moreover, if the term 'treaty application' is understood as the possibility of treaty termination or amendment by subsequent custom,[56] this is not strictly speaking an intertemporal problem. Intertemporal law as usually defined consists of determining the temporal application of different rules that have succeeded one another in time. The development of custom in conflict with a prior treaty raises a different issue, that of determining whether the later rule has succeeded the earlier one at a given point in time.[57]

---

[56] Ibid., at 9–10.

[57] See the discussion at 55 *AIDI* (1973), especially M. Sørensen, 'Le Problème dit du droit intertemporel dans l'ordre international', 1, at 10 *et seq.*, 86; see also Karl, *Vertrag*, at 107.

2

An Overview of the Literature

This chapter examines the different ways in which new custom may affect a prior treaty. A treaty may be interpreted in the light of supervening custom that completes or clarifies its provisions. If new custom is incompatible with a prior treaty, two possibilities exist: either the treaty is amended or terminated on account of new custom, or both the treaty and the customary rule are considered to be in force giving rise to conflicting obligations whose order of priority must be established.

The possibility of treaty amendment or termination on account of supervening custom is accepted in the literature, although views differ as to the precise manner in which it takes place. It is sometimes said that supervening custom automatically modifies or terminates a prior incompatible treaty, because the more recent expression of the will of States must be considered as having replaced an earlier one. Other authors suggest that, following the emergence of new custom, a prior incompatible treaty can be terminated if the parties cease to apply it in their *inter se* relations in a manner establishing their consent to let it lapse (*desuetude*). Or new custom can be a ground of treaty termination, especially when its development can be regarded as a fundamental change of the circumstances that constituted an essential basis of the parties' consent to be bound by the treaty.

These possible ways in which new custom may affect a prior treaty are not necessarily mutually exclusive. For instance, if supervening custom is considered to be a ground of termination, it confers upon a party to a prior treaty the right to call for its abrogation. Until this right has been exercised, the treaty rule remains in force, and a tribunal requested to determine the applicable law must decide whether it should give it priority over the customary rule. Or, following the emergence of new custom, the right to call for treaty termination may not need to be exercised because the treaty has been brought to an end in another manner, for instance, by tacit agreement of the parties to let it lapse (*desuetude*).

2.1. TREATY INTERPRETATION IN THE LIGHT OF NEW CUSTOM

According to Article 31, para. 3, of the Vienna Convention on the Law of Treaties, the interpreter of a treaty should take into account *inter alia* any relevant rules of international law applicable in the relations between the parties at the time when the interpretation is made.[1]

It is accepted in the literature that Article 31, para. 3, embodies a generally recognized rule of treaty interpretation. This rule is, however, difficult to reconcile with another general principle of interpretation, the principle of contemporaneity,[2] according to which the terms of a treaty should be given the ordinary meaning they had at the time when the treaty was concluded. The principle of contemporaneity originated in Judge Huber's dictum in the Island of Palmas Arbitration to the effect that 'a juridical fact must be appreciated in the light of the law contemporary with it and not of the law in force at the time when a dispute in regard to it arises or falls to be settled,'[3] and was reiterated in subsequent case law.[4]

The principle of contemporaneity notwithstanding, there is scope for 'the narrow and limited proposition that the evolution of the law can be taken into account in interpreting certain terms in a treaty which are by their very nature expressed in such general terms as to lend themselves to an evolutionary interpretation'.[5] The concepts of the 'territorial sea' and the 'continental shelf', as well as the notions of 'public policy' and 'domestic jurisdiction', are cited as examples of treaty terms falling within that category. Interpretation of these terms in the light of supervening custom is permissible unless it is shown that this would be contrary to the parties' 'intentions and expectations expressed during the negotiations preceding the conclusion of the treaty'.[6]

This view is supported by the case law of international tribunals. In its Advisory Opinion on the Legal Consequences for States of the Continued Presence of South Africa in Namibia, the International Court of Justice took account of supervening legal developments with regard to non-self governing territories when interpreting Article 22 of the Covenant of the League of Nations:

Mindful as it is of the primary necessity of interpreting an instrument in accordance with the intentions of the parties at the time of its conclusion, the Court is bound to take into account the fact that the concepts embodied in Article 22 of the

---

[1] See also Art. 19, para. 1, of the Harvard Draft, 29 *AJIL* (1935), supp. III; 1956 Resolution of the Institute of International Law, 46 *AIDI* (1956), at 359.

[2] See G. Fitzmaurice, 'The Law and Procedure of the International Court of Justice 1951–1954: Treaty Interpretation and other Treaty Points', 33 *BYIL* (1957), 203, at 212, 225–6.

[3] *Rep. Int. Arb. Awards* (1928-II), 829, at 845.

[4] See *US Nationals in Morocco Case*, at 189; *South West Africa Cases*, at 23, §16: 'in order to determine what the rights and obligations of the Parties relative to the Mandate were and are . . . the Court must place itself at the point in time when the Mandates system was being instituted . . . the Court must have regard to the situation as it was at that time . . .'; Namibia Advisory Opinion, 16, at 31: 'Mindful as it is of the primary necessity of interpreting an instrument in accordance with the intentions of the parties at the time of its conclusion . . .'

[5] Sinclair, *The Vienna Convention*, at 140. See also Sir H. Waldock, *YILC* (1964-II), at 9.

[6] Sinclair, *The Vienna Convention*, at 139.

Covenant—'the strenuous conditions of the modern world' and 'the well being and development' of the peoples concerned—were not static, but were by definition evolutionary, as also, therefore, was the concept of the 'sacred trust'. The parties to the Covenant must consequently be deemed to have accepted them as such. That is why, viewing the institutions of 1919, the Court must take into consideration the changes which have occurred in the supervening half-century, and its interpretation cannot remain unaffected by the subsequent development of law, through the Charter of the United Nations and by way of customary law. Moreover, an international instrument has to be interpreted and applied within the framework of the entire legal system prevailing at the time of the interpretation.[7]

Similarly, in the *Aegean Sea Continental Shelf Case* the Court held that, in accordance with modern international law, the term 'disputes relating to . . . territorial status', included in Greece's reservation to her instrument of accession to the 1928 General Act for the Pacific Settlement of Disputes, covered disputes relating to the continental shelf, although this concept was unknown at the time when Greece acceded to the Act:

Once it is established that the expression 'the territorial status of Greece' was used in Greece's instrument of accession as a generic term denoting any matters comprised within the concept of territorial status under general international law, the presumption necessarily arises that its meaning was intended to follow the evolution of the law and to correspond with the meaning attached to the expression by the law in force at any given time . . . this presumption . . . is even more compelling, when it is recalled that the 1928 Act was a convention for the pacific settlement of disputes designed to be of the most general kind and of continuing duration, for it hardly seems conceivable that in such a convention terms like 'domestic jurisdiction' and 'territorial status' were intended to have a fixed content regardless of the subsequent evolution of international law.[8]

In addition to interpreting treaty terms whose meaning was intended to follow the evolution of international law, supervening custom can also be taken into account in order to clarify ambiguities or fill gaps in the treaty text.[9] The role that custom can play in this context is limited by the scope of the treaty provisions that are being interpreted.[10] A treaty provision cannot be 'interpreted' in the light of new customary rules that are

---

[7] ICJ Reports (1971), at 31.

[8] ICJ Reports (1978), at 32. See also *Marckx Case, ECHR* Ser. A, no. 31 (1979), at 19–20, 44, one of a series of cases where the ECJ took account of developments in the domestic law of the Member States of the Council of Europe in interpreting the European Convention on Human Rights. The issue in the *Marckx Case* was whether the guarantees provided by Articles 8 and 14 of the Convention (the right to respect for family life and the prohibition of discrimination on any grounds in respect of the enjoyment of the rights and freedoms set forth in the Convention) extended to 'illegitimate families'.

[9] See e.g. Villiger, *Customary International Law*, at 269–70.

[10] For an overview of the different theories of treaty interpretation, see Sinclair, *The Vienna Convention*, at 114 *et seq.* and the references therein; Fitzmaurice, 'Law and Procedure' (1957), at 204 *et seq.*

contrary to its meaning. Taking account of supervening custom in these circumstances involves in reality the amendment of the treaty.

The line between interpretation and amendment of a treaty may sometimes be blurred and different views may exist as to whether a certain practice can be reconciled with the treaty text.[11] However, legally the two processes are distinct.[12]

This point is particularly important in the context of international adjudication, because international tribunals normally have the power to interpret treaties and not to revise them.[13] If customary law has evolved outside a convention that remains in force as originally drafted, either a tribunal can reconcile new custom with the meaning of the treaty provisions, or, if this is not possible, it must apply the treaty as it stands.[14]

2.2. PRIORITY BETWEEN INCONSISTENT OBLIGATIONS

It is often necessary to decide which of several conflicting rules of international law deriving from the same or different sources and being in force at a particular time must apply to a given situation. In the literature three criteria are used to solve conflicts of this kind: the normative value of the conflicting rules, their relative degree of generality, and the chronological order of their generation.[15]

According to these criteria, the rule which has a higher normative value (*lex superior*) will prevail. This will be the case when one of the rules has the character of *jus cogens*. If the conflicting rules are all expressions of equal authority, then the rule which is more recent (*lex posterior*) or more specific (*lex specialis*) will prevail. A rule can be regarded as *lex specialis*, because it is binding on a few States as opposed to a rule binding *erga omnes* (*lex specialis ratione personae*) or because it 'furnishes, in comparison with

---

[11] See D. P. O'Connell, *The International Law of the Sea*, ed. I. A. Shearer, i (Oxford, 1982), at 47, 531–2 (on whether the 1958 Geneva Convention on the High Seas could be interpreted so as to allow the establishment of fishing zones beyond the territorial sea); Jennings, 'General Course', at 381.

[12] Commentary to Article 38 of the ILC 1966 Draft, *YILC* (1966-II), at 236; G. Scelle, *Théorie juridique de la révision des traités* (Paris, 1936), at 11.

[13] See *Interpretation of Peace Treaties,* ICJ Reports (1950), at 228–9; *US Nationals in Morocco Case*, at 196.

[14] See M. Virally, 'A propos de la *"lex ferenda"'*, in *Mélanges offerts à P. Reuter* (Paris, 1981), 519, at 524–5; H. Lauterpacht, *The Development of International Law by the International Court* (London, 1958), at 155 *et seq.*

[15] Villiger, *Customary International Law*, at 36; M. Bos, 'The Hierarchy among the Recognized Manifestations of International Law', in *Estudios de Derecho Internacional Homenaje al Profesor Miaja de la Muela*, i (Madrid, 1979), 363, at 366; Nguyen Quoc Dinh, P. Dailler, and A. Pellet, *Droit international public* (3rd edn., Paris, 1987), at 107; H. Kelsen, *Principles of International Law* (2nd edn., New York, 1966), at 438.

the *lex generalis*, the deeper, more detailed, perhaps exceptional, regulation of the same subject-matter' (*lex specialis ratione materiae*).[16]

These criteria also apply to the conflict between a treaty rule and a more recent customary rule. It is accepted that there is no generally established hierarchy between treaty and custom, because they both emanate from States and are equivalent expressions of their consent to be bound internationally.[17] As a result, there is no *lex superior* and in case of conflict the customary rule will prevail as *lex posterior*.

On the other hand, opinions differ as to whether a prior but special treaty will prevail over new but more general custom.[18] It is sometimes said that the treaty will always prevail by virtue of the principles *lex posterior generalis non derogat legi priori speciali*. Other authors suggest that the treaty rule will apply only if it can be interpreted as an exception from the general application of the new custom, because it approaches more closely the subject in hand. If this is not possible, the treaty rule should be considered as having been terminated or modified.[19] In this context, it is said that a treaty should not necessarily be regarded as an exception from general custom, simply because it binds a limited number of States.

Article 38 of the ICJ Statute and the Priority between Treaty and Customary Law

Article 38 of the ICJ Statute provides that the Court, whose function is to decide in accordance with international law such disputes as are submitted to it, shall apply to:

(*a*) international conventions;
(*b*) international custom;
(*c*) the general principles of law recognized by civilized nations;
(*d*) ... judicial decisions and teachings of the most highly qualified publicists of the various nations, as subsidiary means for the determination of rules of law.[20]

---

[16] Villiger, *Customary International Law*, at 36; Karl, *Vertrag*, at 94.

[17] See Villiger, *Customary International Law*, at 35; Bos, 'Hierarchy', at 366 *et seq.*; M. Akehurst, 'The Hierarchy of the Sources of International Law', 47 *BYIL* (1974–5), 273, at 275; R. Monaco, 'Observations sur la hiérarchie des sources du droit international', in *Festschrift für H. Mosler* (Berlin, 1983), 599, at 608; Nguyen Quoc Dinh, Dailler, A. Pellet, *Droit international public*, at 106–7.

[18] In favour, Bos, 'Hierarchy', at 366. With reservations, Villiger, *Customary International Law*, at 36, para. 88: 'To the extent that this maxim is intended to enable a treaty with few parties necessarily to override subsequent general customary law, it may be objected that, although treaties may, at times, constitute the *lex specialis* on account of the merits of *jus scriptum*, they will not *necessarily* do so.'   [19] See e.g. Karl, *Vertrag*, at 58–9, 66.

[20] For the history of Article 38, see PCIJ, Advisory Committee of Jurists, *Procès verbaux of the Proceedings of the Committee* (The Hague, 1920), at 344, 337 *et seq.*

Some authors consider that the order in which the sources of international law are enumerated in Article 38 of the ICJ Statute reflects a logical preference for the application of treaties to a particular dispute: 'The rights and duties of States are determined, in the first instance, by their agreement as expressed in treaties ... When a controversy arises between two or more States with regard to a matter regulated by a treaty, it is natural that the parties should invoke and that the adjudicating agency should apply, in the first instance, the provisions of the treaty in question.'[21] As a result, 'the hierarchy of sources of international law, as indicated in the Statute of the International Court, provides an authoritative initial basis for the application of international law'.[22]

Although it is accepted that the binding force of conventional and customary rules is the same, priority is given to treaties for practical considerations: 'For the judge, however, the difference in application of conventional and customary rules is enormous. Suffice it to mention, for instance, the much greater precision and ease of determination of content and range of validity in the case of conventional rules and, in consequence, the much stronger, by comparison with other rules, persuasive impact for the Court and the parties.'[23]

International tribunals have in several cases applied treaties that conflicted with more recent customary rules.[24] The treaties in question may have been more specific than the new custom. However, the decisions do not always mention the specific character of the treaty as the reason for which it was given priority over more recent custom.

The tendency of tribunals to apply treaties in the first instance may indeed be motivated by practical considerations. The application of a treaty has obvious advantages because of the clarity and ease of determination of the written rule. Moreover, it is often difficult to establish the relative degree of generality of different rules in order to be able to decide which is the *lex specialis*. Tribunals may also be reluctant to disregard the binding character of treaty obligations that have not been terminated or modified by the parties, because they attach importance to the principle of *pacta sunt servanda* and the need to ensure treaty stability.[25]

---

[21] Lauterpacht, *International Law*, i, at 86–7; C. Parry, *The Sources and Evidences of International Law* (Manchester, 1965), at 28, 33–4.

[22] Lauterpacht, *International Law*, i, at 88.

[23] Wolfke, *Custom in Present International Law*, at 98; M. Sørensen, *Les Sources du droit international* (Copenhague, 1946), at 249.

[24] Some of these cases are examined in Ch. 5.

[25] Schwarzenberger, *International Law I*, i, at 56: 'The difficulties which might arise have been solved pragmatically by way of unquestioned assumptions, reliance on the typical intentions of parties to treaties, and emphasis on the binding character of treaty obligations ... This attitude secures preference for rules stemming from the law-creating process of treaties in each case in which the parties to international engagements have expressed their intention beyond any shadow of doubt'; also at 57–8.

2.3. TREATY TERMINATION OR REVISION FOLLOWING THE DEVELOPMENT OF NEW CUSTOM

2.3.1. Succession of Rules

A number of authors suggest that new customary law may terminate or modify a prior treaty rule, because custom and treaties are sources of international law of equal value. It will be recalled that normative equivalence is also one of the criteria used in the literature for the solution of conflicts between a treaty rule and a more recent customary rule both of which are regarded to be in force and in operation.

Termination of one rule by another and priority of one rule over the other in the context of their application to a concrete case are two different possible ways in which supervening custom may affect prior treaties. The two possibilities are theoretically distinct. Either the treaty rule is considered to have ceased to exist as a result of the formation of new custom, in which case no real conflict arises, because only the customary rule remains in force, or both rules are considered to be in force and it must be decided which of the two will apply.[26]

The same distinction is made in the case of a treaty regulating the same subject-matter as a prior treaty. Two separate Articles of the Vienna Convention apply to this issue, Article 59 dealing with the termination or suspension of the operation of a treaty implied by the conclusion of a later treaty and Article 30, para. 3, dealing with the application of successive treaties relating to the same subject-matter.[27] While the practical effects of Article 30 are 'temporarily to negative and in that way suspend the operation of the incompatible provisions of the earlier treaty so long as the later treaty is in force',[28] a different situation is considered to arise when the treaty is terminated according to Article 59, because 'then there are not two sets of incompatible treaty provisions in force and in operation, but only those of the later treaty'.[29]

The Literature

The possibility of treaty termination by new custom is easily accepted by writers who consider that customary law is based on the tacit agreement of States. Under this view, conventional and customary rules have the same normative basis, because they are simply different ways of expressing a

---

[26] See e.g. Villiger, *Customary International Law*, at 36, 216 *et seq.*; Bos, 'Hierarchy', at 362–3; Karl, *Vertrag*, at 58–9, 61, 66; Nguyen Quoc Dinh, 'Evolution de la jurisprudence de la Cour Internationale de la Haye relative au problème de la hiérarchie des normes conventionelles', in *Mélanges offerts à Marcel Waline*, i (1974), 215, at 218.

[27] See ILC Commentary to the 1966 Draft, *YILC* (1966-II), at 253.

[28] Ibid., at 216.   [29] Ibid., at 253.

State's consent to be legally bound. As a result, one legal situation may be substituted for another, if the will of States has changed accordingly.[30]

The interchangeability of treaties and customary law is not, however, necessarily premised on the theory that custom constitutes a tacit agreement between States. It is also accepted on the basis that the relationship between the treaty and custom is not hierarchical.[31] A treaty rule and a customary rule have the same legal value, because they both emanate from States.[32] The international legal order is largely decentralized and there is no international legislator imposing its will on individual States. As a result, States are free to regulate their relations as they see fit, and to change them, if they so wish, by replacing an existing treaty rule by new customary law or *vice versa*.[33]

Once it is accepted that treaties and customary law have the same value as sources of international law, treaty termination or modification on account of new customary law is the consequence of the application of the *lex posterior* rule. Provided that neither of the rules involved has the character of *jus cogens*, the older provision must be considered as having been abandoned, because it no longer reflects the will of States.[34] In these circumstances, substitution can take place between rules deriving either from the same or from different sources of international law. A new customary rule may thus replace either a prior customary or a prior treaty rule.

Termination or modification of a treaty is usually regarded as taking place automatically, once it has been established that a more recent and conflicting customary rule has been formed that binds *all* parties to the treaty.[35] Other

---

[30] See G. I. Tunkin, 'International Law in the International System', 147 *RC* (1975-IV), 1, at 136; K. Strupp, 'Les Règles générales du droit de la paix', 47 *RC* (1934-I), 258, at 315; S. Séfériades, 'Aperçus sur la coutume juridique internationale', 43 *RGDIP* (1936), 129, at 195.

[31] See Cassese, *International Law*, at 180: 'A new customary rule can supplant a treaty in view of their complete interchangeability flowing from their equality as sources of international law.' See also Capotorti, 'L'Extinction', at 516; P. Reuter, *Introduction au Droit des Traités* (Paris, 1985) at 117, no. 205; A. J. P. Tammes, 'Interaction of the Sources of International Law', 10 *NILR* (1963), 225, at 229; J. H. W. Verzijl, *International Law in Historical Perspective*, i (Leiden, 1968), at 85; P. de Visscher, 'Cours général de droit international public', 136 *RC* (1972-II), 1, at 79.

[32] See e.g. Virally, 'Sources', at 168; 'Cours général de droit international public: Panorama du droit international contemporain', 183 *RC* (1983-V), 9, at 170; P. Heilborn, 'Les Sources du droit international', 11 *RC* (1926-I), 1, at 29.

[33] See P. Reuter, 'Principes de droit international public', 103 *RC* (1961 II), 425, at 483: 'Il découle des caractères propres à la société internationale que l'ordre juridique est très mal hiérarchisé: c'est la conséquence directe de son état anarchique'; Cassese, *International Law*, at 169; Nguyen Quoc Dinh, Dailler, and Pellet, *Droit international public*, at 106.

[34] See e.g. Rousseau, *Droit International Public*, i, §283, p. 343: 'la règle incompatible ... est la règle la plus ancienne; et si elle est abandonnée ... c'est parce qu'elle a cessée de refléter l'accord de volontés des sujets des droits, la plus grande 'positivité' internationale appartenant à la règle la plus récente'; Capotorti, 'L'Extinction', at 516; Monaco, 'Observations', at 609; Reuter, 'Principes', at 484; Cassese, *International Law*, at 180.

[35] See Capotorti, 'L'Extinction', at 516; F. Castberg, 'La Méthodologie du Droit International Public', 43 *RC* (1933-I), at 313; Nguyen Quoc Dinh, Dailler, and Pellet, *Droit international*

authors accept that treaty termination or modification by new customary law is *in principle* possible, because treaties are not intrinsically superior to custom. However, actual termination or modification takes place to the extent that the parties do not apply the treaty rule in their *inter se* relations (*desuetude*), a process that may be completed over a period of time.[36]

Lex posterior v. *lex specialis*

A prior treaty rule may be more special than new customary law, either because it binds a few States (*lex specialis ratione personae*) or because it provides a more detailed regulation of the same subject-matter (*lex specialis ratione materiae*). In cases where supervening general custom is incompatible with a prior special treaty, there is disagreement as to which rule, the more recent or the more general, should prevail.

Some authors take the view that the *lex posterior* always repeals the *lex prior*, even if the prior rule is more specific.[37] Others suggest that the *lex specialis* rule limits the scope of the application of the *lex posterior*: a later law, general in character, does not repeal an earlier law that is special in character (*lex posterior generalis non derogat legi priori speciali*).[38]

If the special character of a rule is determined on the basis of its more specific subject-matter, the *lex posterior generalis non derogat legi priori speciali* principle states the obvious—namely, that States are free to conclude agreements designed to meet special circumstances in derogation from general custom. A prior treaty that was intended to be an exception from the general regulation of the subject-matter will, therefore, remain in force as originally drafted, notwithstanding any subsequent developments in custom. By contrast, a treaty regarded as special by virtue of the limited number of States bound by it should not necessarily prevail over supervening custom that is binding *erga omnes*.[39]

2.3.2. Treaty Termination by *desuetude*

A number of authors state that new customary law may modify, or even terminate a prior incompatible treaty by *desuetude*. Before examining this literature, we shall briefly analyse the notion of *desuetude* in general.

---

public, at 285; Verzijl, *International Law*, i, at 85; Séfériades, 'Aperçus', at 195; Heilborn, 'Sources', at 29.

[36] See Rousseau, *Droit international public*, i, at §283, p. 343; R.-J. Dupuis, 'Coutume sage et coutume sauvage', in *Mélanges offerts à Ch. Rousseau* (Paris, 1974), 75, at 81–2; P. Guggenheim, *Traité de droit international public*, i (Geneva, 1967), at 113, 225; Nguyen Quoc Dinh, Dailler, and Pellet, *Droit international public*, at 285.

[37] R. Monaco, 'Cours général de droit international public', 125 *RC* (1968-III), 93, at 214; 'Observations', at 609. See also Castberg, 'La Méthodologie', at 338.

[38] See Bos, 'Hierarchy', at 364–6; Cassese, *International Law*, at 180; A. Verdross and B. Simma, *Universelles Völkerrecht* (Berlin, 1984), at 414.

[39] See Karl, *Vertrag*, at 89–90.

(a) Desuetude *in General*

It is generally considered that a treaty falls into *desuetude* when its non-application by the parties over a period of time establishes their consent to let it lapse.[40] In order to regard the treaty as having been terminated, mere lapse of time, however long, is not sufficient. In addition, the States party to the treaty must have failed to invoke it in situations where they would have been expected to do so, or they must have acquiesced in conduct constituting prima facie a treaty violation.[41]

In the Yuille, Shortridge and Co. Arbitration between Great Britain and Portugal,[42] Portugal argued that Article 7 of the Anglo-Portuguese Treaty of Alliance of 1654 had fallen into *desuetude*, because British subjects had failed to invoke it over a long period of time. The tribunal held that the failure of individuals to rely on a right under the treaty was not sufficient to prove *desuetude*, but failure by the British Government to intervene on behalf of its citizens was required instead.[43] However, the tribunal accepted the possibility that treaties may be terminated by *desuetude*: 'il est certain qu'il appartient aux gouvernements d'abroger expressément un traité ou d'en suspendre l'usage, ce qui devra être regardé par leurs sujets comme une désuétude dérogeant au traité.'[44]

Desuetude Based on Implied Consent

Desuetude is usually described in the literature as treaty termination based on the parties' *implied consent*.[45] This was the view adopted by the International Law Commission when it considered whether *desuetude* should be recognized as a distinct ground of treaty termination:

> while 'obsolescence' or '*desuetude*' may be a factual cause for the termination of a treaty, the legal basis of such termination, when it occurs, is the consent of the parties which is to be implied from their conduct in relation to the treaty. In the Commission's view, therefore, cases of 'obsolescence' or '*desuetude*' may be considered as covered by [Article 54, para. b] under which a treaty may be terminated at any time by the consent of all the parties.[46]

International tribunals also use the term *desuetude* to describe treaty termination by the implied consent of the parties. In the *Nuclear Tests Case*

---

[40] The term desuetude is borrowed from the theory of customary law: see Schwarzenberger, *International Law I*, i, at 535.

[41] See McNair, *Law of Treaties*, at 516, 518; E. Giraud, 'Modification et terminaison des traités collectifs', 49 *AIDI* (1961-I), 5, at 50.

[42] A. Lapradelle and N. Politis, *Recueil des arbitrages internationaux* (Paris, 1932), ii, at 101.

[43] Ibid., at 105.   [44] Ibid.

[45] Brownlie, *Principles*, at 617–18; Schwarzenberger, *International Law I*, i, at 537; R. Plender, 'The Role of Consent in the Termination of Treaties', 57 *BYIL* (1986), 133, at 138 *et seq*.

[46] *YILC* (1966-II), at 237.

Australia requested the International Court of Justice to order interim measures of protection on the basis of Article 41 of its Statute and subsidiarily on Article 33 of the General Act of 1928 for the Pacific Settlement of Disputes.[47] France alleged that the General Act had fallen into *desuetude* since the demise of the League of Nations system and that this view of the matter was confirmed by the conduct of States parties to the Act.[48]

The Court examined the request for interim measures only on the basis of Article 41 of its Statute[49] and did not decide whether the General Act had fallen into *desuetude*.[50] However, members of the Court stated in their dissenting opinions that the legal basis for the termination of a treaty by *desuetude* was the consent of the parties implied from their conduct in relation to the treaty. Judges Oneyama, Dillard, Jiménez de Aréchaga, and Sir Humphrey Waldock thus rejected France's contention that the 1928 Act was no longer in force, because it was impossible 'to conclude from the conduct of the parties in relation to the 1928 Act, and more especially from that of France prior to the filling of the Application in this case, their consent to abandon the Act'.[51]

In the *Aegean Sea Continental Shelf Case*[52] Turkey challenged the Court's jurisdiction on the grounds that the General Act of 1928 was no longer in force. The Court did not examine whether the the General Act was still in force, because it lacked jurisdiction on other grounds.[53] However, Judge de Castro and Judge *ad hoc* Stasinopoulos observed in their dissenting opinions that the Act was still in force, because the parties 'had not evinced the will to cease to be parties to it'.[54]

Desuetude Based on Supervening Custom

It is sometimes said that the legal basis of treaty termination by *desuetude* is the formation of supervening custom ('negative' custom). The parties no longer apply a treaty or some of its provisions without giving rise to protests over a period of time sufficient to consider that a custom has been formed, and during that period they become convinced that their behaviour is legitimate.[55] The new custom is 'negative', because it merely leads to the abrogation of the treaty rule.

If *desuetude* is based on the formation of supervening custom, a separate

---

[47] *League of Nations Treaty Series*, vol. 93, 343.   [48] ICJ Reports (1973), 99, at 102.
[49] Ibid., at 103.   [50] ICJ Reports (1974), at 253.
[51] Ibid., at 338. See also dissenting opinion of Judge Barwick, at 405, 416; dissenting opinion of Judge de Castro, at 381.
[52] ICJ Reports (1978), at 1.   [53] Ibid., at 17, 37.   [54] Ibid., at 72, 62.
[55] Capotorti, 'L'Extinction', at 517; Karl, *Vertrag*, at 259 *et seq.*; F. Berber, *Lehrbuch des Völkerrechts*, i (Munich, 1975), at 492; J. Leca, *Les Techniques de révision des conventions internationales* (Paris, 1961), at 262; M. R. Pinto, 'Prescription en droit international', 87 *RC* (1955-I), 390, at 431.

legal basis of treaty termination by custom is needed, in order to avoid circular arguments of the kind: customary law may terminate a treaty by means of *desuetude, desuetude* may terminate a treaty on account of the development of supervening custom. This separate legal basis can, for instance, be found in the normative equivalence of the two sources of international law.[56]

Desuetude Compared to Treaty Modification by Subsequent Practice

According to the 1963 United States *v.* France Air Transport Services Agreement Arbitration,[57] the conduct of the parties in the application of the agreement may be taken into account 'as a possible source of a subsequent modification, arising out of certain actions or certain attitudes, having a bearing on the juridical situation of the parties and on the rights that each of them could properly claim'. This would be the case when 'express or implied consent has been given to a certain claim or to the exercise of a certain activity' or when 'an attitude—whether it can rightly or not be described as a form of tacit consent—certainly has the same effects on the juridical situation between the parties as consent properly speaking would have'.[58]

The International Law Commission Draft on the Law of Treaties also provided that a treaty may be modified by subsequent practice of the parties in the application of the treaty establishing their agreement to that effect.[59] Although this provision was not included in the text of the Vienna Convention, treaty modification by subsequent practice of the parties is generally considered to be a rule of customary law.[60]

As in the case of *desuetude*, treaty modification by subsequent practice of the parties is explained either in terms of the the parties' consent[61] or in terms of the emergence of new special custom.[62] In our view, it is more appropriate in these circumstances to speak of treaty modification by implied consent for the following reason. Practice followed by some of the parties and accepted by others in the course of the application of their agreement is treaty-oriented, because it is motivated by the intention to modify the conventional rule and not to create a derogation from general custom. Consequently, it does not establish the existence of special custom

[56] See Capotorti, 'L'Extinction', at 516; Karl, *Vertrag*, at 265–6; A. Poch de Caviades, 'De la clause *rebus sic stantibus* et clause de révision dans les conventions internationales', 118 *RC* (1966-II), 109, at 135–6.

[57] 38 *ILR* (1969), 182, at 249.   [58] Ibid.

[59] See Article 68 of the 1964 Draft, *YILC* (1964-II), at 198; Article 38 of the 1966 Draft, *YILC* (1966-II), at 236.

[60] For an analysis of treaty modification by subsequent practice, see Karl, *Vertrag*.

[61] See Article 68 of the 1964 ILC Draft, *YILC* (1964-II), at 198; ILC Commentary to Article 38 of the Final Draft, *YILC* (1966-II), at 236; Villiger, *Customary International Law*, at 211.

[62] See e.g. Karl, *Vertrag*, at 109; Tunkin, *Theory of International Law*, at 144; *YILC* (1966-I), pt. II, at 165, 220–1; Wolfke, *Custom in Present International Law*, at 105.

without separate proof of an *opinio juris*.[63] For the same reason, *desuetude* is also more appropriately described as treaty termination by implied consent.[64]

Desuetude extinguishes a treaty rule, while treaty modification by subsequent practice involves both the *desuetude* of the prior rule and its replacement by a new one. In this sense, authors sometimes use the term *desuetude* broadly to describe both situations.[65] When reference is made to treaty termination by *desuetude* in this book, it will be understood as applying *mutatis mutandis* to treaty modification by subsequent practice.

(b) New Customary Law and the desuetude of Treaties

A number of authors[66] take the view that customary law may terminate a prior treaty by *desuetude*, in cases where the parties no longer apply the treaty in a manner that evidence their agreement to let it lapse: 'A new rule of customary law will supersede inconsistent obligations created by earlier agreement if the parties so intend and the intention is clearly manifested,[67] in which case the earlier provision in the agreement is deemed to have expired by mutual agreement or by *desuetude*.'[68]

In this context it is sometimes suggested that treaty termination as a result of the subsequent growth of a conflicting custom can take place *only* by *desuetude*, for which a high standard of proof is set:

just as there is a presumption against the establishment of new customary rules which conflict with pre-existing customary rules, so there is a presumption against the replacement of customary rules by treaties and *vice versa* . . . subsequent custom can terminate a treaty only when there is clear evidence that that is what the parties intend.

The clearest evidence that the treaty has been replaced by a subsequent conflicting customary rule is to be found in statements by the parties recognizing that this has occurred . . . In the absence of express statements concerning termination . . . evidence can only be provided by abundant and consistent practice . . .

In all cases, what counts is the practice followed *inter se* by the parties to the treaty; the practice which they follow in their dealings with States which are not parties to the treaty, and the practice of the latter States, may give rise to a rule

---

[63] Villiger, *Customary International Law*, at 34; E. Giraud, 'Modification et terminaison des traités collectifs', 49 *AIDI* (1961-I), 5, at 59. See also Briggs, *YILC* (1966-I), pt. II, at 221, paras. 31–2; Yasseen, para. 37; Reuter, para. 39; Rosenne, at 220, para. 28; Jiménez de Aréchaga, para. 29.

[64] See e.g. Bos, 'Hierarchy', at 366.   [65] Karl, *Vertrag*, at 257.

[66] See e.g. Guggenheim, *Traité*, at 113, 225; de Visscher, 'Cours général', at 79; Heilborn, 'Sources', at 29; Schwarzenberger, *International Law I*, i, at 535.

[67] *US Restatement of the Law of Foreign Relations* (Washington, 1986), i. 102, comment (*j*).

[68] Ibid., reporter's note 4.

of customary rule, but such a rule has no effect on the treaty unless it is followed by the parties to the treaty in their relations with one another.[69]

Under this view, treaty termination does not automatically follow the formation of new conflicting custom, even if it binds all parties. In addition, it must be shown that the parties' conduct evidences their specific intent to terminate or modify the treaty.

The following example illustrates how a treaty can be regarded as having been terminated by *desuetude* subsequent to the development of supervening custom. When the European Community proclaimed a 200-mile exclusive economic zone, Spanish vessels had fishing rights in the area between six and twelve miles off the coasts of a number of EC Member States by virtue of prior treaties. Spain and the EC concluded a new fisheries agreement adapted to the evolution of the customary law of the sea. Even before the conclusion of this agreement, the EC had set up and started implementing with the co-operation of the Spanish authorities a new licensing regime for Spanish vessels fishing within the EC 200-mile zone. In these circumstances, it could be considered that the prior fisheries treaties had been abrogated by supervening custom permitting States to exercise exclusive rights of fishing up to 200 miles from the coastline: by co-operating with the Community in the implementation of the new fisheries regime, Spain could be regarded as having tacitly agreed to the abrogation of her earlier treaty rights.[70]

Strictly speaking, in cases where *desuetude* takes place, the treaty is not terminated by new customary law but by tacit consent. In this context, it is accidental or immaterial that supervening custom has developed, because the legal basis of treaty termination is the tacit agreement of the parties.

There may be cases where a treaty is in conflict with supervening custom, but no evidence of the parties' specific intent to abrogate it can be found. Consider, for instance, the following situation. State A has declared a 200-mile exclusive fishery limit off its coasts in accordance with new custom on fisheries jurisdiction, but has not in any manner indicated its consent to the abrogation of its pre-existing treaty rights to fish within 200 miles off the coasts of other States. Cases of this kind are likely to arise because the generation of new customary law is not treaty-oriented. A State's consent to be bound by new custom will not, therefore, always be

---

[69] Akehurst, 'Hierarchy', at 275–6. Cf. O'Connell *International Law of the Sea*, ed. Shearer, i. at 46–7: 'since treaties can only fall into *desuetude* if the parties so intend,' a rule of the Law of the Sea which is set forth in a treaty is not easily subverted by the progress of customary law. But . . . it can be modified, especially where its stability is a matter of inference rather than of textual prescription'; Rosenne, *Developments*, at 9 n. 11.

[70] M. Akehurst, note on the *Burgoa Case, BYIL* (1981), at 355–6; note on *Tome, BYIL* (1982), at 327 n. 9. For an analysis of these cases, see below, Ch. 5.

accompanied by evidence of specific intent to abrogate any prior inconsistent treaty provisions.

In these cases *desuetude* cannot be established, and the abrogation of prior treaty rights can take place only if supervening custom *per se* is a ground of termination. Some authors consider that *desuetude* is only one of several ways in which customary law can terminate or modify a prior treaty.[71] If this is the case, the treaty may be abrogated either because the parties decide to let it lapse with a view to adapting it to new custom, or because one of the parties exercises the right to call for its abrogation.

Is *desuetude* Inherent in the Creation of New Custom?

It is sometimes suggested in the literature that the development of supervening custom that binds the parties to a prior treaty necessarily involves the *desuetude* of any conflicting treaty rules:

[A customary rule] creates a legal obligation for States to follow that one particular rule. Inherent in such obligation is, logically, the duty to abstain from applying another rule, whether customary or conventional, on the same subject-matter; otherwise, it would no longer be an obligation to follow one rule. . . . the obligation to adhere only to the customary rule is essential, since it entails and ensures that the latter shall command the necessary general and uniform State practice. If States adhere to other rules on the same subject-matter, the instances of practice will no longer suffice as evidence of the continuous existence of a new general customary rule. As a result, modification includes, and implies, *desuetude* of the conventional rule.[72]

Under this view, the conventional rule is considered to have passed out of use and fallen into *desuetude* if it is shown that new conflicting custom has developed. There is no need for the parties to express an intent or take specific measures to terminate the treaty: 'at that stage, denunciation clauses, or other formal means provided for amending or terminating the convention will have become irrelevant; failure to invoke them produces inconclusive results, since the conventional rule is *ex hypothesi* no longer in force.[73]

In our view, it is doubtful whether new custom necessarily implies a duty to abstain from applying another conventional rule on the same subject-matter. New customary law is created as a result of a consensus to change the general rules governing relations between States. The review of existing treaty rights and obligations is not part of this process and the *opinio juris* required for the formation of new custom does not establish an intent to abrogate prior treaty provisions.

Moreover, supervening custom and a prior conflicting treaty can exist in

---

[71] See e.g. Giraud, 'Modification', at 49–50.

[72] Villiger, *Customary International Law*, at 216. See also Karl, *Vertrag*, at 257.

[73] Villiger, *Customary International Law*.

parallel if the parties to the treaty wish to continue applying the conventional rule in their *inter se* relations. There is 'certainly room for a small conventional subsystem as a *lex prior specialis* alongside a general (incompatible) customary rule'.[74] It is, therefore, not appropriate to consider that treaty termination automatically follows the formation of new conflicting custom.

2.3.3. New Customary Law as a Ground of Treaty Termination or Revision

(a) Jus cogens

Under the Vienna Convention, 'if a new peremptory norm of general international law emerges, any existing treaty which is in conflict with that norm becomes void and terminates' (Article 64). For the purposes of the Convention, a peremptory norm of general international law, i.e. a rule of *jus cogens*,[75] is defined as 'a norm accepted and recognized by the international community of States as a whole as a norm from which no derogation is permitted and which can be modified only by a subsequent norm of general international law having the same character' (Article 53).[76] In order for a rule to become *jus cogens*, the international community as a whole[77] must, therefore, regard it not only as binding, but also as a rule from which States are not allowed to derogate by agreement.

The inclusion of the concept of *jus cogens* in the Vienna Convention was criticized in the literature.[78] It was feared that the notion of 'higher law',

[74] Ibid., at 217.

[75] See L. A. Alexidze, 'Legal Nature of *jus cogens* in Contemporary International Law', 172 *RC* (1981-III), at 219; Brownlie, *Principles*, at 512; J. A. Frowein, '*Jus cogens*', in *Max Planck Encyclopedia of Public International Law*, vii (1984), at 327; Guggenheim, *Traité*, at 128; K. Marek, 'Contribution à l'étude du *jus cogens* en droit international', in *Recueil d'études en droit en hommage à Paul Guggenheim* (Geneva, 1968), at 426; A. Gomez Robledo, 'Le *jus cogens* international: Sa genèse, sa nature, ses fonctions', 172 RC (1981-III), at 9; P. Reuter, *Introduction au droit des traités* (1972), at 118 *et seq.*; C. L. Rozakis, *The Concept of* jus cogens *in the Law of Treaties* (Amsterdam, 1976); G. Schwarzenberger, 'International "jus cogens"', 43 *Texas Law Review* (1965), at 455; *International Law and Order* (London, 1971), at 27; Sinclair, *The Vienna Convention*, at 203; J. Sztucki, Jus cogens *and the Vienna Convention on the Law of Treaties* (Vienna, 1974); M. Virally, 'Réflexions sur le *jus cogens*', 12 *AFDI* (1966), at 5; '*Cours général*', at 175; C. de Visscher, 'Positivisme et *jus cogens*', 75 *RGDIP* (1971), at 5.

[76] See proposal of Finland, Greece, and Spain at the Vienna Conference, *Conference Records*, First Session, 52nd Meeting (Evrigenis).

[77] But not necessarily every single State; see statement of the Chairman of the Drafting Committee (Yasseen), introducing to the Committee of the Whole the text of Article 53, *Official Records*, First Session, A/CONF. 39/11, 472. As to whether persistent objectors are bound by rules of *jus cogens*, in favour, Brownlie, *Principles*, at 514, Rozakis, *Concept*, at 78, U. Scheuner, 'Conflict of Treaty Provisions with a Peremptory Norm of General International Law and its Consequences', 27 *ZaöRV* (1967), 520, at 531; *contra*, G. J. H. van Hoof, *Rethinking the Sources of International Law* (1983), at 160 *et seq.*; K. Wolfke, '*Jus cogens* in International Law', 6 *PYIL* (1974), 145, at 149.

[78] See e.g. Schwarzenberger, *International Law and Order*, at 39–40, 50, 53; de Visscher, 'Positivisme', at 9; Marek, 'Contribution'.

which found little support in State practice or the case law of international tribunals,[79] had strong natural-law connotations and would be difficult to reconcile with positivism.

The International Law Commission, on the other hand, took the view that international law contained imperative norms[80] whose generation was compatible with positivism, because it was based on State practice.[81] At the Vienna Conference, the provisions on *jus cogens* were adopted by a substantial majority of States,[82] and the criticisms voiced by some related mainly to the procedures for the settlement of disputes concerning *jus cogens*.[83]

However, the notion of *jus cogens* still remains controversial.[84] Opinions are sharply divided on the subject, especially when it comes down to specifying whether a particular rule has the character of *jus cogens*.[85]

A rule of *jus cogens* can manifest itself in different forms, written or unwritten.[86] However, there is a clear distinction between a peremptory rule based on State practice and an ordinary customary rule. A peremptory rule is not simply binding but also a rule from which no derogations by agreement are allowed, while an ordinary customary rule admits exceptions in the form of special rules and regimes.

In view of the differences between peremptory norms and ordinary custom, it is generally accepted that Article 64 does not apply to treaty termination by new custom other than *jus cogens*. Treaty termination pursuant to Article 64 is seen as the logical consequence of the character of *jus cogens* as 'an overriding rule depriving any act or situation which is in conflict with it of legality'.[87] Ordinary custom does not have the same character and its effect on prior incompatible treaties needs to be addressed separately.

(b) Fundamental Change of Circumstances

A number of authors take the view that in certain circumstances treaty termination by new customary law may be the result of the application of

[79] Capotorti, 'L'Extinction', at 521.

[80] *YILC* (1966-II), at 247: 'the view that . . . there is no rule of international law from which States can not at their own free will contract out has become increasingly difficult to sustain.'

[81] See statements by Sir Waldock in *YILC* (1963-II), at 75, and at the Vienna Conference, A/CONF. 39/11, at 356.

[82] Article 53 was adopted by 87 votes to 8 (Australia, Belgium, France, Liechtenstein, Luxembourg, Monaco, Switzerland, and Turkey) with 12 abstentions and Article 64 by 84 votes to 8 (same as before) with 16 abstentions, Doc. A/CONF. 39/11/Add. 1, at 107, 125.

[83] With the exception of Turkey, Australia, Belgium, and Switzerland.

[84] See Sinclair, *The Vienna Convention*, at 24: 'The mystery of *jus cogens* remains a mystery . . . it has some of the attributes of the Cheshire Cat which has the disconcerting habit of vanishing and then reappearing to deliver further words of wisdom.'

[85] See ibid., at 215 *et seq.* For examples of rules of *jus cogens*, see *YILC* (1966-II), at 248 (the UN provisions on the use of force, the prohibition of trade in slaves, piracy, or genocide, the principle of self-determination); see also Judge Ammoun's separate opinion in the *Barcelona Traction Company Case*, ICJ Reports (1970), at 304.

[86] *YILC* (1966-II), at 248.   [87] Ibid., at 261.

the *rebus sic stantibus* rule. Examples of the application of the rule cited in the literature include the effect of developments in the law of the sea on the 1964 London Fisheries Convention[88] and the 1961 Exchange of Notes governing the fishery relations between the United Kingdom and Iceland,[89] and the effect of the UN provisions regarding human rights on the minorities treaties.[90]

This view finds support in the holding of the International Court of Justice in the *Fisheries Jurisdiction Case* to the effect that in principle 'changes in the law may under certain conditions constitute valid grounds for invoking a change of circumstances affecting the duration of a treaty'.[91] It is based on the assumption that the changed circumstances constituting the essential basis of the consent of the parties to be bound by the treaty can be not only factual but also circumstances of law.[92]

It is considered that legal changes may bring the treaty to an end under the same conditions required for the application of the *rebus sic stantibus* rule in general. These are contained in Article 62 of the Vienna Convention, which the International Court of Justice regarded as 'in many respects, a codification of existing customary law' on the subject of treaty termination on account of a fundamental change of circumstances.

Article 62 provides that

a fundamental change of circumstances which has occurred with regard to those existing at the time of the conclusion of a treaty and which was not foreseen by the parties, may not be invoked as a ground for terminating or withdrawing from the treaty unless:

(a) the existence of those circumstances constituted an essential basis of the consent of the parties to be bound by the treaty; and
(b) the effect of the change is radically to transform the extent of obligations still to be performed under the treaty . . .[93]

---

[88] H. G Schermers, note on *A.-G.* v. *Burgoa*, 18 *Common Market Law Review* (1981), 227, at 230; Ch. Vallée, 'Sur quelques poursuites engagées contre les pêcheurs espagnols ayant pratiqué la pêche dans les eaux territoriales ou dans la zone économique de la France', 83 *RGDIP* (1979), 220, at 231; Ch. Philip, note on *Arbelaiz–Emazabel Tome* v. *Procureur de la République*; *Procureur de la République* v. *Yurrita. AFDI* (1981), 322, at 327. *Contra*, R. R. Churchill and N. G. Foster, 'The Spanish Fishermen's Cases', 36 *ICLQ* (1987), 504 at 515.

[89] S. A. Tiewul, 'The Fisheries Jurisdiction Case and the Ghost of *rebus sic stantibus*', 6 *New York University Journal of International Law and Politics* (1973), at 455.

[90] 'Study of the Legal Validity of the Undertakings concerning Minorities', undertaken by the Secretariat-General of the United Nations, UN Doc. E/CN. 4/367, 7 Apr. 1950; Jiménez de Aréchaga, 'General Course', at 75–6.

[91] *Fisheries Jurisdiction Case,* ICJ Reports (1973), at 18. For an analysis of the case, see Ch. 5.   [92] Jiménez de Aréchaga, 'General Course'.

[93] For treaty revision on account of a fundamental change of circumstances, see ILC Commentary to the final Draft, *YILC* (1966-II), at 275; Sir H. Waldock, *YILC* (1963-I), at 157; Reuter, P. Reuter, *Introduction au droit des traités* (Paris, 1985), at 156–7; Rousseau, *Droit international public*, at 207, 229–30; *Principes généraux de droit international public* (Paris 1944), i, at 590.

The decision of the ILC to omit the issue of treaty modification by new custom from its final Draft on the law of treaties[94] revived interest in Article 62 as a legal basis of treaty termination on account of new customary law. Although the text of Article 62 does not limit itself to factual circumstances, it is not clear from the *travaux préparatoires* of the Vienna Convention whether it was intended to cover legal changes as well.[95] Initially, Article 62 provided that an essential change in the circumstances forming the basis of the treaty must have taken place 'with respect to *a fact or state of facts* which existed when the treaty was entered into'.[96] This expression was changed to '*a fact or situation* existing at the time when the treaty was entered into',[97] until the term 'circumstances' was finally used in the 1966 ILC Draft[98] and in the text of the Convention.

In our view, the significance of these drafting changes is uncertain. If anything, since the question of treaty termination or modification on account of legal changes was addressed separately when the Convention was drafted, it was probably not envisaged that Article 62 would serve as a vehicle for the adaptation of treaties to new custom.[99] This conclusion would be consistent with the negative formulation of Article 62, which was intended to emphasize that the application of the *rebus sic stantibus* rule should be exceptional.[100]

The possibility of using Article 62 to cover treaty termination by new custom becomes even more doubtful when the specific requirements for the application of the *rebus sic stantibus* rule are examined. In the *Fisheries Jurisdiction Case*, the International Court of Justice held that, in order for the *rebus sic stantibus* rule to apply, the legal changes must be far-reaching enough to alter the contractual balance of rights and obligations. This would be the case, if the changed circumstances had increased 'the burden of the obligations to be executed to the extent of rendering the performance something essentially different from that originally undertaken'.[101]

In the *Fisheries Jurisdiction Case* it was held that the evolution of the law of the sea had not altered the balance of rights and obligations of the fisheries agreement in question, because one of its aims was specifically to provide for a compulsory settlement mechanism in cases of disputes arising out of a change in the law.[102] It is possible that this condition will also not be met in other cases of conflict between custom and a prior

---

[94] See below, Ch. 6.   [95] Ibid.

[96] Article 22 of Waldock's Second Report on the Law of Treaties, *YILC* (1963-II), at 249 *et seq*. Cf. Article 22, para. 2 of Fitzmaurice's Second Report, *YILC* (1957-II), at 32–3.

[97] Article 44, *YILC* (1966-II), at 207.

[98] Article 59, *YILC* (1966-II), at 256; see also *YILC* (1966-I, pt. I), at 130.

[99] See Nguyen Quoc Dinh, Dailler, and Pellet, *Droit international public*, at 285; Poch de Caviades, 'Clause *rebus sic stantibus*', at 136.

[100] ILC Commentary to the Final Draft, *YILC* (1966-II), at 259; see also Sir Humphrey Waldock, *YILC* (1966-I), pt. I, at 85–6; Tunkin, *YILC* (1963-I), at 155.

[101] *Fisheries Jurisdiction Case* (1973), para. 43, at 21.   [102] See Ch. 6.

treaty. Consider, for instance, the effect of the evolution of the law of the sea on the 1964 London Fisheries Convention, which is cited as an example of the application of the *rebus sic stantibus* rule. The Convention gave fishing rights to vessels of third countries within a twelve-mile zone from the coasts of EC Members States. Following the development of new custom permitting coastal States to exclude third countries from the exploitation of fishery resources beyond twelve and up to 200 miles from the coasts, the parallel existence of the prior treaty and the new custom created an anomalous situation. However, strictly speaking, the burden of the treaty obligations under the 1964 Convention did not increase as a result of the development of the new custom.

A distinction should, in our view, be made between those cases where a treaty provision is in conflict with more recent custom and those cases in particular where the change of the general law affects the implementation of a treaty. The question of the application of the *rebus sic stantibus* rules arises only in respect of the second category of cases.

The Theory of the Implied Term

According to the theory of the 'implied term', a change of circumstances brings a treaty to an end only when it can be established that the parties would have envisaged to terminate the treaty, if they had foreseen the changes:

What puts an end to the treaty is the disappearance of the foundation upon which it rests; or if we prefer to put the matter subjectively, the treaty is ended because we can infer from its terms that the parties, though they have not said expressly what was to happen in the event which has occurrred, would, if they had foreseen it, have said that the treaty ought to lapse. In short the *clausula* is a rule of construction . . . attempting not to defeat but to fulfil the intention, or as the English cases call it the 'presumed intention' of the parties.[103]

If this theory were adopted, a change in customary law could be regarded as a fundamental change of circumstances affecting the continued validity of the treaty only if this was the intention of the parties. In any event, the ILC rejected the theory of the 'implied term' in the belief that it would increase the risk of subjective interpretations of the *rebus sic stantibus* rule, and decided to formulate the conditions of application Article 62 in objective terms.[104]

---

[103] See Grotius, *De jure belli ac pacis: The Classics of International Law*, trans. W. Kelsey, 3 vols. (1925), bk. II, ch. XVI on Interpretation, XXV, XXII, at 423; Brierly, *The Law of Nations*, ed Waldock, 336–7; C. Hill, 'The Doctrine of *rebus sic stantibus*', 3 *The University of Missouri Studies* (1934), 2, at 8–9; O. J. Lissitzyn, 'Treaties and Changed Circumstances', 61 *AJIL* (1967), 895, at 896.

[104] *YILC* (1966-II), at 258. On the subjective elements of the present formulation of Article 62, see Lissitzyn, 'Treaties', at 898.

2.4. CONCLUSION

Although the literature accepts the possibility of treaty termination or modification as a result of the emergence of new custom, opinions differ as to its legal basis. It is suggested by some that the parties' consent can be the only legal basis of treaty termination or modification following the development of new custom, while others consider that a prior incompatible treaty can be brought to an end or revised as a result of the application of a rule of general international law. In the latter case, termination or modification can occur either automatically or as a result of the act of one party exercising a power conferred to it by general law.

Despite their disagreement about the precise legal basis and method of treaty termination or revision on account of supervening custom, it can be said that all these different approaches share the same concern—that is, how to adapt obsolete agreements to changed conditions without undermining the principle of *pacta sunt servanda*. In this context each approach takes account of the intention of the contracting parties to a varying degree. In cases where treaty termination is based on *desuetude*, intention is the only determining factor. By contrast, other approaches base termination on objective elements flowing from the character of the international legal system or from notions of justice, and the parties' intention becomes relevant when their ability to create special treaty regimes is discussed.

3

State Practice: The Impact of the New Law of the Sea on Prior Fisheries Agreements

In this century customary international law regarding fishery limits underwent considerable changes leading to the recognition of extended fishing zones first of twelve and subsequently of 200 miles. These developments called into question the continued validity of fisheries agreements concluded under the old legal regime.

This chapter reviews a number of instances from State practice in this field that illustrate the untenability of treaty law in the face of general legal developments.

3.1. THE EVOLUTION OF THE GENERAL LAW ON FISHERIES JURISDICTION

In the late eighteenth century the range of cannons from the shore was generally considered as the outer limit within which coastal States could exercise sovereign rights in the areas adjacent to their coastal belt. In 1794 the United Stated adopted, for neutrality purposes, three miles as the supposed equivalent of the maximum range of cannons from the shore. This was the first step towards what became in State practice the general limit for the territorial sea and the exercise of fisheries jurisdiction.

A number of conventions concluded in the nineteenth and in the early twentieth century—such as the 1818 Anglo-American Convention, the 1839 Anglo-French Convention, the 1882 North Sea Fisheries Convention, and the 1901 Anglo-Danish Fisheries Agreement[1]—reinforced this trend by setting three miles as the limit of the territorial sea in general or for fishing purposes in particular. Moreover, legislation in various jurisdictions excluded foreigners from fishing within three miles from the coast or at least in the State's territorial waters.[2] As a result, by the end of the nineteenth century, the distinction was clearly made in State practice between an area of exclusive fisheries jurisdiction of the coastal State extending, in the absence of special agreement, up to three miles from the shore and, beyond that, the area of the high seas where fishing was free for all.

---

[1] See below, this chapter. For similar conventions of the same period, see G. Gidel, *Le Droit international public de la mer*, iii (1934), at 69 *et seq.*

[2] See O'Connell, *International Law of the Sea*, ed. Shearer, i, at 520 *et seq.*

State practice in the twentieth century moved in the direction of increasing exclusive fishery limits. Especially after the 1940s and 1950s States made claims to preferential or exclusive fishing rights in areas adjacent to their coasts beyond the traditional three-mile limit. Overexploitation of fishery resources and the need to conserve stocks, especially but not exclusively in cases where the local population was dependent on fishing, were the main reasons for these claims.

The solution to the problem of extended fisheries jurisdiction was originally sought in increasing the limits of the territorial sea. The question of the extent of fisheries jurisdiction became, however, gradually separated from the notion of the territorial sea, and State practice developed instead towards the creation of adjacent zones of exclusive fisheries jurisdiction.

Claims for extended fishery zones were opposed by some States. When the First Conference on the Law of the Sea was convened in Geneva in 1958 it was not possible to reach agreement on the extent of coastal State jurisdiction over its offshore fisheries. Fishing was not included among the powers of the coastal State within its twelve-mile contiguous zone. A US 6-plus-6 proposal[3] provided for six miles as the maximum breadth of the territorial sea and for coastal State exclusive fishing rights and fisheries jurisdiction within a twelve-mile zone, subject to the right of habitual foreign fishermen to continue fishing in the outer six miles of the zone. This proposal was not finally adopted, being seven votes short of the required two-thirds majority.[4]

An Icelandic proposal calling for preferential treatment of the coastal State in situations where the local population was exceptionally dependent on coastal fisheries equally failed to obtain the majority required for adoption by the Conference. However, in the end a resolution was adopted urging fishing nations to co-operate with the coastal State in order to establish measures that would recognize the preferential requirements of the coastal State and at the same time take account of the interests of other States.[5]

The general trend towards an extended fisheries jurisdiction became more apparent at the 1960 Conference, where proposals based on the idea of fishery zones beyond the three-mile limit were favoured by a considerable number of States. One of these proposals put forward by the United States and Canada provided for six miles as the maximum breadth of the territorial sea and for twelve miles as the limit of coastal State exclusive fisheries jurisdiction. The rights of habitual fishermen in the six-to-twelve-mile zone would gradually be phased out.[6] None of the proposals put

---

[3] A/CONF. 13/C.1/L.159/Rev. 2.

[4] 45 votes in favour, 33 against, and 7 abstentions, see UNCLOS *II, Plenary Meetings* (A/CONF. 13/38), 39.

[5] A/CONF. 13/L.56, UNCLOS *I, Official Records*, ii. 144.

[6] A/CONF. 1/L.11; amended by Brazil, Cuba, and Uruguay, A/CONF. 1/L.12; one vote short of the required majority for adoption: 54 votes in favour, 28 against, and 5 abstentions.

forward at the Conference attained the required two-thirds majority for adoption.

Despite the failure of the two Geneva Conferences to agree on a new limit for fisheries jurisdiction, the three-mile rule for fisheries purposes continued to be eroded in State practice. On the basis of the generality of State practice in the 1960s, the International Court of Justice concluded in the 1974 *Fisheries Jurisdiction Case* involving Iceland and the United Kingdom that the concept of a twelve-mile fishery zone, within which a State was entitled to claim fisheries jurisdiction independently of its territorial sea, had become customary law.[7] Moreover, the concept of preferential fishing rights of the coastal State in situations where the local population was especially dependent on coastal fisheries had also become generally accepted in State practice. These preferential fishing rights should be implemented by agreement between all States concerned and, in case of disagreement, by recourse to the means for the peaceful settlement of disputes provided in Article 33 of the United Nations Charter.[8]

Following the judgment of the Court, State practice continued to evolve towards the creation of wider areas of exclusive fisheries jurisdiction. By 1978, thirty-eight coastal States had claimed 200-mile exclusive economic zones and another twenty-three, including the United States, the USSR, and the United Kingdom, had adopted a 200-mile exclusive fishery zone. On the basis of the consensus emerging from the the Third UN Law of the Sea Conference, the text of the 1982 Law of the Sea Convention provided for a 200-mile exclusive economic zone within which the coastal state had sovereign rights for the purpose of exploring and exploiting, conserving and managing the living and non-living resources of the sea (Articles 55–75). With regard to fishing in particular, the coastal State was given exploitation rights to the extent of its capacity to harvest. The coastal State could determine which other States would have access to the surplus of the allowable catch taking into account all relevant factors, including the significance of the living resources of the area to the economy of the coastal State concerned and its other national interests, the situation of landlocked or geographically disadvantaged States, and the need to minimize economic dislocation in States whose nationals had habitually fished in the area or had made substantial efforts in research and identification of stocks (Article 62). The management of highly migratory species (Article 64) and of marine mammals (Articles 65 and 120) was made subject to specific international considerations.

It is generally accepted that the right of the coastal State to exercise exclusive jurisdiction over fisheries within 200 miles from its shores has become in State practice the new rule of customary international law. In

---

[7] ICJ Reports (1974), at para. 52.   [8] Ibid., at para. 57.

the 1982 *Continental Shelf Case* (*Tunisia* v. *Libya*) the ICJ observed that the 200-mile exclusive economic zone 'may be regarded as part of modern international law'.[9] More recently, in the 1985 *Continental Shelf Case* (*Libya* v. *Malta*), it was in the Court's view 'incontestable that the institution of the exclusive economic zone . . . is shown by State practice to have become a part of customary law'.[10]

3.2. FISHERIES IN THE NORTH PACIFIC (RUSSIA–JAPAN)

The Original Treaties

Under the 1905 Treaty of Peace between Russia and Japan,[11] Russia engaged 'to arrange with Japan for granting to Japanese subjects rights of fishery along the coasts of the Russian possessions in the Japan, Okhotsk and Bering Seas'.[12] The 1905 Treaty contained no provision for termination or denunciation.

In implementation of the 1905 Treaty, a fisheries convention was signed in 1907,[13] by virtue of which Russia granted to Japanese subjects 'the right to catch, to take and to prepare all kinds of fish and aquatic products, except fur seals and sea otters along the coasts of the Russian possessions in the Japan, Okhotsk and Bering Seas', excluding a number of rivers and inlets enumerated in Annex I of the Convention (Article I).

The Convention stated that it applied to the Russian territorial waters,[14] without, however, specifying their outer limit. Under Article IX Japanese and Russian subjects were placed on an equal footing with regard to laws, regulations, or ordinances, in force or to be enacted, concerning all fisheries matters. Russia engaged to inform the Japanese Government of any such laws and regulations six months before their entry into force. The Treaty was subject to revision or renewal by common agreement of the parties after twelve years from its entry into force.

The Dispute

In 1911 Russia enacted a 'Law Establishing Rules for Sea-Fishing'[15] in the Pacific applicable to a distance of twelve miles from the coasts. Within this area fishing was allowed only 'with an arrangement of special permits'.

---

[9] ICJ Reports (1982), at 74.
[10] ICJ Reports (1985), at para. 34. See also *Gulf of Maine Case*, ICJ Reports (1984), at para. 94.
[11] Treaty of Portsmouth of 23 Aug. 1905, 98 *Br. & For. State Papers* (1904–5), at 735.
[12] Article XI.
[13] Fishery Treaty of 15 July 1907, 101 *Br. & For. State Papers* (1907–8), at 453.
[14] See Annex I, at 457.
[15] Law of 29 May 1911, Enclosure in Despatch from Mr Wheeler, US Chargé d'affaires at Petersburg to the Secretary of State, *For. Relations of the US* (1912), at 1302–3.

The 1911 Law was notified to the Japanese Government pursuant to the provisions of the 1907 Treaty.

Russia's ultimate goal was to exercise control over fisheries within twelve miles from all her coasts,[16] and she had already claimed jurisdiction for customs purposes in that area by a 1909 Customs Law.[17] The Russian position was that general international law did not contain a generally accepted rule relating to the extent of territorial waters. As a result, in the absence of treaty provisions to the contrary, the determination of the limits within which jurisdiction over the marginal seas could be exercised was a question of domestic regulation,[18] subject only to the possibility of effective control from the land. This was to be determined by the range of the cannon from the shores, which at that time extended to twelve miles.[19]

Japan, a strong advocate of three miles as the maximum limit of a State's coastal jurisdiction, protested against the 1911 Law. She contended that the Law was contrary not only to international law, but also to the spirit of the 1907 Russo-Japanese Fishery Agreement.[20]

Russia was determined to maintain the twelve-mile limit for fisheries purposes as a general policy, but agreed to hold discussions with Japan in view of the particularities of her case.[21] Although, in her view, the new twelve-mile limit did not conflict with international law,[22] she conceded that the 1911 Law did not abrogate nor alter Japan's rights under the 1907 Convention. Japanese vessels were consequently allowed to continue fishing in their traditional grounds between three and twelve miles from the coasts.[23]

After the expiry of the 1907 Convention in 1919, fishing by Japanese vessels in Russian waters was carried out on the basis of provisional fisheries arrangements. In 1925 a Convention of Friendship and Economic Co-operation intended to establish the basic rules of the relations between Japan and the Soviet Government[24] dealt with all international agreements concluded before the Communist Revolution. The USSR agreed that the 1905 Fisheries Treaty of Portsmouth should remain in force[25] and that the

[16] Ibid., at 1304. The United Kingdom protested against Russia's efforts to enforce a twelve-mile fisheries limit in the White Sea and off Archangel, ibid., at 1298, 1304.

[17] See Enclosure in Despatch from the US Ambassador to the Secretary of State, ibid., at 1288–9; for UK protests, ibid., at 1287, 1288.

[18] Ibid., at 1305; with regard to customs supervision, ibid., at 1288.

[19] Ibid., at 1299, 1305.   [20] Ibid., at 1305.

[21] Statements by the Russian Minister of Foreign Affairs to the US Ambassador, ibid., at 1305.

[22] Enclosure in Despatch from the US Chargé d'affaires to the American Secretary of State, ibid., at 1308.

[23] 4 *Whiteman's Digest in International Law*, at 1148; Z. Ohira, 'Fishery Problems between Soviet Russia and Japan', 2 *Japanese Annual of International Law* (1958), at 1.

[24] Convention of 20 Jan. 1925, 122 *Br. & For. State Papers* (1925), at 894.

[25] Article 2, para. 1.

1907 Agreement should be revised to take into consideration such changes in the general conditions as may have occurred since its conclusion.[26]

A fisheries agreement modelled upon the 1907 Convention was signed on 23 January 1928.[27] It granted Japanese subjects fishing rights off the Russian coasts in the Japan, Okhotsk, and Behring Seas, but reduced the number of bays and inlets open to Japanese fishing. The agreement stated that it did not apply to the high seas,[28] but did not specify the extent of Russia's territorial waters.

The exercise of the fishing rights granted by the 1928 Agreement was the subject of numerous disputes between the two countries. Their outcome was the gradual reduction of Japanese fishing activities off the Russian coasts.[29] In 1936, when the agreement expired in accordance with its terms, it was extended by a *modus vivendi* for one year, and then on each succeeding year by other temporary arrangements which further reduced Japanese fishing rights. More restrictions were imposed by a five-year fisheries agreement concluded in March 1944.[30]

The erosion of Japanese fishing rights continued after the Second World War, when the general trend towards a twelve-mile fishery limit gained momentum, and the USSR became more assertive in her claims over a wider territorial sea. In the end Japan lost her fishing rights in Soviet waters granted by the Treaty of Portsmouth.[31]

Conclusions

Two stages of the dispute can be distinguished. Until 1919 fisheries relations between the parties were governed by the 1907 Agreement concluded in implementation of the Portsmouth Convention. After 1919, when the 1907 Agreement came to an end, the Portsmouth Convention continued to be in force, but the fishing rights it granted to Japan were gradually adjusted following developments in the general law on fisheries.

When the dispute first arose, the precise scope of the 1907 Agreement was a matter of controversy between the parties. Japan's claim that the extension of Russia's fishing zone was contrary to the spirit of the 1907 Agreement reflected the view that the agreement indirectly prevented Russia from claiming jurisdiction beyond three miles from her coasts. Although the Agreement did not define the extent of Russia's 'territorial waters', it could have been interpreted as setting the outer limit of the parties' exclusive fisheries jurisdiction at three miles, because this was the generally accepted rule at the time of its conclusion.

By contrast, according to a different interpretation of the provisions of

---

[26] Article 3.   [27] 129 *Br. & For. State Papers* (1928-II), at 769.
[28] See Annex I, at 775, 776.   [29] Ohira, 'Fishery Problems', at 4.
[30] Mentioned in 4 *Whiteman's Digest in International Law*, at 1149.
[31] Ohira, 'Fishery Problems', at 9.

the 1907 Agreement, the treaty grant of fishing rights to Japan was meant to apply in the area over which Russia could claim exclusive fisheries jurisdiction from time to time. As a result, the Agreement did not prevent a future extension of Russia's fishery limit beyond three miles in accordance with general international law, but only safeguarded Japan's fishing rights in that area. Presumably on the basis of this interpretation, Russia argued that the 1907 Agreement was compatible with the introduction of the twelve-mile limit and allowed Japan to continue fishing in the area between three and twelve miles from her coasts.

While the validity of Russia's jurisdictional claims was initially doubtful under general international law,[32] subsequently claims to fisheries jurisdiction beyond three miles became more and more frequent in State practice. When the 1907 Treaty expired in 1919, the Treaty of Portsmouth remained in force as the basis of the fisheries relations between the parties. The Treaty provided that Russia had to grant Japan fishing rights in her territorial waters by means of appropriate implementation agreements. The USSR agreed to reflect in the implementation agreement replacing the 1907 Treaty any changes in the general conditions that may have occurred in the meantime. Changes in the general law were not specifically mentioned in this respect, but it is significant that the gradual reduction and eventual disappearance of Japanese fishing rights in Russian waters paralleled the degree of general recognition of the twelve-mile limit.

3.3. FISHERIES OFF THE FAEROE ISLANDS (UNITED KINGDOM–DENMARK)

The United Kingdom and Denmark were parties to a 1901 Convention regulating fisheries outside the Danish territorial waters off the Faeroe Islands and Iceland.[33] The Convention provided that Danish subjects would enjoy the exclusive right of fishery within a distance of three miles from the coasts of the said islands. As amended in 1955,[34] it was not open to unilateral denunciation until 1965.

In 1957 the Danish Government decided to extend its exclusive fisheries jurisdiction around the Faeroe Islands from three to twelve miles. At the same time it notified the United Kingdom of its wish to reopen negotiations

---

[32] Compensation was given by Russia to a number of UK vessels arrested for fishing in the White Sea between three and twelve miles from the coasts following the introduction of the 1911 Law; see P. C. Jessup, *The Law of Territorial Waters and Maritime Jurisdiction* (New York, 1927), at 30.

[33] Signed at London on 24 June 1901, *Br. & For. State Papers* (1900–1), 29 *et seq.*

[34] Exchange of notes of 22 April 1955, *Br. & For. State Papers* (1955–6), 78 *et seq.*, at 80, para. 5.

concerning the Faeroese fishery limit.[35] Denmark stated that, '*from a long-term point of view*, the present state of affairs with regard to the fishery limits round the Faeroe Islands was untenable' and 'the Faeroese authorities were *justified in expecting to obtain an expansion of the fishing territory*' (emphasis added). The United Kingdom agreed in principle to open discussions with a view to revising the 1901 Agreement but suggested that the actual revision should be deferred until the results of the 1958 Geneva conference on the Law of the Sea were made known.[36] The negotiations were as a result postponed.

At the 1958 Conference Denmark supported a general extension of territorial waters up to six miles and the establishment of special fishing zones up to twelve miles in cases where the local population was exceptionally dependent on offshore fisheries, a principle which she advocated with the Faeroe Islands in mind.[37] After the end of the Conference and despite the failure to agree on the extent of coastal Sate fisheries jurisdiction, Denmark contended that State practice outside the Conference was developing towards the general recognition of fishery zones beyond a distance of three miles from the coasts: 'the negotiations at the Conference clearly revealed that *the trend towards an extension of the territorial waters, which has been noticeable in recent years, is gathering momentum*. If adopted, several of the proposals submitted to the conference would have resulted in a right to extend the present fishing territory round the Faeroe Islands very considerably' (emphasis added).[38]

A different legal argument in support of the revision of the 1901/1955 Agreement was put forward by the local Assembly of the Faeroe Islands (Lagting). In a resolution calling for the extension of fishery limits around the islands to twelve nautical miles as from 1 September 1958,[39] the Lagting stated that, 'after Iceland decided to extend the fishery limits to twelve nautical miles as from September 1, 1958, this fact altered the assumptions underlying the question of fishery limits to such a material degree that the Faeroe Islands must be regarded as having been released from the [1901/1955] convention'.[40] The Lagting feared that if Iceland finally succeeded in enforcing her claim to a twelve-mile fishing zone, the result would probably be greater exploitation by foreign trawlers of the Faeroese fishing grounds.[41]

To the extent that this argument was an allusion to the *rebus sic stantibus* rule, its validity was doubtful, if only because a fundamental change of circumstances does not automatically release a party from its treaty obligations.

---

[35] Danish memorandum of 25 June 1957, mentioned in the Danish memorandum of 18 June 1958, *ICLQ* (1959), at 171.

[36] Ibid., at 172.   [37] Danish memorandum of 18 June 1958, ibid., at 172.

[38] Ibid., at 171.   [39] Ibid.   [40] Ibid.

[41] *Keesing's*, 16489C; *ICLQ* (1959), 172. See also statement by the Faeroese Chief Minister, *Keesing's*, ibid.

This issue was not, in any event, discussed, because, according to the United Kingdom, the unilateral extension by Iceland of her fishery limit to twelve miles was unlawful under international law and consequently could not have altered the assumptions underlying the question of fishery limits, as alleged by the Lagting Resolution.[42]

The United Kingdom rejected the Danish demands for the revision of the 1901/1955 Agreement, arguing that under general international law the limit of territorial waters and of exclusive fisheries jurisdiction remained three miles from the coasts.[43] The alleged trend towards the establishment of extended fishery zones beyond the three-mile limit was not supported by State practice. In particular, the proposals that received the broadest measure of support by the States participating in the 1958 Conference 'would grant less to the Faeroes than the Faeroese Lagting has declared its intention of taking by unilateral action'.[44] The Conference recommended measures other than the establishment of special fishery zones in cases where the local population was exceptionally dependent on fisheries, and the US proposal, which received the greatest measure of support, recognized historic fishing rights such as those enjoyed by the United Kingdom.[45] A revision of the 1901 Agreement to accommodate Denmark's demands would encounter practical difficulties, because its terms would not automatically be accepted by other governments.[46]

Talks between the parties were, however, resumed in London on 12 September 1958 and the two governments exchanged views 'on the implications for the fisheries around the Faeroe islands of the Geneva Conference on the Law of the Sea and subsequent developments'.[47] In April 1959 the two parties agreed on a 'temporary regulation of fishing pending the entry into force of a general convention regulating the breadth of the territorial sea and fishery limits'.[48]

The 1959 Agreement prevented British vessels from fishing in an area of approximately six miles from the coasts off the Faeroe Islands (Article I), while between six and twelve miles, vessels which had historically fished around the islands were allowed to continue fishing in their traditional grounds (Article II). The agreement was inspired by the US 6-plus-6 proposal,[49] which was seven votes short of the two-thirds majority required for adoption at the 1958 Geneva Conference.[50]

---

[42] Reply by the United Kingdom to the Danish memorandum, 2 July 1958, *ICLQ* (1959), at 173.

[43] See statement of the UK representative in the Sixth Committee of the United Nations, 18 Nov. 1958, 9 *ICLQ* (1960), at 279.

[44] *ICLQ* (1959), at 175.   [45] Ibid., at 174.   [46] Ibid.   [47] *Keesing's*, 16489C.

[48] Exchange of notes of 27 Apr. 1959, 337 *UNTS*, at 416.

[49] A/CONF. 13/C.1/L.159/Rev. 2.

[50] 45 votes in favour, 33 against, and 7 abstentions, see *UN Conference on the Law of the Sea II, Plenary Meetings* (A/CONF. 13/38), 39.

The agreement was temporary in the hope that the Second UN Conference due to be held in 1960[51] would solve the question of fishery limits. In view of the forthcoming Conference the parties stated in the 1959 Exchange of Notes that 'nothing in the present agreement shall be deemed to prejudice the views held by either government as to the delimitation and the limits in international law of territorial waters or of exclusive jurisdiction in fishery matters'.[52] Following the failure of the Conference to reach agreement on the extent of the territorial sea, Denmark denounced the 1959 Agreement on 28 April 1962 and adopted a twelve-mile limit around the Faeroe Islands from 11 March 1964 despite Britain's protests.

This is an incident where claims for the revision of an international agreement were based on the evolution of the general law on fishery jurisdiction. Although the trend towards fishery zones beyond three miles had not probably yet become a generally recognized rule of customary law, it was alleged to be a sufficient ground for the revision of the 1901 Agreement.

This argument was made on the assumption that general customary law would inevitably evolve in a certain manner, and, as a result, was open to criticisms based on a different view of the present state of the law and its evolution. Negotiations between the parties were postponed in the hope that the legal uncertainties with regard to fishery limits would eventually be clarified.

It is significant, in this respect, that the United Kingdom did not claim that, irrespective of the evolution of the general law, the 1901/1955 treaty should in any event prevail as special law between the parties. This argument would be of no use after 1965, when the treaty was open to denunciation in accordance with its terms, but one would expect it to play some role in the preceding negotiations between the parties. In the end Denmark extended its fishery limit before 1965, after her efforts to reach a permanent settlement had failed and on the assumption that there was substantial support in state practice for the establishment of fishery zones beyond three miles.

3.4. FISHERIES IN THE NORTH ATLANTIC AND THE 1964 LONDON FISHERIES CONVENTION

In 1963, following the failure of the Second Geneva Conference on the Law of the Sea to reach agreement on the breadth of the territorial sea, Great Britain called a conference to discuss fisheries problems in the North Atlantic, including the question of fishery limits. At the same time and 'in

---

[51] GA Resolution VIII of 27 Apr. 1958, Doc. A/CONF. 13/L.56.   [52] Article VII.

order to regain freedom of action regarding the extent of fishery limits'[53] Britain gave notice of 'her intention to terminate her participation'[54] in the 1882 North Sea Fisheries Convention and the 1843 Fisheries Regulations issued pursuant to the 1839 Anglo-French Fishery Convention.

Both agreements adopted three miles as the outer limit of the parties' exclusive right of fishery in the waters adjacent to their coasts. By the 1839 Anglo-French Convention[55] it was agreed that French and British subjects would enjoy the exclusive right of fishery within a distance of three miles off the coasts of their respective countries.[56] The objective of the 1882 North Sea Fisheries Convention[57] was to regulate fisheries outside the territorial waters of the contracting parties.[58] For this purpose it set the outer limit of the parties' exclusive right of fishery at three miles from their respective coasts.[59]

Lord Privy Seal, Edward Heath, announcing in the House of Commons the British decision to terminate both fisheries conventions,[60] explained that there was an urgent need to re-examine the whole complex of fishery problems, because 'many of the international agreements regarding fisheries and our related legislation are very old and *many of their provisions are consequently obsolete*'.[61] He referred to the recent extensions by many countries of their fisheries jurisdiction beyond the three-mile limit and concluded that, '*in the present state of international law*, [the British Government] would be justified in no longer denying to British fishermen some extension of their exclusive rights in their own coastal waters' (emphasis added).[62]

Britain gave notice of termination of the 1882 Convention in accordance with its terms (Article XXXIX). However, the 1839 Anglo-French Convention contained no provisions for unilateral denunciation and France announced her intention to protest against Britain's action.[63] On the other hand, France was not adverse to a general revision of fishery limits through negotiations with all parties concerned[64] and agreed to seek a common solution to the problem by participating in the North Atlantic Fisheries

---

[53] Announcement of the Lord Privy Seal, Edward Heath, in the House of Commons, 29 Apr. 1963, 676 *HC Deb.* (5th ser.), col. 717.　　　　　　　　　　　　　　[54] Ibid.

[55] Convention for Defining and Regulating the Limits of the Exclusive Right of Oyster and other Fishery on the Coasts of Great Britain and France, signed at Paris, 2 Aug. 1839, 27 *Br. & For. State Papers* (1838–9), at 983 *et seq.*　　　　　　　　　　　　　　[56] Article IX.

[57] Signed at the Hague on 6 May 1882 between Germany, Belgium, Denmark, France, Great Britain, and the Netherlands, 73 *Br. & For. State Papers*, at 39.

[58] Article I.　　　[59] Article II.　　　[60] 676 *HC Deb.* (5th ser.), cols. 715 *et seq.*

[61] Ibid., col. 716.　　　[62] Ibid., col. 717.

[63] See statement by the French Minister of Transport and Public Works before the National Committee on Fisheries, see *The Times*, 4 May 1963; *RGDIP* (1963), at 643.

[64] D. H. N Johnson, 'European Fishery Limits', in *Developments in the Law of the Sea: 1958–1964* (British Institute of International and Comparative Law Special Publication, No. 6; 1965), 48 at 55.

Conference convened in London between 3 December 1963 and 2 March 1964.

The States participating in the Conference (Austria, Belgium, Denmark, France, Germany, Iceland, Ireland, Italy, Luxembourg, the Netherlands, Norway, Portugal, Spain, Sweden, Switzerland, and the United Kingdom) had different views as to the fishery limit that should be adopted.[65] Britain favoured an extension of the three-mile limit for fisheries jurisdiction, provided that traditional fishing rights were safeguarded, and claimed that this solution was in accordance with existing international law. Britain would extend its fishery limits beyond three miles, if the conference could not reach agreement on a new limit.[66] Iceland and Norway refused to accept fishery zones of less than twelve miles. The EC Member States, especially France, Germany, Belgium, and the Netherlands, took the position that under international law the maximum limit of a State's exclusive jurisdiction over fisheries was three miles and were unwilling to accept extended fishery zones.

The Conference finally reached agreement[67] on a fisheries regime of 'a permanent character'[68] that was incorporated in the 1964 Fisheries Convention. The Convention recognized the right of each contracting party to establish a fishery zone up to a distance of six miles from the coasts, within which it would enjoy the exclusive right to fish and exclusive jurisdiction over fisheries (Article 1, para. 1, in combination with Article 2). Within a belt between six and twelve miles from the coasts, the right to fish would be exercised only by the coastal State and by such other contracting parties the vessels of which had habitually fished in that belt between 1 January 1953 and 31 December 1962 (Article 3). The coastal state alone had the power to regulate fisheries in the six-to-twelve-mile zone, provided that there was no discrimination against the vessels of the other contracting parties (Article 5). The Convention guaranteed most-favoured-nation treatment to all contracting parties with regard to fishing rights in the twelve-mile zone (Article 8). It would be of unlimited duration, but denunciation would be possible after twenty years from its entry into force (Article 15).

The basis of the negotiations of the parties was the text of the joint

---

[65] D. Vignes, 'La Conférence européenne sur la pêche et le droit de la mer', *AFDI* (1964), 670, at 674–75.

[66] See opening statement by the British Representative at the London Conference, *Keesing's*, 19950A.

[67] Final Act of the European Fisheries Conference, containing the European Fisheries Convention of 1964, Protocol of Provisional Application and Agreements as to Transitional Rights, 58 *AJIL* (1964), at 1068, 1070, 1078, 1079; A. Boyer, 'La Notion d'eaux territoriales et la convention de Londres du 9 mai 1964', 69 *RGDIP* (1965), 1051, at 1063 *et seq.* Johnson, 'European Fishery Limits', 48, esp. at 55 *et seq.*, 61 *et seq.*; C. A. Fleisher, 'Norway's Policy on Fisheries', in *Developments in the Law of the Sea*, 92, at 93, 106 *et seq.*; Vignes, 'Conférence', at 670 *et seq.*   [68] Preamble to the Convention.

US–Canada 6-plus-6 proposal, which had failed by one vote to attain the required two-thirds majority at the 1960 Law of the Sea Conference.[69] The final text of the Convention was, however, inspired by the 6-plus-6 US proposal, short by seven votes of the necessary two-thirds majority at the 1958 Law of the Sea Conference, which safeguarded the rights of habitual fishermen in the six-to-twelve-mile zone. In contrast to both proposals, the London Convention determined the fishery limit but not the maximum breadth of the territorial sea, because agreement on this issue could not be reached at the Conference.[70]

The Convention provided for a phase-out period in the inner six miles of the twelve-mile fishing zone in order to allow fishermen who had habitually fished in the area to adapt themselves to their exclusion from that belt. In implementation of this provision, Great Britain allowed French, German, Irish, and Dutch fishing vessels to continue fishing up to three miles from the coast until 31 December 1965, and until 31 December 1966 in cases where straight baselines or bay-closing lines in excess of ten miles were drawn.[71]

It is interesting to note that the Convention did not distinguish in this respect between France, whose fishing rights were derived from the 1839 Convention, an international instrument of a permanent character, and the other countries, which claimed only traditional fishing rights based on usage. As a result of these arrangements, France no longer enjoyed the right to fish within three miles of the British coasts, except in certain areas specifically mentioned in Article 10, para. *d*, of the Convention, namely Granville Bay and the Minquiers and Ecréhous.

Granville Bay and the Minquiers and Ecréhous were treated as special cases even under the old conventional regime, the former by virtue of a Declaration made on 20 December 1928[72] and the latter by virtue of a Fisheries Agreement concluded between France and Great Britain on 30 January 1951.[73] The London Convention simply maintained in this respect a special regime, which the parties themselves had created in the past in derogation from general law. This arrangement was compatible with the creation of a new *general* fishing limit between the two countries.[74]

During the second reading of the new Fishery Limits Bill in Parliament[75] the British Minister of Agriculture, Fisheries, and Food explained that the 1883 Sea Fisheries Act that the Bill proposed to amend by

---

[69] See above.　　[70] See Vignes, 'Conférence', at 686–7.

[71] Agreement as to transitional rights, Article 1.　　[72] 1929 *UKTS*, No. 2, Cmd. 3254.

[73] 1952 *UKTS*, No. 4, Cmd. 8444.

[74] See the Exchange of Notes between France and the United Kingdom concerning the status of previous fisheries agreements between the two countries, 10 Apr. 1964 (Cmd. 2363).

[75] 696 *HC Deb.* (1963–4), cols. 944–1027. The Fisheries Limits Act entered into force on 30 Sept. 1964, SI 1964, No. 1553 (C. 20).

giving statutory effect to the principle of a 3-mile limit, introduced no innovation, but merely confirmed a situation then generally accepted in international law ... The 3-mile limit became generally, if not universally established during the last century, but since the last war it has become more and more challenged with an increasing number of states claiming wider fisheries jurisdiction for themselves.[76]

The Government had to change its thinking about the fishing limits, because, *inter alia,*

the practice of the states showed that it was *no longer realistic to regard three miles as the limit beyond which fisheries jurisdiction could not be recognised in international law. This is because so many States have extended their limits*... It was in these circumstances that Her Majesty's Government came to the conclusion that some extension of limits should no longer be denied to our own fishermen.... To that end we took steps a little more than a year ago to terminate certain treaty obligations, dating from the last century, so as to gain freedom of action for ourselves in this respect. (emphasis added)[77]

In the present case claims for the revision of the fishery limit were made on the basis of the evolution of the general law on fisheries and despite the existence of prior treaties restricting the United Kingdom's freedom of action with regard to the extent of its fishery limits. France, a party to a prior treaty of unlimited duration, objected to the unilateral termination of the 1839 Convention by the United Kingdom but agreed to participate in negotiations leading to a new treaty regime reflecting the supervening developments in the general law.

3.5. THE RENEGOTIATION OF FISHING RIGHTS IN CANADIAN WATERS[78]

3.5.1. The Establishment of a Twelve-Mile Fishery Zone

On 4 June 1963 the Canadian Prime Minister announced in the House of Commons that his Government intended to adopt a twelve-mile exclusive fishery zone, in order to prevent third countries from depleting Canada's fishery resources: 'in similar circumstances, an increasing number of countries have felt themselves compelled to abandon the three-mile limit. All told, more than 40 countries have already extended their territorial limits, and more than 50 countries their fisheries limits beyond three miles.'[79]

The proposed extension would affect a number of countries fishing in

---

[76] 696 *HC Deb.* (1963–4), col. 944.   [77] Ibid., col. 945; see also col. 952.
[78] See A. E. Gotlieb, 'The Canadian Contribution to the Concept of a Fishing Zone in International Law', 2 *CYIL* (1964), at 55; J.-Y. Morin, 'La Zone de pêche exclusive du Canada', ibid., at 77.   [79] *CYIL* (1964), at 288–90.

the waters off Canada's coasts. Two of these countries, the United States and France, enjoyed fishing rights by virtue of perpetual treaties concluded in the nineteenth and in the early twentieth century.

By virtue of the 1818 Convention of Commerce with Great Britain[80] the United States enjoyed 'for ever, in common with the subjects of His Britannic Majesty the liberty to take fish of every kind' on certain parts of the coast of Newfoundland and of the coast of Labrador (Article I). In return the United States 'renounced for ever the liberty heretofore enjoyed or claimed by the inhabitants thereof to take, dry or cure fish on or within three miles' off any other coasts not included in the agreement. The 1818 Convention was the first international agreement establishing three miles from the coast as the boundary between the area of exclusive coastal State fisheries jurisdiction and the high seas, where fishing was free for all. It set the pattern for the diplomatic negotiations leading to the adoption of the 1839 Anglo-French Convention and the 1882 North Sea Fisheries Convention.[81]

France derived its fishing rights in the Canadian territorial waters from a Convention concluded in 1904 with Great Britain.[82] Under the Convention France renounced the right to fish and dry fish on the French shore, which she enjoyed by virtue of Article XIII of the 1713 Treaty of Utrecht,[83] and retained in return the right to fish in the territorial waters off the coast of Newfoundland and between Cape St. John and Cape Ray passing by the north, on an equal footing with British subjects. The Convention did not specify the extent of Canada's territorial waters and contained no provision for denunciation.

It was announced that the proposed extension of Canada's fisheries jurisdiction would take into account the historic and treaty fishing rights of France and the United States.[84] By contrast, traditional fishing rights claimed by other countries on the basis of usage were 'not quite the same'.[85]

The Canadian Territorial Sea and Fishing Zones Act enacted in 1964[86] provided for a three-mile territorial sea and for an exclusive fishing zone extending up to nine miles from the outer limit of the territorial waters.

---

[80] Signed in London on 20 Oct. 1818, 6 *Br. & For. State Papers* (1818–19), at 3 *et seq.* See also fisheries agreement regulating the liberties granted by the 1818 Convention signed on 20 July 1912, 105 *Br. & For. State Papers*, at 284 *et seq.*

[81] For the history of the agreement, see O'Connell, *International Law of the Sea*, ed. Shearer, i, at 133–4, 513–14.

[82] Respecting Newfoundland and West and Central Africa, signed on 8 Apr. 1904, 97 *Br. & For. State Papers*, 31 *et seq.* On the history of the Convention, see O'Connell *International Law of the Sea*, ed. Shearer, i, at 511.

[83] See 35 *Br. & For. State Papers*, at 843, as confirmed or modified by subsequent provisions, namely the 1763 Treaty of Paris, *Hertslet's Commercial Treaties*, i, at 238, art. 5, and the 1783 Treaty of Versailles, 1 *Br. & For. State Papers*, at 424.

[84] Statement made by the Canadian Prime Minister, *CYIL* (1964), at 289.

[85] Ibid., at 290.   [86] 3 *ILM* (1964), at 922.

The Coastal Fisheries Protection Act of the same year[87] exempted from the application of the Fisheries Act a number of countries fishing in Canadian waters, namely the United States of America, France, Britain, Portugal, Spain, Italy, Norway, and Denmark, as an interim measure until the conclusion of their ongoing negotiations with Canada. Canada's intention was to allow US and French vessels to continue fishing in their traditional grounds within the twelve-mile zone and to exclude all other traditional fishermen from that area, after a phase-out period, which would give them time to adjust to the new regime.[88]

The United States followed suit in 1966 by establishing its own exclusive fishing zone to a distance of nine miles from the outer limit of the territorial sea, subject to the continuation of such traditional fishing by foreign States and their nationals as may be recognized by the United States.[89] The position of the Department of State was that the creation of the zone 'would not be contrary to international law', because of recent developments in State practice: 'since the 1960 Law of the Sea Conference there has been a trend toward the establishment of a twelve-mile fisheries rule in international practice . . . Such actions have no doubt been accelerated by the support for the proposals made at the Geneva Law of the Sea Conference in 1958 and 1960 of a fisheries zone totalling twelve miles as part of a package designed to achieve international agreement on the territorial sea.'[90]

The creation of twelve-mile fishing zones by the United States and Canada was followed by the signature of a two-year fishery agreement in 1970,[91] which allowed nationals of each country to continue fishing between three and twelve miles from the coasts of the other, except for certain species of fish. Nothing in the agreement was to prejudice the claims or views of either party concerning fisheries jurisdiction or territorial waters nor affect bilateral or multilateral agreements to which either government was a party.

3.5.2. The Establishment of a Twelve-Mile Territorial Sea

In 1970 a bill was introduced in Parliament providing for the extension of Canada's territorial waters to twelve miles from the baselines. Canada alleged that international law provided a sound basis for the proposed

[87] 3 *ILM* (1964), at 925.

[88] Statement of the Canadian Minister of State for External Affairs, *HC Deb.* (Can.), 20 May 1964, at 3410–11; ibid., 4 June 1969, repr. in *CYIL* (1970), at 347: 'Apart from traditional fishing rights, the United States and France also have treaty rights off Canada's coasts and these rights will of course be respected.'   [89] 61 *AJIL* (1967), at 658.

[90] Department of State, letter of the Assistant Secretary for Congressional relations to the Chairman of the US Senate Committee on Commerce, 60 *AJIL* (1966), at 831–2.

[91] Signed on 20 Apr. 1970, 21 *US Treaties and Other International Agreements*, at 1283.

extension, because the twelve-mile limit for the territorial sea was generally acceptable, or at least it was certain that the law was developing in that direction: 'this is following some almost sixty nations of the world which have done that. We are absolutely certain that international law is moving from the three to the twelve mile limit ... the law exists, it may be developing from three miles to twelve, but the law exists.'[92]

The United States protested against Canada's action, on the grounds that unilateral extensions of jurisdiction on the high seas were contrary to international law.[93] The United States would be willing to accept the twelve-mile limit for territorial waters only as part of an agreed international treaty also providing for freedom of passage through and over international straits.

In reply to the United States, Canada reaffirmed her position that customary law allowed such extensions. She referred to the establishment of territorial seas of twelve miles or more by some forty-five States as 'overwhelming evidence of the fact that international law can be and is developed by State practice'.[94]

Following the enactment of the Territorial Sea and Fishing Zones Act of 1970[95] Canada announced its intention to conclude the negotiations started in 1964 with countries whose nationals had fished in Canadian waters with a view to phasing out their fishing activities in the twelve-mile territorial sea.[96] On 27 March 1972 four phasing-out agreements were signed with Denmark, France, Portugal, and Britain.[97] As explained above, out of the four States only France enjoyed fishing rights in Canadian waters by virtue of prior treaties. In view of the adoption by Canada of 'certain measures relating to the delimitation of the territorial sea and fishing zones' and in order to *'adapt to present circumstances* the mutual relations [of the parties] in fishery matters',[98] France renounced its treaty rights in the 1972 Agreement that was intended to supersede all prior treaties relating to fishing by French nationals off the Atlantic coast of Canada. In return, in the event of a modification of the juridical regime of the waters situated beyond the present limits of Canada's territorial sea and fishing zones, Canada would be obliged to allow French nationals to continue fishing in these waters subject to conservation measures. The parties agreed that no

---

[92] Statement by the Canadian Prime Minister, ibid., at 601. Cf. the Prime Minister's statement in respect of an Arctic Pollution Bill, 9 *ILM* (1970), at 543, which would apply to a distance of 100 miles from the coasts: 'In the other case, where no law exists or where law is clearly insufficient, there is no international law applying to the Arctic seas ... we are prepared to help it develop by taking steps on our own.'
[93] Statement released by the State Department on 15 Apr. 1970, *CYIL* (1971), at 288.
[94] *CYIL* (1971), at 290.   [95] 26 June 1970, 9 *ILM* (1970), at 553.
[96] 10 *ILM* (1971), at 438.
[97] UN Legislative Series, *National Legislation and Treaties relating to the Law of the Sea* (1974), ST/LEG/SER.B/16, at 567, 570, 572, 575.
[98] Preamble to the 1972 Agreement.

provision of their agreement would prejudice their views and future claims on fisheries or territorial waters, or other agreements to which either government was a party.

The 1972 Agreement allowed French vessels to fish in Canada's three-to-twelve-mile zone in the Gulf of St Lawrence only until 1986. Exceptionally, and in view of the special situation of Saint-Pierre and Miquelon, vessels registered there were allowed to continue fishing in their traditional grounds off the coasts of Newfoundland. Up to ten trawlers registered in Saint-Pierre and Miquelon were allowed to continue fishing along the coasts of Newfoundland, Nova Scotia, and in the Gulf of St Lawrence (Article 4).

On 24 April 1972 Canada and the United States signed an Exchange of Notes[99] that renewed the above-mentioned 1970 fisheries Agreement between the two countries for one year. Another one-year agreement was concluded on 15 June 1973[100] granting each party fishing rights in the exclusive fishing zone of the other in the area between three and twelve miles from the coasts, without any prejudice to the views or claims of the parties concerning fisheries matters.[101]

3.5.3. The Establishment of the 200-Mile Fishing Zone

The Territorial Sea and Fishing Zones Act of 1964 that extended Canada's territorial waters to twelve miles from the coasts also enabled the Executive to create fishing zones beyond twelve miles.[102] Already in 1970[103] new areas of extended fisheries jurisdiction had been established by drawing 'fisheries closing lines' across the entrances to the Gulf of St Lawrence, the Bay of Fundy, Queen Charlotte Sound, and Dixon Entrance–Hecate Strait.[104] On 1 November 1976 Canada extended her fishing zone on both the Atlantic and the Pacific Coasts to 200 miles from the baselines by an Order-in-Council pursuant to the 1964 Act.[105]

Canada claimed that the proclamation of 200-mile fishing zones was in conformity with international law. In particular, a State's sovereign right

---

[99] 23 *US Treaties and Other International Agreements*, at 623.
[100] UN Legislative Series (1976), ST/LEG/SER.B/18, at 580.   [101] Article 7.
[102] See *CYIL* (1971), at 293; see also statement made by the Canadian Secretary for External Affairs to the House of Commons, ibid., at 286.
[103] 26 Dec. 1970, 10 *ILM* (1971), at 438.
[104] See statement of the Canadian Minister of Fisheries and Forestry on 18 Dec. 1970, 10 *ILM* (1971), at 437; *Keesing's*, 24521A. For US protests against Canada's action, see statement of 18 Dec. 1970, 10 *ILM* (1971), at 441.
[105] 110 CAN. GAZ., EXTRA MP. 101 (1 Nov. 1976), repr. in M. H. Nordquist and Choon Ho Park, *North America and Asia-Pacific and the Development of the Law of the Sea* (1981-I), I.C.2, at 12.

to manage the living resources of the sea in a 200-mile zone adjacent to its coasts was part of the consensus emerging at the Law of the Sea Conference.[106] Moreover,

a number of countries have enacted, or are soon to enact, 200-mile zones, including Mexico, Norway, Denmark, France, the U.K. and the U.S.A. . . . Altogether, there are now some 50 states which have already, or will soon establish extended fisheries zones beyond twelve miles, and in many cases as far as 200 miles. Thus, *from the standpoint of both emerging treaty law and cumulative state practices there is a sound basis in international law for the action Canada has taken* to protect the living resources in waters contiguous to its shoreline. (emphasis added)[107]

Already in 1975 the Canadian government had instructed its officials to conduct bilateral negotiations with major fishing States operating off the Canadian coasts with a view to arranging the terms and conditions of their access to any fisheries surplus within Canada's 200-mile zone so that 'a smooth transition to the new regime of extended Canadian fisheries jurisdiction' could be achieved.[108]

Canada's policy to seek treaty adjustment to new custom did not apply with regard to the above-mentioned 1972 French-Canadian Fisheries Agreement. Canada conceded that the special fishing rights the Agreement granted to vessels from Saint-Pierre and Miquelon were not modified by the establishment of the new Canadian fishery zones.[109] Canada also acknowledged that French vessels in general had the right to continue fishing in the new zones in accordance with all applicable rules and regulations, in view of an express provision to that effect in the 1972 Agreement relating to the eventual extension of Canada's fisheries jurisdiction.[110]

In 1977 the United States established a 200-mile fishery conservation zone off its coasts (Fishery and Conservation and Management Act of 1976). A new fisheries agreement was consequently signed in order to take into account the extension of both countries' fisheries jurisdiction.[111] The Agreement regulated fishing by nationals of each Contracting Party in the areas falling under the fisheries jurisdiction of the other, and allowed traditional fishermen to continue their fishing operations in accordance with existing patterns. The 1977 Agreement was renewed by a 1978 Convention, which was provisionally implemented until June 1988.

---

[106] Statement by the Canadian Secretary of State for External Affairs, *HC Deb.* (Can.), 19 Nov. 1976, at 1189–90, repr. in *CYIL* (1977), at 357.

[107] Ibid.; also *HC Deb.* (Can.), 4 June 1976, at 14164–5, repr. in *CYIL* (1977), at 355; press statement by the Secretary of State for External Affairs and the Minister of Fisheries and the Environment, 2 Nov. 1976, repr. in *CYIL* (1977), at 328.

[108] *HC Deb.* (Can.), 4 June 1976.

[109] *HC Deb.* (Can.), 19 Nov. 1976, at 1189–90, repr. in *CYIL* (1977), at 360.

[110] Ibid.   [111] Fishery Agreement of 24 Feb. 1977, 16 *ILM* (1977), at 590.

Conclusion

The extension by Canada of her exclusive fisheries jurisdiction beyond three miles ran counter to treaty provisions governing her relations with the United States. It will be recalled that the 1818 Treaty set at three miles the parties' exclusive fishery limit and beyond that point fishing was free for all. Canada based her right to extend her fisheries jurisdiction on new customary law, and the existence of her prior treaty commitment proved to be no obstacle in this respect.

On the other hand, Canada conceded that the United States could make a stronger claim for special treatment compared to other countries that based their fishing rights only on usage. Consequently, although the old treaties could not remain in their original form, Canada was prepared to revise them in order to give US vessels some fishing rights, to which they would not necessarily be entitled under the new customary law. Accordingly, new arrangements were made allowing US fishermen to continue their operations in the areas between three and twelve miles from Canada's coasts.

The 1904 Convention, which was the basis of France's fishing rights in the area, did not determine the limit of Canada's fisheries jurisdiction but simply granted fishing rights in Canada's 'territorial waters'. The meaning of this expression is not clear. If it was intended to cover 'any waters then or in future considered by international law to be under Canadian sovereignty', France's fishing rights should not be affected by Canada's extension of jurisdiction. By contrast, if the agreement referred to 'territorial waters as then understood and delimited in international law', it indirectly set three miles as the outer limit of the parties' fisheries jurisdiction, as did the 1818 Treaty with the United States.

In fact, initially Canada suggested that French and US treaty rights should be treated in the same way. In the end, unlike the United States, France was given fishing rights within three to twelve miles only for a limited period of time, but in return obtained Canada's commitment that, in the event of a future extension of jurisdiction, her fisheries rights beyond twelve miles would not be affected.

In any event, irrespective of the particular solution adapted in respect to each country, in both cases it was considered necessary to re-examine the old treaties in the light of legal developments and adjust them after a suitable transitional period.

3.6. US PARTICIPATION IN INTERNATIONAL FISHERY COMMISSIONS

By the Fishery Conservation and Management Act of 1976[112] the United States asserted exclusive management and conservation authority for all fishery except highly migratory species within 200 miles from its coasts and for all anadromous species and continental shelf resources beyond 200 miles. The Act gave foreigners access to any surplus within the 200-mile zone on the basis of international fishery agreements to be concluded between the United States and third countries, and only after specific permission of the Secretary of Commerce for each fishing vessel.

Section 202 of the Act provided for the renegotiation of prior incompatible treaties. The United States would withdraw from any such treaty, in accordance with its provisions, if renegotiations did not take place within a reasonable period of time.

There were a number of international agreements falling within the scope of the provisions of the Act.[113] We shall examine four agreements that established international fishery management and conservation bodies, and were either amended to conform to the new regime of the 200-mile fishery zones or were subject to demands for revision on that basis.[114]

Two of these agreements, namely the International Convention for North-West Atlantic Fisheries (ICNAF)[115] and the 1952 International Convention for the High Seas Fisheries of the North Pacific Ocean between the United States, Canada, and Japan[116] related to high-seas fisheries that fell under US jurisdiction as a result of the 1976 Act. Both agreements were amended in order to accommodate new legal principles regarding the establishment of exclusive economic zones in the first case and jurisdiction over anadromous species in the second. These new principles were embodied in the 1982 Law of the Sea Convention, which, although not yet in force, could be a source of rights and obligations to the extent that it codified or generated customary law.

The other incidents we shall examine were attempts to effect the revision of two international tuna conservation agreements, namely the Convention for the Establishment of an Inter-American Tropical Tuna Commission

[112] 28 Feb. 1977, P. L. 94–265 (90 STAT. 331), repr. at 70 *AJIL* (1976), at 624. See W. T. Burke, 'US Fishery Management and the New Law of the Sea', 76 *AJIL* (1982), at 24.

[113] K. Grzybowski, 'The US Fishery Conservation and Management Act 1976: A Plan for Diplomatic Action', 28 *ICLQ* (1979), 685, at 698.

[114] On the impact of the creation of the exclusive economic zone on international fisheries commissions, see D. J. Attard, *The Exclusive Economic Zone in International Law* (Oxford, 1987), ch. 5; J. E. Carroz, 'Institutional Aspects of Fishery Management under the New Regime of the Oceans', 21 *San Diego Law Review* (1984), at 513; R. R. Churchill and A. V. Lowe, *The Law of the Sea* (2nd edn., Manchester, 1988), ch. 16; B. Kwiatowska, *The 200-Mile Exclusive Economic Zone in the New Law of the Sea* (Dordrecht, 1989), ch. II.

[115] No. 2053, 157 *UNTS* 158.   [116] No. 2770, 205 *UNTS* 80.

(IATTC)[117] and the International Convention on the Conservation of Atlantic Tunas (ICCAT).[118] The 1976 Act exempted tuna from domestic jurisdiction[119] and provided that the United States would not recognize any claims to fishery conservation zones, unless the State concerned accepted that highly migratory species should be managed on the basis of international fishery agreements.

US policy with regard to tuna clashed with the claims of the large majority of States that asserted jurisdiction over all living resources of the exclusive economic zone, including all highly migratory species,[120] in line with the Law of the Sea Convention.[121] Two of these States, Mexico and Costa Rica, tried to bring about the amendment of the IATTC in accordance with the new principles relating to tuna conservation as reflected in the text of the 1982 Law of the Sea Convention. The Convention provides for co-operation between the coastal State and other States whose nationals fish in the region with a view to ensuring conservation and optimum utilization of highly migratory species, both within and beyond the exclusive economic zone. Similar, although less pronounced, attempts were also made within the framework of the International Commission for the Conservation of Atlantic Tuna.

All four Conventions contained provisions for denunciation or withdrawal. However, withdrawal from an international fisheries organization, without ensuring that alternative regulatory arrangements concerning fishing in the Convention area are made, will not always be a satisfactory solution. The aim of the parties would often be to replace the conventional regime by a new system, and any provisions for withdrawal or denunciation may be used as a means of exerting pressure on the other parties. In the examples we shall examine, claims for the revision of the old regime were indeed made and were specifically based on the incompatibility of the prior treaties with new custom.

3.6.1. The International Commission on North-West Atlantic Fisheries[122]

The Convention establishing the International Commission for the North-West Atlantic Fisheries (ICNAF) regulated fishing in the waters of the

---

[117] No. 1041, 80 *UNTS* 4.   [118] No. 9587, 673 *UNTS* 63.

[119] See sect. 3(14). See also the Reagan Proclamation on the Exclusive Economic Zone, 10 Mar. 1983, 22 *ILM* (1983), at 461.

[120] See FAO Legal Study No. 26, 'The UN Convention on the Law of the Sea: Impact on Tuna Regulation' (1982), at 5 *et seq.*   [121] See Article 64 of the Convention.

[122] See Carroz, 'Institutional Aspects of Fishery Management', at 519; J. L. Meseguer, 'Le Régime juridique de l'exploitation des stocks conjoints de poissons au delà de 200 miles', 28 *AFDI* (1982), at 885; E. L. Miles and W.T. Burke, 'Pressures on the United Nations Convention on the Law of the Sea of 1982 Arising from New Fisheries Conflicts: The Problem of Straddling Stocks', 20 *ODILJ* (1989), 343, at 344.

North-West Atlantic outside the territorial sea. ICNAF was responsible for gathering and analysing information relating to the conservation of fisheries in the Convention area and for submitting proposals for conservation measures for joint action by the parties. These measures had to be adopted by agreement of all the parties and were designed to maintain the fish stocks in the area at a level permitting the maximum sustainable catch.

The United States withdrew from ICNAF on 22 June 1976, pursuant to the 1976 Act.[123] Following Canada's decision to extend its fisheries jurisdiction to 200 miles by 1 January 1977, Canada also gave formal notice of her intention to withdraw from the Convention, with effect from 31 December 1976. Canada stated that 'new multilateral arrangements would be needed to bring ICNAF *into line with the new jurisdictional realities*'[124] but was willing to continue to play an active role in the work of the Commission, in the hope that the necessary adjustments to the conventional regime would be made.[125]

At Canada's initiative a Conference was convened in 1977 with a view to amending ICNAF on the basis of the new general law on fisheries. The outcome of the Conference was the 1978 Convention on Future Multilateral Co-operation in the North-West Atlantic Fisheries.[126] The new treaty noted that the coastal States of the North-West Atlantic had, 'in accordance with relevant principles of international law', extended their fisheries jurisdiction to areas up to 200 miles from the baselines.[127] 'Desiring to promote the conservation and optimum utilisation of the fishery resources of the [area] within a framework appropriate to the regime of extended coastal State jurisdiction',[128] the signatories set up a new organization, the North-West Atlantic Fisheries Organization (NAFO), to replace the ICNAF Commission.

While the provisions of ICNAF reflected the classic distinction between territorial waters and high seas, the NAFO Convention adopted for regulatory purposes 200 miles as the outer limit of the coastal State fisheries jurisdiction, in line with recent legal developments. The functions of the Commission were amended to take account of the new principles relating to the conservation and management of fishery resources.

NAFO was entrusted with the co-ordination of scientific research relating to fisheries over the whole area of the North-West Atlantic. It was responsible for the management and conservation of fisheries within the so-called 'regulatory area',[129] that is the waters of the North Atlantic beyond 200

---

[123] 76 *Dept. of State Bulletin*, at 80.
[124] Statement of the Canadian Secretary of State for External Affairs, *HC Deb*. (Can.), 4 June 1976, at 14164–5, repr. in *CYIL* (1977), at 355.
[125] *HC Deb*. (Can.), 19 Nov. 1976, at 1189–90, repr. in *CYIL* (1977), at 358.
[126] *OJ* (1978), C271/17.   [127] Preamble to the 1978 Convention.
[128] Ibid.   [129] Article XI.

miles from the coasts. Its functions included the allocation of catches and the adoption of international measures of control and enforcement. The Commission would seek to ensure that its proposals relating to stocks migrating between the 200-mile zones and the high seas were consistent with any relevant measures taken by the coastal State within its area of jurisdiction (Article XI, para. 3). The interests of member countries whose vessels had traditionally fished in the regulatory area would be one among many criteria the Commission would take into account in formulating its proposals designed to achieve optimum utilization of the fishery resources of the area.

3.6.2. The International North Pacific Fisheries Commission

The International North Pacific Fisheries Commission (INPFC)[130] set up by the 1952 International Convention for the High Seas Fisheries of the North Pacific Ocean was also amended to take account of developments in coastal State jurisdiction under general international law.

The Commission was responsible for promoting and co-ordinating scientific studies relating to the conservation of halibut, herring, and salmon in the high-seas area of the North Pacific and for recommending conservation measures to be carried out by the parties through the enactment of the necessary laws and regulations. The 1952 Convention was based on the principle of abstention—that is, the contracting parties agreed to abstain from fishing for a certain species of fish outside territorial waters, in cases where another contracting party had been substantially engaged in its exploitation, had subjected it to an effective conservation programme, and was making maximum use of the existing stocks upon a sustainable yield basis.

While the provisions of the 1952 Convention gave equal weight to the State of origin and to the State engaging in high-seas salmon fisheries, new principles of international law reflected in the 1982 Law of the Sea Convention vest primary authority in the State of origin. According to Article 66 of the Convention, States in whose rivers anadromous stocks originate shall have the primary interest in and responsibility for them. Fishing for anadromous stocks is allowed only landward of the outer limits of the exclusive economic zone, except in cases where this would result in economic dislocation for a State other than the State of origin. Where fishing in the high seas is allowed, the States concerned shall consult about the terms and conditions of such fishing, giving due regard to the conservation

---

[130] See Carroz, 'Institutional Aspects of Fishery Management', at 523; E. L. Miles, 'The Evolution of Fisheries Policy and Regional Commissions in the North Pacific under the Impact of Extended Coastal State Jurisdiction', in *The Law and the Sea: Essays in Memory of J. Carroz* (Rome, 1987), at 139.

requirements of the coastal State of origin. Enforcement in the high seas shall be by agreement between the State of origin and the other States concerned.

In view of these developments, the United States gave notice in February 1977 of its intent to withdraw from INPFC in one year, unless the Convention was renegotiated. Negotiations on a revised Convention began in October 1977. 'Taking into account that each of the Contracting Parties had established new fishery jurisdiction in the Convention area' and 'acknowledging that certain provisions of the Convention are not compatible with such jurisdiction',[131] the three member countries amended the 1952 Convention by a 1978 Protocol.[132]

The revised Convention maintained the 1952 Commission but redefined its functions. The most important changes introduced in this respect were the following: the Convention no longer mentioned the principle of abstention, and the Commission was entrusted generally with recommending changes in the regulation of salmon fishing in the area. In addition, the Commission was responsible for the promotion and co-ordination of studies regarding anadromous as well as non-anadromous species in the Convention area.

Although the revised Convention still applied to all waters of the North Pacific 'other than territorial waters', it took account of the creation of 200-mile fishery zones for enforcement purposes. The new text thus provided that within the 200-mile zone the Convention would be enforced by each coastal State member to the Convention in accordance with its domestic law, and outside 200 miles a system of reciprocal inspection was established.

3.6.3. The Inter-American Tropical Tuna Commission

The IATTC[133] was established by a 1948 Convention between the United States and Costa Rica, to which Mexico adhered in 1964. The IATTC was originally established in order to study and research all matters relating to the conservation of species of tuna in the waters of the Eastern Pacific and to recommend from time to time proposals for joint action to the parties with a view to maintaining the tuna population at a level permitting the maximum sustainable catch.

In 1962 the Commission created a Yellowfin Regulated Area comprising

---

[131] Preamble to the 1978 Protocol.

[132] 25 Apr. 1978, *TIAS* 9242, 30 *US Treaties and Other International Agreements* (1978–9), i, at 1096.

[133] A. Székely, 'Implementing the New Law of the Sea: The Mexican Experience', in B. J. Rothschild (ed.), *Global Fisheries: Perspectives for the 1980s* (New York, 1983), 51, esp. at 65 *et seq.*; S. O'Malley Wade, 'A Proposal to Include Tunas in US Fishery Jurisdiction', 16 *ODILJ* (1986), at 255.

a zone of more than 500 nautical square miles, extending in some sections up to more than 1,000 miles from the coastlines, within which it exercised a conservation function. Within that area the Commission set a global maximum catch quota for yellowfin tuna for every season which was carried out on a first-come, first-served basis. From 1969 onwards special allocations were authorized during the closed season in favour of small or newly built vessels from developing member States.

At the 1975 annual meeting of the IATTC Mexico announced her intention to call for a special conference in order to adjust the existing conservation regime to the new law of the sea. According to the consensus emerging from the Third UN Law of the Sea Conference, the coastal State had the right to establish a 200-mile exclusive economic zone, within which it could exercise sovereign rights for exploring, exploiting, conserving and managing all resources, including tuna.

Under the new regime the conservation and management of highly migratory species should be a matter of co-operation, through appropriate regional organizations, in existence or to be established. In Mexico's view, the ICCAT in its present form was not an appropriate organization for the conservation of tuna, because it was based on the regime of freedom of fishing. A new organization had to replace it based on the new rules of the game as formulated at the UN Conference.

Mexico convinced the IATTC Commissioners to entrust the Director of Investigations of the Commission, Dr J. Joseph, with drafting a paper on the revision alternatives available to the parties, including the new concepts emerging from the UN Conference. The Report was prepared by J. Joseph and J. W. Greenough and was distributed to the members of the Organization at the 1976 Meeting of the IATTC.

A plenipotentiary Conference co-sponsored by Mexico and Costa Rica was convened in 1977 in San Jose in order to discuss the possibility of revision of the existing IATTC regime. Mexico and Costa Rica submitted a joint proposal based on one of the alternatives contained in the Joseph and Greenough Report. It provided for the establishment of a new organization that would replace the IATTC. Under the new regime, a maximum global quota for yellowfin would be set. The coastal State would be guaranteed a part of this quota, equal to the concentration of the resource within its zone, while other States would have access to any surplus in exchange for the payment of a fee.

The United States took the position that tuna was not subject to the sovereign rights of the coastal State in its exclusive economic zone. Accordingly it rejected the joint proposal, and especially the concept of the concentration of the resource. The United States did not favour the replacement of the IATTC by a new organization and proposed instead formulas aiming at amending the IATTC in a way that would ensure continuity with the existing regime. Negotiations continued over the next two and a half years, but the parties failed to reach an agreement. Mexico denounced the IATTC Convention with effect from 8 November 1978 and Costa Rica soon followed suit.

In March 1983 Costa Rica, Panama, and the United States signed the Eastern Pacific Ocean Tuna Fishing Agreement,[134] a temporary licensing agreement allowing fishing for a fee in the area of the Agreement and providing for disbursement by the parties in proportion to the volume of tuna taken within 200 miles from the coasts. In recognition of the transitory character of the 1983 Agreement, the contracting parties resolved to continue efforts towards the establishment of a new regional regime of guaranteed quotas for the coastal State based upon, *inter alia*, the criterion of resource concentration of tuna.[135]

3.6.4. The International Commission for the Conservation of Atlantic Tuna

The International Commission for the Conservation of Atlantic Tuna (ICCAT) was set up by the 1966 Convention on the Conservation of Atlantic Tuna applicable to all waters of the Atlantic. Under the Convention the Commission would be responsible for the study of tuna and such other species of fish not under investigation by another fisheries organization and for the preparation of recommendations designed to maintain the population of tuna at levels permitting the maximum sustainable catch. The contracting parties agreed to take all action necessary for the enforcement of the Convention and to collaborate with each other with a view to setting up a system of international enforcement to be applied to the Convention area outside the territorial sea and any other waters in which a State is entitled under international law to exercise jurisdiction over fisheries. Withdrawal from the Convention was possible after ten years from its entry into force, and termination could be effected at any time thereafter by agreement of the majority of the parties.

The Commission was confronted with demands for revision with a view to accommodating ICCAT to the new concepts of the Law of the Sea as embodied in the 1982 Law of the Sea Convention. In November 1982 Portugal suggested that the Convention should be amended, because its underlying philosophy was inconsistent with the provisions of the 1982

---

[134] FAO Fisheries Report No. 293 (1983), 189 *et seq.*

[135] Cf. the agreement on Eastern Pacific Tuna signed on 21 July 1989 by Ecuador, Mexico, Peru, Nicaragua, and El Salvador, giving coastal States responsibility for the conservation and management of their exclusive-economic-zone resources; see J.-F. Pulvenis, 'Vers une emprise des états riverains sur la haute mer au titre des grands migrateurs? Le Régime international de la pêche au thon dans le Pacifique Oriental', 35 *AFDI* (1989), at 791 *et seq.*

Convention relating to the rights of the coastal State over the living resources of the exclusive economic zone (Article 64 in combination with Articles 56, 61, and 62).[136] The new legal regime applicable to tuna fishing was based on the combination of two elements incorporated in Article 64 of the 1982 Law of the Sea Convention, that is international co-operation and coastal State jurisdiction over the living resources of its exclusive economic zone. In the following year the President of ICCAT, Dr L. Koffi, referred to the introduction of the concept of the exclusive economic zone and to the generalization of 200 miles as the outer jurisdictional limit of the coastal State. He suggested that it would be appropriate for the Commission to consider seriously the delicate question of the implications of the evolution of the law of the Sea on the ICCAT regime.[137]

3.7. SPANISH FISHING RIGHTS IN EUROPEAN COMMUNITY WATERS

The Hague Resolution adopted on 3 November 1976 by the Council of the European Community provided that the EC Member States would by concerted action extend the limits of their fishing zones off their North Atlantic and North Sea coasts to 200 miles, as from 1 January 1977.[138] The measures to be adopted to this end would be based 'on the guidelines which are emerging within the Third United Nations Conference on the Law of the Sea'. The Council instructed the Commission to start negotiations with third countries in order to regulate the access of their fishing vessels to the resources of the EC 200-mile zone after 1 January 1977 and to ensure that Community fishermen retain or obtain fishing rights in foreign waters.

When the Hague Resolution was adopted, Spanish vessels had fishing rights between six and twelve miles off the coasts of EC Member States by virtue of the 1964 London Fisheries Convention[139] and a 1967 Franco-Spanish Agreement[140] concluded in implementation of the London

---

[136] *Report of the International Convention on the Conservation of Atlantic Tunas* (1982–3), pt. I, at 61–2.

[137] Ibid., pt. II; J. L. Meseguer, 'La cooperación internacional para la ordenación del atun en el Oceano Atlantico', in *The Law and the Sea: Essays in Memory of J. Carroz* (Rome, 1987), at 121 *et seq.*

[138] Council Resolution of 3 Nov. 1976 on Certain External Aspects of the Creation of a 200-Mile Fishing Zone in the Community with effect from 1 Jan. 1977, *OJ* (1981), C105/1.

[139] 516 *UNTS*, 206, signed by Austria, Belgium, Denmark, France, the Federal Republic of Germany, Ireland, Italy, Luxembourg, the Netherlands, Portugal, Spain, and Sweden; subject to denunciation after 15 Mar. 1986.

[140] General Fisheries Agreement of 20 Mar. 1967, 712 *UNTS*, at 365. Article I(*b*) of the Agreement provides that: 'In the belt between 6 and 12 miles along the French coasts, Spanish nationals shall enjoy in perpetuity the right to fish: (i) for all species on the Atlantic coast from the mouth of the Bidassoa to the parallel of the northern extremity of Belle-Ile; (ii) for all species on the Mediterranean coast, from the border to Cape Leucate.'

Convention. Spain was also a party to the 1958 Geneva Convention on Fishing and Conservation of the Living Resources of the High Seas,[141] which prevented a coastal State from unilaterally adopting 'in any area of the high seas adjacent to its territorial sea' conservation measures discriminating in form or in fact against foreign fishermen.

The relevance of Spain's treaty rights to the determination of the future fisheries regime that would apply in the Community area soon became a matter of controversy. The Community argued that the old agreements had been superseded by recent legal developments in the law of the sea and should be renegotiated. Spain reserved her rights under the 1958 Geneva Convention and the 1964 London Convention and claimed that the establishment of the new EC fishing zones and the adoption of unilateral conservation measures were not opposable to her inasmuch as they were contrary to both general international law and to treaties in force.[142]

Spain was willing to start negotiations with the Community with a view to concluding a fisheries agreement that would maintain the traditional Spanish catches in the extended Community zones. If a fisheries agreement were not concluded before 1 January 1977, when the Hague Resolution would come into force, it was the opinion of the Spanish Government that the prior *status quo* ought to be maintained in conformity with the existing rules of international law.

The Commission's view of the current state of international law was that the 200-mile fishing limit had been generally accepted in State practice and that new principles regarding the regulation of fisheries in the new zones had emerged during the discussions at the Law of the Sea Conference.[143] On this basis, access by third countries to the resources of the Community's fishing zones should be possible only after mutual agreement and on the basis of reciprocity.[144] Since the Community's fishing interests in Spain's fishing zone were not substantial, the extent of fishing rights to be granted to Spanish fishermen in the Community zones was limited. All other fishing rights should gradually be phased out.[145]

---

[141] 599 *UNTS* 285.

[142] Note of 15 Nov. 1976 to the EC, mentioned in J. L. Meseguer, 'La politica pesquera de la CEE ante el derecho internacional: Relaciones hispano-communitarias', *Revista de las instituciones europeas* (Madrid, 1977), 701, at 718 n. 60; J. D. Gonzales Campos, 'Las Relaciones entre España y la CEE en materia de pesca', in F. Leita and T. Scovazi, *Il regime della pesca nella Communità Economica Europea* (Studi e Documenti sul Diritto Internazionale del Mare, 4; Milan, 1979), 133, at 144. See also the Commission's written observations to the *Arbelaiz–Emazabel Case, ECR* (1981), at 2974.

[143] See Explanatory Memorandum and Directives for Negotiations with Non-Member Countries on the Conservation of Resources and the Exploitation of Fishing Grounds, attached to COM(76) 500 final, at 1, 4; Communication by the Commission to the Council of 23 Sept. 1976, COM(76) 500 final, at 2; Communication by the Commission to the Council of 18 Feb. 1976, COM(76) 59 final, at 9.

[144] Explanatory Memorandum, COM(76) 500, at 3–4.   [145] Ibid., at 13–14.

The Commission omitted any reference to Spain's treaty rights in the Community's fishing zones, implying that it was not prepared to take them into account in the new fisheries arrangements with Spain. This attitude reflected the position that the rules contained in the 1958 and 1964 Conventions were rendered obsolete by new general customary law that emerged from State practice following the Third UN Conference on the Law of the Sea.[146]

Spain was among the advocates of the 200-mile economic zone at the Third UN Conference, but only on condition that preferential access to the resources of the new zones should be given to vessels of third countries that had traditionally fished in that area.[147] In her view, the new general principles regarding the regulation of fisheries within the 200-mile fishing zone invoked by the Community as a basis for the solution of the dispute had not yet become generally accepted customary law.[148] As a result, the only relevant rules in force were the provisions of the 1958 and 1964 Conventions.

Negotiations with Spain started in December 1976 with a view to concluding a new fisheries treaty. The drafts prepared by the EC were based on the assumption that Spain would renounce the fishing rights she enjoyed under the 1964 Convention.[149] Spain accepted in principle the criterion of reciprocity advocated by the EC as a basis for the conclusion of a new fisheries treaty. However, she was not prepared to agree to the phasing-out of Spanish fishing operations between six and twelve miles from the Community coasts and wanted to reserve the possibility of invoking her prior treaty rights in the future.[150]

On 15 April 1980 Spain and the EC signed a framework agreement[151] setting out the conditions under which each party would have access to the 200-mile fishing zone of the other. The agreement applied provisionally from the date of signature until 22 May 1981, when it entered definitely into force. It affirmed that the extension of coastal State jurisdiction over areas of biological resources should be conducted pursuant to and in accordance with the principles of international law and took account of the work of the Third UN Conference on the Law of the Sea and the establishment by the contracting parties of 200-mile fishing zones.[152] It was to remain in force for five years initially[153] and would be re-examined upon

---

[146] See Meseguer, 'La politica pesquera', at 719; Gonzales Campos, 'Relaciones', at 146–7.

[147] See J. L. Meseguer, 'La IIIe Conferencia sobre Derecho del Mar: Posición española en materia de pesca maritima', 30 *Revista española de derecho internacional* (1977), at 387–3.

[148] See Meseguer, 'La politica pesquera', at 717–18.

[149] See J. L. Meseguer, 'Accord de pêche entre l'Espagne et la CEE', 23 *Revue du Marché Commun* (1980), 527, at 527–9.

[150] Gonzales Campos, 'Relaciones', at 150; Meseguer, 'Accord', at 529.

[151] *OJ* (1980), L322/4.   [152] See Preamble to the Agreement.

[153] Article 12, para. 2.

the conclusion of the UN negotiations on a new Law of the Sea Treaty.[154] In view of the ongoing negotiations at the UN Conference, the agreement provided that its provisions would not affect or prejudice the position of either party with respect to questions relating to the Law of the Sea (Article 10).

The 1980 Agreement did not expressly terminate prior fisheries treaties between the parties. Article 1, para. 2, however, provided that the 1980 Agreement would not affect the 1959 Franco-Spanish Agreement regulating fishing in the Bidassoa waters and in the Bay of Figuer, which implied that the agreement would supersede all other prior fisheries arrangements, including the 1964 London Convention and the 1967 Franco-Spanish Agreement. Moreover, as provided by Article 1, para. 1, the agreement was meant to 'establish the principles and rules which will govern, *in all respects*, the fishing activities of vessels of either Party within the fishing zones falling under the jurisdiction of the other' (emphasis added).[155]

The issue of Spain's fishing rights in Community waters resurfaced during the negotiations preceding her accession to the Community.[156] Spain invoked her rights under the 1967 Franco-Spanish fisheries Agreement and contended that they were not affected by he 1980 Agreement.[157] She also challenged the validity of a number of EC regulations adopted by the Council both before the conclusion of the 1980 Agreement and during the course of its implementation, which introduced a system of compulsory licensing applicable to fishing by Spanish vessels over the whole area of the 200-mile Community exclusive economic zone.[158] These regulations disregarded Spain's prior treaty rights in the twelve-mile zone off the French coast. Spain contended that the new internal regime of the EC regulating the access of her fishing vessels to Community waters should take account of the traditional Spanish catches in that area before 1 January 1977, when the 200-mile Community exclusive economic zone came into force.

The position of the EC was that Spain's treaty rights had been acquired in a different international legal context, which was now a thing of the past as a result of the general acceptance of 200-mile fishing zones as a rule of customary law.[159] Consequently, they would not have to be taken into account when determining Spain's participation in the Community's fisheries regime.

---

[154] Article 13.   [155] *Contra* Meseguer, 'Accord', at 532.

[156] Started on 5 Feb. 1979. The Treaty of Accession was signed on 12 June 1985, *OJ* (1985), L302.

[157] See G. Apollis, 'La Réglementation des activités halieutiques dans l'Acte d'adhésion de l'Espagne et du Portugal au Traité C.E.E.', 31 *AFDI* (1985), 837, esp. at 842 *et seq.*, 857 *et seq.*

[158] See Council Regulation 746/77 of 5 Apr. 1977, *OJ* L90/8; Regulation 1416/77 of 28 June 1977, *OJ* L160/18; Regulation 1709/77 of 26 July 1977, *OJ* L189/8.

[159] See Apollis, 'Réglementation', at 843.

Annex 1 of the Act of Accession allowed Spanish vessels to fish in the six to twelve-mile French zone in the Mediterranean only, where the Hague Resolution did *not* apply. On the other hand, in the Atlantic, where the EC fishing zone extended to 200-miles from the coast, the Act of Accession granted to Spanish vessels limited fishing rights with regard to sardine and anchovy for certain times of the year only. These limited fishing rights, which had also been granted by a number of EC regulations in the past,[160] were regarded as an exceptional concession on grounds of continuity of an existing practice. Spain's claims were not met in other respects.

3.8. THE FISHERIES DISPUTE BETWEEN MOROCCO AND SPAIN

In 1969 Spain and Morocco concluded a permanent fisheries convention[161] regarding fishing by their nationals in the territorial waters of the other party. Under the 1969 Agreement and for the purpose of its application, the limit of the territorial sea was set at twelve miles from the baselines. Within that zone the nationals of each party were allowed to fish subject to the terms of the convention. The agreement provided for the right to initiate negotiations with a view to an eventual revision of the convention ten years after its entry into force. It also stipulated that any future extension of the territorial waters of the parties in conformity with international law would not modify the conventional regime unless it was otherwise agreed by the two countries.

In 1972 the exercise of Spain's fishing rights under the 1969 Agreement[162] became a matter of controversy. During the first half of that year over a 100 Spanish fishing vessels were reported to have been seized by the Moroccans and King Hassan informed the Spanish Government of his country's intention to abrogate the 1969 Agreement.

Following unofficial reports that Morocco intended to extend its fishery limits from twelve to seventy miles off its coasts, the Spanish Government stated that it would not recognize such an extension.[163] However, by

---

[160] Regulations 3598/82, L375/45 (subsequently extended by Reg. 709/83, L83/9, Reg. 598/84, L67/1, Reg. 7/85, L1/64) authorizing Spanish vessels to fish between twelve and 188 miles off the Atlantic up to the limit of their quota, and only by way of exception between six and twelve miles for sardine or anchovy.

[161] Signed at Fès on 4 Jan. 1969, UN Legislative Series, *National Legislation and Treaties Relating to the Law of the Sea* (1974), ST/LEG/SER.B/16, at 512, repr. from *Royaume du Maroc, Bulletin Officiel* (28 May 1969), 571–4.

[162] *Keesing's* (1973), 25866A; Chronique des Faits Internationaux, *RGDIP* (1974), 513.

[163] Speech of 5 Feb. 1973 by the Spanish Minister of Commerce. Spain had established a six-mile exclusive fishery zone and recognized historic fishing rights of foreign vessels between six and twelve miles from the coasts; see *Act Concerning the Extension of Spanish Territorial Waters to 12 Miles for Fishing Purposes* of 8 Apr. 1967, UN Legislative Series, ST/LEG/SER.B/15, at 668.

legislation published on 9 March 1973[164] Morocco established an exclusive fishing zone beyond its twelve-mile territorial sea and up to seventy miles from the baselines. Morocco's sovereignty over the natural resources of its exclusive fishing zone was affirmed and fishing within that zone was reserved for vessels under Moroccan flag or Moroccan exploitation, 'without prejudice to the principles of international co-operation to which Morocco subscribes, in accordance with its sovereign rights and in respect of its national interest'. Any research or scientific or archeological exploration undertaken by foreigners within the seventy-mile zone required prior permission from the Moroccan authorities.

Following the unilateral abrogation of the 1969 Agreement by Morocco in December 1972, negotiations began with Spain with a view to concluding a new fisheries agreement. The negotiations broke off twice in 1973 because of Morocco's insistence on a maximum of 200 Spanish vessels being allowed in the seventy-mile zone, instead of some 800 which had previously fished there.[165] A fisheries agreement was finally signed in Rabat on 2 January 1974.

The 1974 Agreement set up a framework of co-operation between the parties with regard to fisheries. The two countries agreed to exploit jointly the Moroccan demersal and pelagic species, with the exception of sardines, and Spain engaged to grant financial and technical aid for the development of Morocco's fisheries. Up to 200 Spanish fishing vessels were allowed to fish in the Moroccan waters. These vessels would be chartered by Moroccan companies with mixed Moroccan–Spanish capital. The agreement did not contain an express recognition of the Moroccan seventy-mile limit nor of any other outer limit for the exercise of coastal State fisheries jurisdiction.[166]

Despite this compromise agreement, the dispute between the two countries over the legality of Morocco's seventy-mile fishing zone under general international law continued. In April 1975 a Moroccan gunboat seized two Spanish trawlers for fishing inside the seventy-mile limit, while two Spanish warships sent to the scene succeeded in releasing one of the trawlers and in capturing two Moroccan sailors.[167] The incident was resolved a few days later, when the two Moroccans were exchanged for the Spanish fishermen and the trawler. According to an official Spanish statement, the incident had taken place 'in free waters outside the jurisdiction of either country'.[168]

In 1977 Morocco established a 200-mile fishery zone off its coasts[169] and

---

[164] M. Nordquist *et al.* (eds.), *New Directions in the Law of the Sea*, vii (1980), at 166.
[165] *Keesing's* (1974), 26324A.
[166] Nordquist *et al.* (eds.), *New Directions in the Law of the Sea*, v (1977), at 18.
[167] *Keesing's* (1975), 27415.   [168] Ibid.
[169] Royal Decree of 15 June 1977, Nordquist *et al.* (eds.), *New Directions in the Law of the Sea*, vii, at 167.

Spain followed suit in 1978.[170] In 1977 Spain had set the limit of her territorial waters at twelve miles from the coasts, 'that being the limit established by most States and considered to be in accordance with prevailing international law'.[171]

On 17 February 1977 a new fisheries agreement was signed[172] allowing Spanish trawlers to fish in the waters off Morocco and the Moroccan sector of the Western Sahara under the Moroccan flag on condition that the boats should be transferred into mixed Moroccan–Spanish ownership within five years. In return Spain granted to Morocco credits to expand its fishing fleet and industry and allowed Moroccan vessels to fish under the Spanish flag in the tuna grounds off the Canary Islands. In defence of the agreement, the Spanish Government referred to the extension of the fishery zones of many countries to 200 miles and the increase in State practice of similar agreements with coastal States.[173]

The 1977 Agreement was never ratified by the Moroccan Parliament. While talks on a revised agreement were in progress, the fishing relations between the two countries were regulated by a series of provisional agreements renewable at six-month intervals. Finally an agreement was signed on 18 August 1983[174] that granted Spain fishing rights in the waters off the coasts of Morocco and of the Western Sahara in return for guarantees and concessional loans. The terms of the 1983 Agreement regarding the size of the Spanish fleet allowed to fish in Moroccan waters and the fees payable to Morocco were less favourable to Spain than the corresponding terms of the 1977 Agreement.

The outcome of the dispute was beneficial to Morocco. Its claim to a seventy-mile fishing zone was upheld, Spain's fishing rights were gradually reduced, and, to the extent that they were retained, concessions had to be made in return.

This is a striking example of a treaty that was successfully challenged only a few years after its entry into force by reason of its incompatibility with general legal developments. Spain's omission to rely on her fishing rights under the 1969 Agreement is all the more surprising, in view of the express provision of Article 7 of the 1969 Agreement to the effect that any future extension of the Moroccan territorial waters in accordance with international law would not affect the conventional regime.

Strictly speaking, Article 7 referred only to the possibility of a future extension of Morocco's *territorial waters* and did not envisage the creation of exclusive fishing zones, which are neither part of the territorial waters nor part of the high seas. On the other hand, it could be argued that the proclamation of a seventy-mile exclusive fishing zone in areas which

---

[170] *Law 15/1978 of 20 Feb. on the Economic Zone*, ST/LEG/SER.B/19, at 250.
[171] *Act No. 10/1977 of 4 Jan. Concerning the Territorial Sea*, ST/LEG/SER.B/19, at 109.
[172] *Keesing's* (1979), 29567.   [173] Ibid.   [174] *Keesing's* (1981), 30716.

previously were part of the high seas, violated the spirit, if not the letter, of the 1969 Agreement.

In any case, the provisions of the Agreement proved to be untenable in the face of the alleged evolution of the general law. The decisive question in this respect was the legality of the seventy-mile zone under general international law and the dispute between the parties focused on this issue.

4

State Practice: Other Examples

This chapter reviews a number of cases from State practice relating to treaty termination or revision in the light of new customary law. The disputes examined belong to different subject-areas and are presented in chronological order, according to the time when they first arose. Their value as precedents varies and is briefly discussed in each case.

4.1. THE EXTRADITION REGIME IN THE EAST INDIES

In 1815 France and Great Britain signed a Convention regulating various matters relative to their possessions in the East Indies.[1] In Article 9 of the Convention France and Great Britain engaged to extradite any person who, after being prosecuted for crimes committed or civil debts contracted within the territory of one of the parties, sought refuge in the territory of the other. The Convention was intended to be permanent, no modification being allowed without the consent of both parties.[2]

In 1843 Great Britain and France signed a general convention providing for the extradition of persons accused of committing one of a limited number of crimes.[3] The 1815 Convention continued to apply in the East Indies *qua lex specialis*.

In 1876 the 1843 Agreement was replaced by a new general extradition convention,[4] which introduced a number of important innovations: there was no longer an obligation to extradite a State's own nationals (Article 1) or any person accused of having committed a political offence (Article 5); the number of crimes for which there was a duty to extradite was significantly increased (Article 3); and no person could be extradited, if he had already been judged for the same offence by the extraditing State (Article 10).

The object of the 1876 Convention was to bring the 1843 Agreement into line with the evolution of the general international law on the extradition of criminals.[5] The following legal developments which had taken place since 1843 were reflected in the text of the 1876 Convention:[6] first,

---

[1] Convention of 7 March 1815, De Clerq, *Recueil Des Traités de la France*, ii, at 452.
[2] Article 10.   [3] De Clerq, v, at 2.
[4] Convention of 14 Aug. 1876, De Clerq, xi, at 454.
[5] Statement by French Minister of Foreign Affairs, 14 Aug. 1876, ibid., at 475.
[6] Ibid., at 463 *et seq.*

States began to view extradition as a general duty to one another involving principally common criminals; secondly, procedural guarantees aiming at the protection of the individual were imposed on the extraditing State; thirdly, according to the practice of the majority of States, only non-political crimes constituted extraditable offences and a State was not obliged to extradite its own nationals.

Effects of the Legal Changes on the Application of the East Indies Extradition Arrangements

The 1876 Convention was not intended to apply to the East Indies, where the 1815 Convention remained in force.[7] This was due to the proximity of the territories of the parties and of their slaves in the East Indies, which made extradition necessary even for less serious crimes than those enumerated in the 1876 Convention.[8]

One would thus expect that, after 1876, the 1815 Convention would apply to the East Indies in derogation of the regime introduced by the 1876 Convention, especially in the following two respects: first, the 1815 Convention provided for the extradition of all offences, whether civil or criminal; secondly, its wording was wide enough—'tous les Européens ou autres quelconques contre qui il sera procédé en justice'—to encompass the extradition of a State's own nationals. However, this would not be the case, because the parties to the 1815 Convention had already modified it in practice by restricting its application to criminal offences only and by refraining from extraditing their own nationals, unless they were members of the indigenous population.[9]

It was argued that in this case a treaty was modified by *desuetude*. In the light of developments in the general law on extradition, the 1815 Convention lost its *raison d'être* and was consequently amended by implied consent of the parties.[10] Indeed, when a treaty becomes incompatible with new general law, it is possible that the parties will not expressly terminate it or revise it, as the case may be, but will either let it lapse or derogate from its provisions in practice. In these circumstances, *desuetude* takes place in recognition of the need to adapt an obsolete treaty to general legal changes.

In the present case, some of the legal developments in the law of extradition could have been incorporated in the 1815 Convention through an appropriate interpretation of its provision.[11] However, this would not be possible at least with regard to civil offences, because the Convention expressly included them in the extraditable offences.

In the early twentieth century the 1815 Convention was abandoned

---

[7] Article 16. [8] De Clerq, xi, at 473. [9] Ibid.
[10] L. Holz, 'L'Extradition entre l'Inde française et l'Empire anglo-indien', 17 *RGDIP* (1910), at 449; Rousseau, *Principes*, at 553. [11] See Holz, 'L'Extradition', at 465.

by the parties in its entirety and instead the 1876 Convention applied to extradition matters in the East Indies.[12]

4.2. THE TREATY ON THE PANAMA CANAL

The Panama Canal Treaty was signed in 1903.[13] It granted the United States 'in perpetuity the use, occupation and control of a zone of land and land under water for the construction, maintenance, operation, sanitation and protection' of the Panama Canal (Article 11) as well as 'all the rights, power and authority . . . which the United States would possess and exercise as if it were the sovereign . . . to the entire exclusion of the exercise by the Republic of Panama of any such rights, power or authority' (Article 111). Panama agreed not to impose any taxes on equipment or employees in the service of the Canal Company (Article X).

These provisions deprived Panama of significant benefits deriving from the operation of the Canal in return merely for a lump sum, an annuity (Article XIV), and an undertaking by the United States to secure the integrity of the Panamanian Republic (Article 1).[14] Panama's dissatisfaction with the terms of the 1903 Treaty and the circumstances in which it was concluded[15] led to a long dispute with the United States regarding the legal status of the Canal Zone.

The 1903 Treaty was revised in 1936[16] and in 1955[17] by mutual consent of the parties.[18] The amount of the annuity payable to Panama was increased, the Canal Zone was recognized as Panamanian territory under the jurisdiction of the United States, and the United States relinquished the right to exercise the power of eminent domain, to intervene in Panama's internal affairs, and to use or occupy land outside the Canal Zone. Panama obtained the exclusive right to levy taxes on all Panamanians working in the Zone and understandings were reached ensuring equal wages and equal opportunities to Panamanian workers as well as competitive opportunities to Panamanian businesses.

---

[12] Rousseau, *Principes*. See also Decision of 22 July 1937 of the Cour d'Appel of Aix in the *Davidson* case, noted by C. Rousseau, *Nouvelle Revue du Droit International Privé* (1937), at 769; *RGDIP* (1939), at 395.

[13] Hay–Bunau-Varilla Treaty of 18 Nov. 1903, 33 Stat. 2234 (1903–5), *UKTS* No. 431.

[14] See letter of Secretary of State Hay to Senator Spooner of 20 Jan. 1904, quoted in D. C. Miner, *The Fight for the Panama Route* (New York, 1966), at 383.

[15] On this history of the negotiations see Ph. Bunau-Varilla, *Panama: The Creation, Destruction and Resurrection* (Paris, 1913); R. R. Baxter and R. D. Caroll, *The Panama Canal* (1965); N. J. Padelford, *The Panama Canal in Peace and War* (New York, 1942).

[16] General Treaty of Friendship and Co-operation of 2 Mar. 1936, 53 Stat. 1807 (1939), *UKTS* No. 945.

[17] Treaty of Mutual Understanding and Co-operation of 25 Jan. 1955, 243 *UNTS* 211.

[18] Letter from Secretary of State Hull to Senator Shipstead, 30 June 1939, MS Dept of State, file 711. 1928/789, quoted in 3 *Whiteman's Digest of International Law*, at 1157; see also preamble and Article I of the 1955 Treaty.

Despite the two revisions of the 1903 Treaty, Panama remained dissatisfied with the legal regime applicable to the Canal Zone. In 1964 riots erupted in the Zone and Panama severed diplomatic relations with the United States. When diplomatic relations were resumed, the two countries agreed to appoint special ambassadors with a view to reaching a 'just and fair agreement' which would eliminate the causes of conflict between them.[19]

Panama's argument was that the 1903 Treaty, besides having been imposed on it against its interests,[20] was incompatible with new principles of international law and should be revised accordingly. Already in 1960 Panama's ambassador to the United States had claimed that 'in the light of legal principles a lease for an indefinite period of time is inadmissible'.[21] More clearly in 1962 Panama argued in the United Nations that the 1903 Treaty was concluded at a time 'when colonies and the occupation of small countries by powerful ones was a common practice in the world, that is to say, by a treaty which does not conform *to the principles, precepts and rules of law*, justice and international morality which are universally accepted today' (emphasis added).[22] The Treaty was 'iniquitous' and 'prejudicial to its dignity as a sovereign State' and should therefore be revised.[23]

Negotiations for the revision of the Treaty were resumed between Panama and the United States in 1971. Panama brought its case before the Security Council in 1973[24] and insisted on 'effective sovereignty and complete jurisdiction over its entire territory as basic points of a new treaty for the Panama Canal'. At Panama's request a special series of meetings was held in Panama City to discuss the issue of revision.

New Customary Law and the Abrogation of the 1903 Treaty

Panama argued that the Treaty was incompatible with

the principles of international law concerning friendly relations and co-operation among States, and particularly those pertaining to respect for the territorial integrity and political independence of States, non-intervention, equality of rights and self-determination of peoples, the sovereign equality of States, the elimination of all forms of foreign domination, the right of peoples and nations to permanent sovereignty over their natural resources, and international co-operation in the economic and social development of all nations.[25]

Some of these principles, such as the principles of respect for the territorial integrity and political independence of States, non-intervention, equality of rights and self-determination of peoples, and sovereign equality

---

[19] 50 *Dept. State Bull.* (1964), at 656.
[20] *Sec. Council Official Records* (1964), 1086th Meeting, at 7.
[21] Cited in 3 *Whiteman's Digest of International Law*, at 1152.
[22] 17 *UN GAOR* (1962), Plenary Meetings, 113. [23] Ibid.
[24] 28 *Sec. Council Official Records* (1973), 1684th Meeting, at 4.
[25] Ibid., 1704th Meeting, at 6–7; see also 1702nd Meeting, at 5.

of States, were proclaimed by the UN Charter[26] and reiterated or made
more specific by UN Resolutions. Others, such as the concept of a State's
permanent sovereignty over its natural resources, were not contained in
the Charter but were the product of General Assembly Resolutions.[27]

Most of these principles are generally regarded as forming part of general
international law[28] and Panama and the other States involved in the discussions relied on their customary law character. It was thus argued that
the Treaty had been made obsolete by the emergence of a new international legal order, consisting of a whole body of norms and principles,
which, although at least partly originating in the Charter provisions,[29] had
subsequently become customary law. Some of these principles were new,
while others existed in traditional international law, but had changed with
time.[30]

During the UN meetings there was general agreement that the revision
of the 1903 Treaty was necessary in order 'to write off and cancel one of
those historical mortgages and to do so by bringing to bear the entire body
of ideas, principles and norms that the international community has evolved
over the last decades'.[31] Its provisions were no longer valid 'in the light of
international law and the Charter of the United Nations'[32] and should be

[26] See Articles 1–2, 55–6.
[27] For examples of UN Resolutions reiterating Charter principles or proclaiming new
international law principles, see Panama, 1702nd Meeting, at 4; 1704th Meeting, at 6–7; Peru,
ibid., 1696th Meeting, at 3; Kenya, 1700th Meeting, at 4. See also the draft resolution submitted by Peru on behalf of Peru, Panama, and Yugoslavia, 1700th Meeting, at 21.
[28] See e.g. the Declaration on Friendly Relations and Co-operation among States adopted
without a dissenting vote, Resolution 2625 (XXV) of 24 Oct. 1970, 25 *GAOR* Supp. No. 28
(A/8028), 122–4: 'The Principles of the Charter which are embodied in this Declaration
constitute basic principles of international law ...'. See also *Case Concerning Military and
Paramilitary Activities in and against Nicaragua*, Merits, ICJ Reports (1986), at 99–101, 107;
Jiménez de Aréchaga, 'General Course', at 32; R. Rosenstock, 'The Declaration on Principles of International Law concerning Friendly Relations', 65 *AJIL* (1971), 713, at 714–15; B.
Sloan, 'General Assembly Resolutions Revisited', 58 *BYIL* (1987), 39, at 88; Tunkin, *Theory
of International Law* at 175–6.
[29] The incorporation of a rule in a treaty does not exclude the possibility of its parallel
existence and application *qua* customary law, see *Case Concerning Military and Paramilitary
Activities in and Against Nicaragua*, Merits, at 92 *et seq.*, esp. paras. 175, 177 *et seq.*
[30] For an overview see Cassese, *International Law*, at 127 *et seq.*
[31] El Salvador, 1697th Meeting, at 6.
[32] Cuba, 1696th Meeting, at 21. See also the Secretary-General of the United Nations,
ibid., 1701st Meeting, at 2; Colombia, 1696th Meeting., at 15: 'the readjustment of old situations inherited from the past century' was necessary, because their continuation would be
contrary to the 'new international order'; Peru, 1701st Meeting, at 5: the Treaty 'is completely
out of the spirit of the age and the principles of international law ... it should be abrogated
and a new treaty should emerge as soon as possible whereby Panama's effective sovereignty
and total jurisdiction over all its territory will be vindicated'; Canada, 1700th Meeting., at 18:
'reviewing developments since the first Convention 70 years ago, it is clear that, as the poet
said, the old order changeth, yielding place to new'; the United Kingdom, 1701st Meeting.,
at 13: 'I share the feeling that ... the present agreement is in certain respects anachronistic
and in urgent need of revision.'

'brought up to date with present-day realities and international concepts'.[33] The perpetuity clause had 'neither moral nor juridical justification', because it subjected Panama 'to jurisdictional limitations which are as unjust as they are anachronistic'.[34]

The abrogation of the 1903 Treaty and its replacement by a new treaty was a matter of negotiations between the parties.[35] Following recognition by the United States that 'the relationship originally defined in the 1903 Convention needs to be brought into line with the realities of the world today',[36] a draft Resolution[37] proposed to take note of the willingness of the parties to the 1903 Treaty to abrogate it and conclude a 'new, just and fair treaty ... which would fulfil Panama's legitimate aspirations and guarantee full respect for Panama's effective sovereignty over all of its territory'. Although the United States agreed 'on the need to replace the 1903 Convention by a totally new instrument reflecting a new spirit',[38] it voted against the draft Resolution, because it was 'cast in the form of sweeping generalities when we know that the real difficulties lie in the application of those generalities'.[39]

In 1974 Panama and the United States announced eight fundamental principles to serve as a guide in the negotiations on a new treaty, including the elimination of the concept of perpetuity, the termination of United States jurisdiction in the Canal Zone, interim joint administration, and eventual assumption by Panama of total responsibility for the operation of the Canal.[40] In the same year the US Secretary of State stated that, in view of the 'profoundly transformed legal environment', the arrangements concerning the Panama Canal which 'may have been suitable 70 years ago to both parties must be adjusted to the realities of the contemporary world'.[41] In a joint report on the ongoing negotiations submitted to the Organization of American States in June 1976 the two countries agreed to work towards the conclusion of a treaty in line with the evolution experienced by the international community and 'the principles and objectives of the Charter of the United Nations'.[42]

Two new treaties were signed in 1977, the Panama Canal Treaty and the Treaty Concerning the Permanent Neutrality and Operation of the Panama Canal.[43] The Canal Treaty superseded all prior agreements concerning the Panama Canal and expressly recognized Panama as the territorial sovereign.

---

[33] Australia, 1699th Meeting, at 14.
[34] Panama, 1704th Meeting, at 6; see also Argentina, ibid., at 8.
[35] See e.g. Indonesia, 1699th Meeting, at 9; Peru, 1701st Meeting, at 5; Canada, 1700th Meeting, at 13.   [36] 1701st Meeting, at 16.
[37] Proposed by Panama, Guinea, India, Indonesia, Kenya, Peru, Sudan, and Yugoslavia, UN Doc. S/10931/Rev. 1, 21 Mar. 1973.
[38] 1704th Meeting, at 8.   [39] Ibid.   [40] 70 *Dept of State Bull.* (1974), at 184.
[41] Ibid., at 181.   [42] 75 *Dept of State Bull.* (1976), at 12–13.
[43] 16 *ILM* (1977), at 1022, 1040 respectively.

It granted the United States for the period of its duration, that is until 31 December 1999, and in return for an annuity, the rights necessary for regulating the transit of ships through the Canal and for managing, operating, protecting, and defending it. It provided for an increase in Panama's participation in the operation of the Canal up to the year 2000, after which date Panama would assume total responsibility for the operation and management of the Canal, including the maintenance of any military forces in the Canal Zone.

4.3. THE ABOLITION OF THE CAPITULATIONS

The History of the Capitulations

The privileges granted by Süleyman I to France in 1535[44] formed the basis of the capitulatory regime[45] in Turkey, under which other Powers obtained similar advantages.[46] Although the specific rights established under the Capitulatory treaties varied from case to case, the main features of the regime as it was at the beginning of this century can be summarized as follows. Nationals of the Capitulatory Powers residing in Turkey were subject to the jurisdiction of their own consuls and to the application of their national laws to the exclusion of the Turkish laws and tribunals. As a general rule, consuls were competent in cases involving only foreigners and in matters of personal statute. In cases where the Turkish courts retained jurisdiction, the foreign Powers had the right to intervene in the administration of justice; they were present throughout the proceedings and signed the judgment of the court as a prerequisite to its execution. Foreigners were exempted from taxes other than customs duties.

The Capitulations were initially valid only during the life of the grantor and had to be renewed by each successive Sultan. This situation changed in 1740, when France was granted permanent privileges binding upon the

---

[44] For the text, see J. C. Hurowitz, *Diplomacy in the Near and Middle East*, i (1956), at 1.

[45] P. Fauchille, *Droit international public* (1926), i, pt. III, at 111 *et seq*; A. Heyking, 'L'Exterritorialité et ses applications en Extrême-Orient', 7 *RC* (1925-II), 237, at 304; E. W. Keeton, 'Exterritoriality in International and Comparative Law', 72 *RC* (1948-I), at 287; L. Oppenheim, *International Law* (1905), i, at 439, §418; A. Rechid, 'La Condition des étrangers dans la République de Turquie', 46 *RC* (1933–IV), at 169; Rousseau, *Droit international public*, at 233 *et seq.*; A. Truyol Y Serra, 'L'Expansion de la société internationale aux XIXe et Xe siècles', 116 *RC* (1965-III), as, at 130; Y. Yaotong Tchen, *De la disparition de la jurisdiction consulaire dans certains pays de l'Orient* (Paris, 1931), at 9; J. Zourek, 'Report to the ILC on Consular Intercourse and Immunities', A/CN.4/108, *YILC* (1957-II), at 72.

[46] See the 1830 Treaty of Commerce and Navigation with the US, Hurowitz, *Diplomacy*, at 102; for Britain's capitulatory rights, ibid., at 25, confirmed by the 1809 Treaty of Dardanelles, ibid., at 81. Other Capitulatory Powers were Austria–Hungary, Belgium, Brazil, Denmark, Germany, Greece, Italy, the Netherlands, Norway, Portugal, Russia, Spain, and Sweden.

successor of the grantor[47] and subsequent Capitulatory treaties followed this pattern.

The institution of consuls had its origin in the feudal institution of special magistrates who settled disputes between merchants residing outside their State of origin. Special magistrates as well as their successors, consuls, were the direct consequence of the system of personal laws, which a man 'carried with him like a baggage in whatever part of the world he might be'.[48] In order to promote international trade, States in the East and the West regularly exempted foreign merchants residing in their territory from the application of local laws and the jurisdiction of local tribunals. Instead, foreigners were subject to the jurisdiction of their consuls which applied the laws of the home State. When capitulatory privileges were granted by Süleyman I to France and by later Sultans to other Capitulatory Powers, they were generally regarded as an acceptable concession that did not give rise to an infringement of Turkish sovereignty.

In seventeenth-century Europe States assumed jurisdiction over foreigners residing in their territory. Following the emergence of independent nation States, the concept of personal laws, which was linked to feudal particularism, gave way to the new principle of the territoriality of laws. Consular jurisdiction came to be regarded as incompatible with sovereignty, and the jurisdiction of the host State became generally accepted in mixed cases involving foreigners and non-foreigners as well as in disputes involving foreigners only.

The changes taking place in Europe did not have immediate repercussions on the capitulatory regimes existing in non-European countries, where consuls continued to exercise their traditional functions. The Capitulatory Powers insisted on the continued application of these regimes as an exception justified by the alleged underdeveloped state of the legal systems of non-European nations and their inability to afford adequate protection to foreigners. On the other hand, most host States regarded the survival of the Capitulations as a form of discrimination incompatible with their sovereignty and independence. We shall examine how two of these States, Turkey and Egypt, succeeded in abolishing the Capitulatory rights that foreign nationals enjoyed in their territory.

4.3.1. The Capitulations in Turkey

In 1914 Turkey informed the Capitulatory Powers of her decision to abrogate the Capitulatory treaties and to begin negotiations with a view to

---

[47] For the text, see Le Baron I. de Testa, *Recueil des Traités de la Porte Ottomane avec les Puissances Étrangères* (Paris, 1864), i, at 186.　　　　[48] McNair, *Law of Treaties*, at 662.

concluding new treaties of commerce on the basis of the general principles of international law.[49] Turkey argued that the Capitulatory privileges were 'in complete opposition with the juridical rules of the century and the principle of national sovereignty'.[50] The regime of the Capitulations was 'obsolete and no longer responding to modern needs, even when confined within its true contractual limits'[51] and 'should evidently be submitted to the evolution of time'. The following features of the Capitulatory regime were regarded as particularly objectionable: the intervention of foreigners in the exercise of judiciary power 'which constitutes the most important basis of the sovereignty of State'; the limitation of a State's legislative powers as a result of the non-application of its laws to foreigners residing in its territory; the intervention of foreign States in criminal cases involving its own nationals; the exemption of foreigners from taxes.

The Capitulatory Powers protested against the unilateral denunciation of the Capitulatory treaties,[52] and the matter remained unsettled until 1992, when the Lausanne Conference was convened to discuss the peace arrangements concerning Turkey. In the meantime Austria-Hungary, Germany, and the USSR had consented to the abolition of their Capitulatory rights in Turkey.[53]

The Lausanne Conference

In a Memorandum read on 2 December 1922[54] Turkey argued that her decision to abolish the Capitulations was based on a legitimate right, because 'a treaty may be denounced when it has become incompatible with the common international law of civilised States to which the contracting countries subscribe'.[55] When the Capitulations were granted, the system of personal laws was generally in force and was not considered to be incompatible with the prerogatives of the State.[56] By contrast, 'according to modern legal conceptions, each State, in order to be considered as an independent State, must enjoy, within the limits of its frontiers, a complete and full independence' and 'its laws and institutions must have a completely territorial character'. The concept of the territoriality of laws replaced, 'not only in theory, but also in practice',[57] the system of personal laws, and at

---

[49] *For. Relations of the US* (1914), at 1093.   [50] Ibid. (1092); also (1916), at 968.

[51] Ibid. (1915), at 1302.

[52] See note of 10 Sept. 1914 by the Six Great Powers, *For. Relations of the US* (1914), at 1093; note by the United States (1915), at 1301, 1305. For Turkey's reaction, ibid., at 1304–5; (1916), at 968.

[53] See Treaty of 16 Mar. 1921 between Turkey and the USSR, 118 *Br. & For. State Papers*, at 990: 'holding that the Capitulations regime is incompatible with the full exercise of sovereign rights and the national development of any country...' For the Conference, see *Lausanne Conference on Near Eastern Affairs 1922–1923* (HMSO, London, 1923).

[54] *Lausanne Conference*, at 471 et seq.

[55] Ibid., at 479.   [56] Ibid., at 471.   [57] Ibid., at 472.

the same time a State's right to legislate and to administer justice within its territory became one of the exclusive attributes of sovereignty. The Capitulations were 'an anomaly and an anachronism',[58] and 'plainly contrary to the rules of modern international public law'[59] and to the modern conception of State sovereignty. Their abolition was therefore necessary.[60]

The Capitulatory Powers recognized that the Capitulations were incompatible with the sovereign rights of an independent State under modern international law. There was general agreement that the existing regime should be brought into line with the evolution of the law and the legitimate demands of the Turkish Government.[61]

The new regime should provide adequate guarantees for the protection of foreign nationals to the extent that Turkey's sovereign rights were fully respected.[62] It was accepted, for instance, that the new system of taxation should not discriminate against foreigners, but should not contain special tax privileges, which were a thing of the past.[63]

The Conference ended with the conclusion of a Peace Treaty[64] based on 'respect for the independence and sovereignty of States' and providing for 'the complete abolition of the capitulations in Turkey in every respect' (Article 28). Turkey agreed to treat nationals of the contracting parties 'in accordance with ordinary international law' in matters of entry, residence, and jurisdiction.[65] In fiscal matters there would be equality of treatment between Turkish and foreign nationals (Articles 8 *et seq.*).

The Capitulatory rights of the United States, which was not a signatory to the Peace Treaty, were abolished by the 1931 Treaty Regarding Matters

---

[58] Ibid.   [59] Ibid., at 469.   [60] Ismet Pasha, ibid., at 468.

[61] See e.g. Marquis Garroni: 'It must be recognised that according to present ideas of law the capitulatory regime is regarded as liable to diminish the sovereign powers of an independent State; and it is intelligible that Turkey should demand the abolition of this regime which had its day' (ibid., at 467) see also Garroni, at 482–3; M. Barrère: 'the task of the Conference was to devise a system more suited to modern requirements in place of the capitulatory system, which was in consonance with archaic ideas' (ibid., at 468); Barrère: 'The French Delegation had agreed to renounce the Capitulations, because they considered that some features of the regime were out of date, and that others—especially these respecting financial obligations—were in part unjust' (ibid., at 492); Sir H. Rumbold: the Allied delegations 'were anxious to devise a substitute compatible with Turkey's sovereign rights' (ibid., at 485); M. Bombard: 'the Capitulatory regime was defective and out of date. Its revision and even its abolition were necessary' (ibid., at 499). See also the preamble to the Draft Convention on the Regime of Foreigners, ibid., at 790.

[62] M. Barrère, ibid., at 468; Marquis Garroni, at 470, 481 *et seq*; Sir H. Rumbold, at 484; Baron Hayashi, at 492; Child, at 494.

[63] Albrecht, 'The Taxation of Aliens under International Law', 24 *BYIL*, at 152 *et seq.*

[64] Treaty of Peace of Lausanne of 24 July 1923 between Britain, France, Italy, Greece, Romania, the Serb–Croat–Slovene State, and Turkey, 117 *Br. & For. State Papers*, at 543, 18 *AJIL* (1924), Supp., at 4 *et seq.*

[65] Convention Respecting Conditions of Residence and Business and Jurisdiction of 24 July 1923, 18 *AJIL* (1924), Supp., at 67, esp. Articles 2 and 15.

of Establishment and Sojourn of American Nationals and Corporations in Turkey.[66] The Treaty, which affirmed the parties' desire to establish their relations 'in accordance with modern international law', provided for most-favoured-nation treatment for their nationals.

The abolition of the Capitulations in Turkey is an example of treaty adaptation to the evolution of general customary law on the basis of negotiations between the contracting parties. It will be recalled that, although the States concerned recognized the substantive validity of Turkey's claims, they protested against Turkey's attempt unilaterally to terminate the Capitulations and insisted on their treaty rights, until the Capitulations were expressly abolished by the 1914 Convention.[67]

Rebus sic stantibus

At the Lausanne Conference Turkey also alleged that she had the right to abrogate the Capitulatory treaties by reason of a fundamental change of circumstances. The purpose for which the Capitulations were concluded was to protect foreigners against the deficiencies of the Turkish legal system, and they had no reason to exist after these deficiencies had been remedied.[68] While Turkey alleged that this change of facts had deprived the treaties of the reason for their existence and given rise to the application of the *rebus sic stantibus* rule, it regarded the evolution of the general international law as a *separate* ground for the abrogation of the Capitulations.[69]

4.3.2. The Capitulations in Egypt

The Capitulatory regime in Egypt was based on the same treaties that applied in Turkey. In 1876 the Capitulatory Powers consented to the transfer of part of the jurisdiction of the Consular Courts to Mixed Courts consisting of foreign and Egyptian judges, with a view to mitigating the consequences of the Capitulatory regime.[70] However, the majority of the judges in the Mixed Courts were foreigners and the Capitulatory privileges remained otherwise intact.

Great Britain was the first of the Capitulatory Powers that expressly

[66] Treaty of 28 Oct. 1931, *Treaties, Conventions, International Acts, Protocols and Agreements between the United States and other Powers* (1923–37), iv, at 4670; see also *Hackworth's Digest of International Law*, V (1943), v. Washington, at 307.

[67] See *Hackworth's Digest*, ii (1941), at 529; M. Barrère, *Lausanne Conference*, at 468; Lord Curzon, at 468–9.

[68] *Lausanne Conference*, at 478. See also Baron Hayashi, at 470; Marquis Garroni, at 482; Sir H. Rumbold, at 485; Lord Curzon, at 496.   [69] Ibid., at 479.

[70] See the *Règlement d'Organisation Judiciaire*, 66 *Br. & For. State Papers*, at 593; *For. Relations of the US* (1874), at 1126–92; J. Y. Brinton, *The Mixed Courts of Egypt* (New Haven, Conn., 1930). For a general study of the Capitulations in Egypt, see J. H. Scott, *The Law Affecting Foreigners in Egypt as a Result of the Capitulations* (Edinburgh, 1907).

[70] *For. Relations of the US* (1937-II), at 615.

recognized in the 1936 Anglo-Egyptian Treaty of Alliance that 'the capitulatory regime now existing in Egypt is no longer in accordance with the spirit of the times and with the present state of Egypt' and agreed to co-operate with Egypt in order to 'bring about speedily its abolition'. The abolition of the Capitulations should involve the removal of all existing restrictions on Egypt's sovereignty relating to the application of her laws to foreigners,[71] including the requirement that the Capitulatory Powers must consent to the application of all Egyptian legislation to their nationals. It should also entail the abolition of the Mixed and Consular Courts after an agreed transitional period.[72]

In 1937 Egypt invited the Capitulatory Powers to a conference held at Montreux on 12 April with a view to abolishing the Capitulations. In Egypt's view it was regrettable that

in spite of a modern political, administrative and economic organization she remained the only country in which there still existed a regime for foreigners based on privileges which were accorded them gratuitously during the sixteenth century for reasons which have entirely disappeared. Now that the Capitulatory Powers have accepted elsewhere and notably in Turkey ... the abolition of the capitulations, this regime *contrary to the principles of modern law*, has continued in Egypt up to the present time ... *constituting an obvious infringement of the sovereignty of the State* and the dignity of the nation. (emphasis added)[73]

In order to end 'such a singular situation' and to develop relations with the Capitulatory Powers 'within the normal framework of rules of common law established by the rights of modern people', Egypt called for the abolition of Capitulations and the transfer of consular jurisdiction to National Courts at the end of a transitional period. Following the abolition of the Capitulations, 'the principles generally accepted in modern legislation', including the principle of equality of treatment, should apply to fiscal and other matters relating to foreigners residing in Egypt.[74]

In accordance with the 1936 Treaty of Alliance, Great Britain supported Egypt in her efforts, for 'it was an *anachronism* that Egypt should under modern conditions continue to be fettered to the extent that she is at present by the capitulations'.[75] In the event that the Capitulations could not be abolished, because the Capitulatory Powers were unduly obstructive, it was by no means clear that the Egyptian Government could not make a good legal case for a right to abolish the Capitulations unilaterally.[76]

The United States shared the view that every reasonable effort should be made to co-operate with the Egyptian Government with a view to abolishing the Capitulations, in order to avoid raising questions as to the

---

[71] Anglo-Egyptian Treaty of Alliance of 26 Aug. 1936, *Br. & For. State Papers* (1936), Article 13 and Annex, para. 1(i).
[72] Ibid., Article 13, para 1(ii).   [73] *For. Relations of the US* (1937-II), at 615–16.
[74] Ibid., at 616.   [75] Ibid., at 622.   [76] Ibid., at 623, 627.

legal right of Egypt to terminate the Capitulations unilaterally—'a right which the Egyptian Government appears to have reserved by the terms of the 1936 Treaty'.[77] It was 'self-evident that the Capitulatory regime in Egypt is an institution which we must acknowledge to be *no longer in accordance with the spirit of the times*' and its termination under proper procedural safeguards would be 'in accordance with the fixed policy of the US Government ... of establishing its relations with foreign countries ... *in accordance with the precepts of modern international law and without seeking to obtain for American Nationals or interests any special privileges or favors*'.[78] The United States gave 'its most unequivocal assurances of the sympathy with which it regards the aims and purposes of Conference' which was proof of Egypt's respect for 'the orderly processes of international law'.[79]

At the Montreux Conference[80] there was general agreement that the abolition of the Capitulations was necessary. The preamble to the Treaty adopted by the Conference[81] affirmed that the Capitulations were 'no longer in harmony with the new situation which Egypt had attained through the progress of its institutions' and that, following their abolition by common agreement, relations among the contracting parties should be based on 'respect for the independence and sovereignty of States and on ordinary international law'. The parties[82] thus agreed to the complete abolition in all respects of the Capitulations in Egypt (Article 1). The Treaty maintained the Mixed Tribunals only for a transitional period (Article 3) and provided for the application of all Egyptian legislation to foreigners, 'subject to the application of the principles of international law' (Article 2, para. 1).

Negotiations *v.* Unilateral Termination

Unlike Turkey, Egypt did not unilaterally declare the Capitulations abolished but initiated negotiations with the States concerned with a view to their abrogation. However, it was the view of the United Kingdom and the United States that, had the Capitulatory Powers refused to negotiate in good faith so that the abolition of the Capitulations by common agreement was made impossible, Egypt could be entitled to denounce the treaties unilaterally.

Although unilateral termination of a treaty incompatible with new custom

---

[77] *For. Relations of the US* (1937-II), at 631–2, and Article 13, para. 4, of the 1936 Treaty.

[78] Memorandum by the Secretary of State to the Minister in Egypt, *For. Relations of the US* (1937-II), at 634.

[79] Draft Statement of the US to be read at the Montreux Conference, ibid., at 639–40.

[80] For the Conference at Montreux, see *Actes de la Conférence des Capitulations*, Montreux, 12 avril–8 mai 1937.

[81] Convention of Montreux of 8 May 1937, 55 *UKTS* (1937), Cmnd. 5630.

[82] These were: Egypt, the United States, Belgium, the United Kingdom, Denmark, Spain, France, Greece, Italy, Norway, the Netherlands, Portugal, and Sweden.

is thus initially unacceptable, it may be justified at a later stage if the other parties have failed to discharge their obligation to negotiate in good faith with a view to terminating the treaty.

This procedure encourages the peaceful settlement of disputes by favouring negotiations as the *initial* course of action. At the same time it ensures that unilateral termination is available as a last resort in cases where the rules of good faith have been breached.

4.4. THE IMPACT OF NEW CUSTOM ON THE VIENNA CLASSIFICATION OF DIPLOMATIC AGENTS

Under the Regulations adopted at the Congress of Vienna in 1815 by Austria, Spain, France, Great Britain, Portugal, Russia, and Sweden,[83] diplomatic agents were divided in three categories: that of ambassadors, legates, or nuncios; that of envoys accredited to sovereigns, having in practice the double title of envoy extraordinary and minister plenipotentiary; and that of chargés d'affaires accredited to Ministers of Foreign Affairs. The class of 'ministers resident' was added to the list by the 1818 Aix-la-Chapelle Protocol[84] as an intermediate category between envoys and chargés d'affaires. Under Article 2 of the Vienna Regulations only ambassadors and their papal equivalents, legates and nuncios, were regarded as personal representatives of their Head of State and were entitled to have access to the Head of the receiving State.

The division of diplomatic agents into classes existed before the adoption of the Vienna Regulations. By the middle of the seventeenth century two classes had become generally recognized in practice—namely, that of ambassadors and that of ordinary envoys called 'residents'—and in the eighteenth century the class of ministers plenipotentiary appeared. However, the question of precedence between the various classes, which was often regarded as reflecting a hierarchy between States, had not been settled before the Congress of Vienna.

The Congress of Vienna originally intended to establish an order of precedence between the Great Powers.[85] This idea was abandoned and the Conference established instead a ranking of diplomatic agents, with ambassadors at the highest level. This indirectly established an order of precedence between States enjoying royal honours and those which did

---

[83] G. F. de Martens, *Nouveau recueil des traités*, ii (1814–15), at 445.

[84] 5 *Br. & For. State Papers*, at 1090.

[85] See E. Satow, *Guide to Diplomatic Practice* (London, 1907), §32, at 21; J. W. Foster, *The Practice of Diplomacy* (Boston and New York, 1906) at 19–20; S. Rosenne (ed.), *League of Nations Committee of Experts for the Progressive Codification of International Law*, ii (New York, 1972), at 409.

not, because at the time of the adoption of the Regulations only the first category of States had the right to send and receive ambassadors.[86]

The Vienna Regulations were not originally considered to be incompatible with the principle of legal equality of States[87] and the classification of diplomatic agents that they introduced became generally accepted in diplomatic practice.[88]

Developments in State practice concerning the appointment of diplomatic agents occurred in the twentieth century. Contrary to the custom that formed the basis of the Vienna Regulations, most States not enjoying royal honours started appointing ambassadors rather than ministers plenipotentiary to represent them, and this trend became prominent after the Second World War. For instance, while in 1822 six States were represented in Great Britain by ambassadors, their number in 1954 rose to 46.[89] Moreover, the Vienna Regulations came to be regarded as no longer compatible with modern perceptions of State equality. It was in application of the principle of equality of States that the USSR tried to establish only one class of diplomatic agents in 1918, by naming all its agents 'plenipotentiary representatives',[90] but her initiative was not followed by other States.

Although the Vienna Regulations were not expressly terminated, they were generally regarded as having been rendered obsolete on account of changes in customary law.[91] In particular, the hierarchy of diplomatic agents that the Regulations introduced was considered to be out of pace with the times, to the extent that it reflected a hierarchy of States. The revision of the classification introduced by the Regulations was proposed in 1927 at the League of Nations, but, because of the lack of general agreement, it did not take place until the 1961 Vienna Convention on Diplomatic Relations was concluded.

4.4.1. The Discussion at the League of Nations

A Report submitted to the League of Nations Committee of Experts for the Progressive Codification of International Law in 1927[92] proposed that the difference in rank between ambassadors, ministers plenipotentiary,

---

[86] L. Oppenheim, *International Law* (1905), i, at §§117, 365.   [87] Ibid., at §117.

[88] L. Oppenheim, *International Law*, 8th edn. ed. H. Lauterpacht (London, 1955), at §364; *Satow's Guide to Diplomatic Practice* (4th edn, London, 1957), at §280. See e.g. the US law of 1 Mar. 1893, 27 *Statutes at Large*, 497, c.182.

[89] See Oppenheim, (8th edn., 1955), at 777 n. 4; *Satow's Guide to Diplomatic Practice* (5th edn., London, 1979), at 83.   [90] See Tunkin, *YILC* (1957-I), at 35, para. 59.

[91] See e.g. Lauterpacht, *International Law*, i, at 88.

[92] See Rosenne (ed.), *League of Nations Committee of Experts for the Progressive Codification of International Law*, ii, at 408.

and ministers resident under the Vienna Regulations should be abolished and a common designation should be given to all three classes.

According to the Report, the hierarchy of States reflected in the hierarchy of diplomatic agents introduced by the Vienna Regulations conflicted with the concept of the equality of States: 'since the League of Nations has inaugurated a system in which the equality of States is a fact, and since international law is developing a new spirit, it would indeed be more than strange if we continued to observe an obsolete tradition which has only survived through the negligence or complacence of the so-called second-class States.'[93] Moreover, in practice States showed 'a definitive intention to abandon the spirit which formed the basis of the 1815 agreement'.[94] Numerous embassies were established between small States, whether monarchic or republican, and ministers resident almost entirely disappeared from diplomatic nomenclature. As result, it was now rare for governments to place in a different rank diplomatic agents to whom they had assigned the same duties and responsibilities.

In reply to the Committee's questionnaire,[95] twelve governments, three of which—namely, Austria, Portugal, and Sweden—were parties to the 1815 Vienna Convention, favoured the proposed revision,[96] because it would be more in keeping with principles of modern international law, and in particular with the principle of the equality of States.[97] However, eleven States were against the Committee's proposal, either because revision was not considered to be feasible[98] or because the distinction between ambassadors and ministers plenipotentiary was not considered to be contrary to the principle of equality of States.[99] As a result, the Committee's proposal was abandoned.[100]

4.4.2. The 1961 Vienna Convention on Diplomatic Relations

The relevance of new customary law to the revision of the Vienna classification was discussed in the context of the codification of law on 'Diplomatic Intercourse and Immunities' by the International Law Commission.[101] The 1961 Vienna Convention on Diplomatic Relations,[102] which was the

---

[93] Ibid., at 410.   [94] Ibid.

[95] Ibid., at 420 *et seq.*   [96] Ibid., at 422–3, 442, and 446 respectively.

[97] Ibid., Brazil, at 425; Switzerland, at 450; see also Austria, at 422; Hungary, at 435; Sweden, at 446.

[98] Great Britain, at 426; France, at 432; Germany, at 432; Japan, at 437; New Zealand, at 439; Norway, at 440; the United States of America at 452.

[99] Belgium, at 424; Spain, at 444–5.

[100] *League of Nations*, V. Legal Questions, 1928. V.4 (Doc. A.15.1928.V), at 6.

[101] See GA Resolution 685(VII) of 5 Dec. 1952, *GAOR*, 8th Session, Supp. No. 9, para. 170.

[102] Signed on 8 Apr. 1961, entered into force on 24 Apr. 1964, 500 *UNTS* (1964), at 95.

result of the ILC work, revised the classification to the extent necessary to make it compatible with State equality.

(a) The Discussion at the ILC

In his 1955 Report,[103] the Special Rapporteur, Mr Sandström, proposed that the distinction between ambassadors and ministers plenipotentiary should be abolished, because it was contrary to the principle of the formal equality of States[104] and to the growing tendency on the part of States to appoint ambassadors rather than ministers plenipotentiary to represent them.[105]

During the ILC discussions there was general agreement that the Commission should take into account the modern perception of the principle of State equality, which was a principle of positive law.[106] It should get rid of the vestiges of 'the special position which the Great Powers then enjoyed in law, as well as in fact', because, according to modern ideas, it resulted in discrimination against certain States.[107]

According to some ILC members, this implied that the distinction between ambassadors and ministers plenipotentiary should be abolished and all diplomatic representatives should have the same title.[108] However, the view prevailed that the existence of different classes of diplomatic agents did not necessarily conflict with State equality, provided that all States could appoint diplomatic agents of all classes.[109]

As a result, 'in harmony with the tendency to claim theoretical equality for all States',[110] the ILC Draft divided heads of mission into three classes—namely, that of ambassadors, legates, or nuncios, that of envoys, ministers, and other persons accredited to heads of State, and that of chargés d'affaires accredited to Ministers for Foreign Affairs. At the same time, Article 14 of the Draft made it clear that, 'except as concerns precedence and etiquette, there shall be no differentiation between heads of mission by reason of their class'.

(b) The Attitude of Governments

In their observations on the ILC Draft, some governments criticized the Commission for maintaining the distinction between ambassadors and

---

[103] A/CN.4/91, *YILC* (1955-II), at 9.   [104] *YILC* (1957-I), at 33, para. 32.

[105] *YILC* (1955-II), at 16; (1957-I), at 33, para. 32.

[106] See e.g. El-Erian, *YILC* (1957-I), at 35, para. 61; Tunkin, at 35, 38, para. 25; Yokota, at 36, para. 70.   [107] François, ibid., at 34–5, para. 56.

[108] François, ibid.; Bartos, at 39, para. 43; at 34, paras, 46–7; (1958-I), at 118, para. 9.

[109] El-Erian, ibid., at 35, para, 61; Hsu, at 35, para 63, at 202, para. 2; Matine Daftary, at 34, para. 52; Tunkin, at 35; Yokota, at 36, para. 70.

[110] Scelle, ibid., at 39, para. 36; Tunkin, at 39, para. 46.

ministers plenipotentiary.[111] The Vienna classification was considered to be outdated and contrary to the principle of the equality of sovereign States, because it distinguished between different categories of diplomatic representatives on the basis of the importance of the sending State.[112] The proposed classification should take account of the general tendency to abolish the distinction between the first two classes of diplomatic agents accredited to heads of State[113] or it should at least be pointed out that all States had the right to appoint all classes of diplomatic agents, as they saw fit.[114]

At the Vienna Conference on Diplomatic Relations (2 March–14 April 1961),[115] two amendments submitted to the Committee of the Whole, one jointly by Mexico and Sweden,[116] and one by Switzerland,[117] proposed that ministers plenipotentiary should not be included in the classes of diplomatic agents mentioned by the Convention. According to Sweden, a party to the Vienna Regulations, although in 1815 the States party to the Regulations aimed at establishing rules of universal scope and validity, the Vienna classification should be revised to reflect changes in world conditions which had occurred in the meantime.[118]

A number of delegates opposed these amendments, because the class of ministers had not completely disappeared and its continued existence was not necessarily contrary to State equality.[119] The Committee of the Whole finally rejected the amendments.[120] As a result, Article 14 of the Vienna Convention maintained the distinction between ambassadors and ministers accredited to the Heads of State, but provided at the same time that there would be no differentiation between heads of mission by reason of their class, except in matters of precedence and etiquette.

It was, therefore, accepted that the classification introduced by the Vienna

---

[111] Norway, 14 *GAOR*, Annexes, Agenda Item 56, at 7; Bulgaria, ibid., at 4.

[112] See Colombia's comments on the ILC Draft at the 6th Committee of the GA, Doc. A/C.6/SR, 13 *GAOR* (1958), 575th Meeting, para. 7; Bulgaria, ibid., 572nd Meeting, at 107; Czechoslovakia, 570th Meeting, at 96.

[113] Switzerland, Doc. A.CN.4/114, *YILC* (1958-II), at 129; Doc. A/4164, 14 *GAOR*, Annexes, Agenda Item 56, at 9; Byelorussian Soviet Republic, 13 *GAOR* (1958), 571st Meeting, at 101; Sweden, Doc. A.CN.4/114, *YILC* (1958-II), at 127; 14 *GAOR*, Annexes, Agenda Item 56, at 8; Finland, *YILC* (1958-II), at 118.   [114] Yugoslavia, *YILC* (1958-II), at 138.

[115] For the records of the Conference, see *Vienna Conference Official Records* (Geneva, 1962), i–ii, Doc. A/CONF. 20/14 and Add. 1.

[116] A/CONF. 20/C.1/L.57 & Add. 1.   [117] A/CONF. 20/C.1/L.108.

[118] Sweden, *Vienna Conference Official Records* (Geneva, 1962), i, Committee of the Whole, 16th Meeting, at 115, para. 29; Mexico, at 115, para. 28; Switzerland, at 115, para. 32. See also Sweden, *GAOR*, 10th Session, 6th Committee, 453rd Meeting, para. 13: the classification 'had been criticized as unrealistic even before the turn of the century' and was in 'urgent need of revision' (Norway, at 115, para. 18).

[119] See e.g. Turkey, ibid., at 116, para. 5; Argentina, at 117, para. 14; China, at 117, para. 8; Iran, at 118, para. 26; Tunisia, at 119, para. 33; Brazil, at 119, para. 35; Italy, at 119, para. 42; Austria, at 119, para, 43; Chile, at 120, para, 47; Ecuador, at 145, para. 22.

[120] *Vienna Conference*, i, Committee of the Whole, 23rd Meeting, at 145, para. 32.

Regulations was obsolete and should be revised to the extent necessary to make it compatible with the principle of equality of States as understood in modern international law. State equality was considered to be incompatible with the assumption behind the Vienna Regulations that there was an order of precedence among States, which was reflected in the rank of their diplomatic representatives. By contrast, the abolition of different classes of diplomatic agents was not considered to be necessary, provided that all States were entitled to appoint representatives of all classes as they saw fit.

The discussions leading to the revision of the Vienna Regulations took place in an institutional framework aiming at the codification of the international law on diplomatic intercourse. For this reason, even States not party to the Regulations could express their views on the compatibility of the classification with new general law, especially since the hierarchy of States reflected in the Regulations discriminated against them.

4.5. THE TERMINATION OF THE 1936 ANGLO-EGYPTIAN TREATY OF ALLIANCE

The 1936 Anglo-Egyptian Treaty of Alliance[121] terminated the military occupation of Egypt by British forces. By way of exception, in view of the importance of the Canal as 'a universal means of communication and as an essential means of communication between the different part of the British Empire', Britain retained the right to station forces in the vicinity of the Suez Canal, until 'such time as the High Contracting Parties agree that the Egyptian army is in a position to ensure by its own resources the liberty and entire security of navigation of the Canal' (Article 8). The Treaty was concluded for an indefinite period and was open to negotiations with a view to its revision after 1956, except for its provisions establishing a perpetual alliance between the parties.

In 1945 Egypt asked that Anglo-Egyptian treaty relations should be reoriented 'in the light of the principles enunciated in the UN Charter'.[122] Egypt argued that the 1936 Treaty was concluded in view of the impending war in Europe and had outlived its purpose.[123] Moreover, the maintenance of military forces in her territory was contrary to the UN Charter and in particular to the principle of sovereign equality.

After negotiations between the two countries had broken down,[124] Egypt submitted the dispute to the Security Council.[125] She argued that the 1936

---

[121] Treaty of Alliance of 26 Aug. 1936, 140 *Br. & For. State Papers* (1962), at 179.
[122] Egyptian Memorandum of 20 Dec. 1945, 2 *Sec. Council Official Records* (1947), at 1747.
[123] Ibid.; also at 1752–3.   [124] Ibid., at 1771, 1868 *et seq.*
[125] Letter of 8 July 1947, ibid., at 1343–5.

Treaty could not bind her any longer, because it was inconsistent with the Charter and a General Assembly Resolution adopted on 14 December 1946[126] as an authoritative interpretation of the Charter provisions.[127] The 1946 Resolution called for the withdrawal without delay of armed forces stationed in the territories of Member States without their consent freely and publicly expressed in treaties or agreements consistent with the Charter.

Egypt requested the Security Council to direct the total and immediate evacuation of British troops from Egypt, including the Sudan, as well as the termination of the administrative regime of the Sudan. Although no Resolution was adopted by the Security Council, the dispute was terminated by the conclusion of the 1953 Agreement concerning self-Determination for the Sudan and the 1954 Agreement concerning the Suez Canal Base,[128] which provided for the withdrawal of all British forces from Egypt over a period of twenty months.

This is an example of treaty termination on account of the evolution of the law, albeit *not* customary law. Egypt argued that the 1936 Treaty was incompatible with the provisions of the UN Charter *qua* treaty law.[129] The Charter provisions were higher law and should prevail pursuant to Article 103 of the Charter.[130] Article 103 provides in this respect that 'in the event of a conflict between the obligations of the Members of the United Nations under the present Charter and their obligations under any other international agreements, their obligations under the present Charter shall prevail'.

4.6. THE IMPACT OF THE CONCEPT OF HUMAN RIGHTS ON THE MINORITIES TREATIES

After the First World War a number of treaties were concluded for the protection of ethnic, linguistic, and religious minorities in certain, mainly European, States.[131] The minorities treaties were designed to attain two

---

[126] UN Doc. S/410, 11 July 1947, *GAOR* 1st Session, Part 2, 65–7.

[127] 2 *Sec. Council Official Records* (1947), at 1343–4, 1753–4.

[128] See UKTS 1953, No. 47, 210 *UNTS*, at 3 respectively.

[129] 2 *Sec. Council Official Records* (1947), at 1344, 1747, 1866, 1868; at 1959; at 1753; Great Britain at 1773.   [130] Ibid., at 1757, 1961, 1863.

[131] See Treaty with Poland of 28 June 1919, 112 *Br. & For. State Papers*, at 232; with Czechoslovakia, Treaty of 10 Sept. 1919, ibid., at 502; with the Serb–Croat–Slovene State, 10 Sept. 1919, ibid., at 514; with Romania, 9 Dec. 1919, ibid., at 538; with Greece, 10 Aug. 1920, 113 *Br. & For. State Papers*, at 471; and additional protocol of 24 July 1923, 117 *Br. & For. State Papers*, at 539; with Austria, Articles 62–9 of the Treaty of Peace of Saint-Germain-en-Laye of 10 Sept. 1919, 112 *Br. & For. State Papers*, at 317; with Bulgaria, Articles 49–59 of the Treaty of Peace of Neuilly of 27 Nov. 1919, ibid., at 781; with Hungary, Articles 54–60 of the Treaty of Peace of Trianon of 4 June 1920, 113 *Br. & For. State Papers*, at 486; with Turkey, Articles 37–45 of the Treaty of Lausanne of 24 July 1923, 117 *Br. & For. State Papers*, at 543. Five other States made appropriate declarations as a condition of their admission to

objectives: first, to ensure that nationals belonging to the protected minority groups would be placed on an equal footing with other nationals of their State; and, secondly, to give minority groups 'special' rights in order to enable them to preserve their separate identity, such as the right to be educated in their own language and the right to establish their own religious institutions.

The minorities regime was solely conventional in character. International customary law did not afford minorities any protection against discrimination or forced assimilation and did not recognize the idea of general protection of human rights.[132] The minorities treaties were placed under the guarantee of the League of Nations and could not be modified without the assent of the majority of the Council of the League.

Although the minorities treaties were never expressly terminated, the prevailing view in the literature was that after the Second World War they were no longer in force, having been superseded by the principle of universal respect for human rights embodied in the UN Charter and the 1948 UN Declaration of Human Rights.[133]

The Principle of Universal Respect for Human Rights

The principle of respect for human rights is proclaimed by the UN Charter. Article 1 of the Charter provides that one of the purposes of the United Nations is international co-operation with a view to 'promoting and encouraging respect for human rights and for fundamental freedoms for all without distinction as to race, sex, language, or religion'. To this end, all States members of the United Nations have pledged to take joint and separate action in co-operation with the Organization (Articles 55 and 56).[134]

Prior to the adoption of the Charter provisions in human rights, a number of declarations of the inter-war period affirmed the will of States to establish a regime for the protection of the rights of man, irrespective of race, sex, language, or religion.[135] The principle of respect for human rights was intended to be an essential foundation of the post-war international order

the League of Nations: Albania in 1921, Lithuania in 1922, Lativia in 1923, Estonia in 1923, and Iraq in 1932.

[132] See Oppenheim, *International Law* (8th edn., 1955), i, at §292.

[133] Ch. Rousseau, *Droit International Public*, ii (Paris, 1974), 758; J. L. Kunz, 'The Present Status of the International Law for the Protection of Minorities', 48 *AJIL* (1954), at 282.

[134] See also preamble to the Charter and Articles 13, 62, and 68.

[135] See joint declaration of the President of the United States and the Prime Minister of Great Britain of 14 Aug. 1941 (the Atlantic Charter), 35 *AJIL* (1941), at 191; joint declaration of the United Nations of Jan. 1942; joint declaration by the USSR, the UK, and the USA, Yalta Conference, Feb. 1945, *The Tehran, Yalta and Potsdam Conferences*, Documents (trans. from the Russian, Moscow, 1969), at 137; Declaration concerning Germany, Potsdam Conference, July–Aug. 1945, ibid., at 322.

and secured almost universal support at the time when the Charter was adopted.[136]

Although both the concept of human rights and the regime for the protection of minorities were based on the principle of non-discrimination, the minorities regime contained in addition special rights for the positive protection of minority groups. More importantly, there was a basic difference in approach between the two systems. The principle of respect for human rights aimed at protecting the *individual* as such, all individuals in all States, while the minorities system safeguarded the rights of minority groups in certain States only.

The Attitude of the States Concerned

At the Paris Peace Conference of 1946, several States referred to the concept of human rights enunciated by the Charter as a fundamental and generally recognized principle of the post-war international legal system.[137] There was agreement at the Conference that the emergence of this concept had changed the point of view from which the problem of minorities should be approached and that, as a result, their legal situation should be reviewed.

On the other hand, views differed as to whether the concept of human rights was incompatible with the idea of the protection of minorities *qua* minorities, as opposed to their protection *qua* individuals. The question was whether 'the minority problem had been wholly absorbed into the larger problem of human righs',[138] especially since the United Nations had not yet committed itself to a definitive position on this issue.[139] Attitudes *vis-à-vis* the minorities treaties varied accordingly.

Hungary, for instance, asserted that the minorities treaties had never been invalidated by any other international agreement and were still

---

[136] For the recognition of this principle as a legal standard, see the *Barcelona Traction Case*, ICJ Reports (1970), at 32; Brownlie, *Principles*, at 598; Lauterpacht, *International Law*, i, at 48, 470–471. 502; iii, at 407 *et seq*; W. McKean, *Equality and Discrimination under International Law* (Oxford, 1983), at 274; Oppenheim, (8th edn., 1955), at paras. 292, 340k.

[137] See e.g. Hungary, note of 20 Nov. 1945, Hungarian Ministry of Foreign Affairs, *Hungary and the Conference of Paris* (Eng. edn., 1947), ii, at 15, to the effect that Czechoslovakia's proposed measures *vis-à-vis* minorities 'violate all generally recognized principles of international law, and the basic human rights accepted by all civilized nations'; statement by the Hungarian Delegation, 30 Sept. 1946, ibid., iv, at 95; statement by the Romanian representative, *Collection of Documents of Paris Conference* (1946), i, at 277 (neither country was at that time a party to the UN Charter or to the Declaration of the United Nations). See also Australia, *Collection of Documents of Paris Conference*, ii, at 65.

[138] See I. Claude, *National Minorities: An International Problem* (New York, 1955), at 154.

[139] See e.g. GA Resolution 217(III) C, *GAOR*, 3rd Session (1948), UN Doc. E/1371; J. P. Humphrey, 'The Sub-Commission on Prevention of Discrimination and Protection of Minorities', 62 *AJIL* (1968), at 869; I. Claude, 'The Nature and Status of Sub-Commission on Prevention of Discrimination and Protection of Minorities', *International Organization* (May 1951), at 300.

binding.[140] She claimed, however, that their revision in the light of developments in the UN law on human rights was necessary. Hungary thus suggested that a new convention should be concluded with a view to guaranteeing certain important minority rights in 'States with a mixed Central and Eastern European population', to the extent that these rights were not covered by the UN Charter and the declarations of principle contained in the Draft Peace Treaties.[141] The procedural aspect of the minorities treaties should also be revised to take account of the new circumstances.[142]

Other States took the position that the principle of respect for the human rights of individuals was incompatible with the idea of special protection of minorities *qua* minorities. These States treated the minorities treaties as though they were already a dead letter. Romania, for instance, refused to 'agree to any system reminiscent of the old minorities statute . . . which imposed minority obligations on one class of States only to the detriment of the principle of the legal equality of States'.[143] After the war, 'the United Nations Charter adopted the broader conception of the international protection of human rights', which established 'a uniform system for all parties, whether majorities or minorities, and protected the man as such, irrespective of race, sex, language or religion'.[144] The emergence of the concept of human rights had changed 'the point of view from which the problem [was] approached'. It was 'in loyal acknowledgment of these principles', and not because of the minorities treaties, that Romania had already guaranteed 'a regime of complete freedom' for all minorities on her territory.[145]

The minorities treaties were not expressly terminated at the Conference. The Peace Treaties signed with the Allied and Associated Powers in 1947 contained human rights provisions, but made no reference to special minority rights.[146] As a result, the issue of the continued validity of the minorities

---

[140] Hungary, note of 20 Nov. 1945; also note by Hungarian Ministry of Foreign Affairs, 11 Dec. 1945, ibid., at 51; preamble to the Draft Treaty on the Protection of Minorities submitted by Hungary to the Paris Conference. 30 Aug. 1946, *Hongrie et la Conférence de la Paix* (French edn., 1947), i, at 142.

[141] Statement of the Hungarian representative of 14 Aug. 1946, C.P. (PLEN), xvii, at 5, *Collection of Documents of Paris Conference* (1946), i, at 300–1. See also Yugoslavia's proposal that the Peace Treaty with Italy should expressly provide for the right of minorities to be educated in their mother tongue, ibid., ii, at 127.

[142] Preamble to the Draft Treaty on the Protection of Minorities submitted by Hungary to the Paris Conference, *Hongrie et la Conférence de la Paix*, i, at 144: 'ont décidé de réviser jusqu'en ses détails et pour le bassin Danubien la procédure de la protection internationale des droits des minorités et de l'individu par la voie d'un remaniement et d'une réadaptation aux circonstances nouvelles des Traités de la protection des minorités . . . conclus à l'issue de la première guerre mondiale.'

[143] Statement by the Romanian representative, 2 Sept. 1946, Doc. CP/ROU/P Doc. 8, p. 13.

[144] Ibid.   [145] *Collection of Documents of Paris Conference*, i, at 277.

[146] Article 3(1) of the Treaty with Romania, No. 645, 42 *UNTS* (1949), 3; see also Article 15 of the Treaty with Italy, No. 747, 49 *UNTS* (1950), 3; Article 2 of the Treaty with Bulgaria, No. 643, 41 *UNTS* (1949), 21; Article 2(1) of the Treaty with Hungary, No. 644, 41 *UNTS* (1949), 135; Article 6 of the Treaty with Finland, No. 645, 49 *UNTS* (1950), 203.

treaties remained controversial.[147] When the ECOSOC considered asking the UN Secretariat to prepare a study on the validity of the minorities treaties, the Russian representative stated that the minorities treaties 'related to conditions which no longer existed' and the basic questions with which they dealt had been undoubtedly solved by the 1947 Peace Treaties and by the UN Charter.[148] Other States reserved their position on this issue and their rights under the minorities treaties.[149]

The UN Study on the Validity of the Minorities Treaties

A study prepared by the UN Secretariat in 1950 at the request of the Commission on Human Rights[150] concluded that 'between 1939 and 1947 circumstances as a whole changed to such an extent that, generally speaking, the system should be considered as having ceased to exist'.[151] One of these changes was the emergence of the idea of a general and universal protection of human rights and fundamental freedoms:

All the international decisions reached since 1944 have been inspired by a different philosophy. The idea of a general and universal protection of human rights and fundamental freedoms is emerging. It is therefore no longer only the minorities in certain countries which receive protection, but all human beings in all countries who receive a certain measure of international protection. Within this system special provisions in favour of certain minorities are still conceivable, but the point of view from which the problem is approached is essentially different from that of 1919.[152]

The emergence of the concept of human rights was a ground for the extinction of the minorities undertakings.[153] According to the study, 'from the strictly legal point of view, the result seems clear in the cases in which the formal liquidation of the war has been completed by the conclusion of peace treaties. The provisions of these treaties and the opinions expressed by the authors of the treaties imply that the former minorities protection regime has ceased to exist so far as concerns the ex-enemy countries with which those treaties have been concluded.'[154] The result would be the same with regard to other States,[155] because, generally speaking, the treaties were considered to be no longer binding and were treated as though they were a 'dead letter'.[156]

There was indeed general agreement at the Peace Conference that the emergence of the concept of human rights had rendered the minorities

---

[147] Belgium, *GAOR*, 3rd Session, 3rd Committee, at 725; Egypt, *ECOSOC Official Records*, 3rd Session, E/CN.4/SR.73, at 5.
[148] *ECOSOC Official Records*, Third Year, 6th Session, 159th Meeting, 2 Feb.–11 Mar. 1948, at 309.   [149] The United Kingdom, ibid.
[150] 'Study of the Legal Validity of the Undertakings concerning Minorities', UN Doc. E/CN.4/367, 7 Apr. 1950.
[151] Ibid., at 71.   [152] Ibid., at 70.   [153] Ibid., at 36–8.
[154] Ibid., at 70.   [155] Ibid.   [156] Ibid., at 27, 39, and Add. 1, at 2.

treaties obsolete. However, views differed as to the precise manner in which termination had actually taken place. Some States believed that the treaties were still in force and claimed that they were subject to termination on grounds of new custom. Others behaved as though termination had already taken place by tacit agreement of all parties concerned.

These are in fact two different ways in which new custom can bring about the abrogation of prior treaties. If new custom was regarded as a ground for the termination of the minorities undertakings, the treaties could be abrogated either by a specific act of one of the parties or by a tacit agreement of all parties to regard them as no longer binding on account of the emergence of the principle of human rights (*desuetude*).[157] In the second case there would be no need for the express termination of the minorities undertakings.[158]

4.7. THE ABROGATION OF AN 'UNEQUAL' TREATY BY CHINA

By Article VII of the 1901 Peking Protocol[159] the US Government acquired the right to use for official purposes the land it occupied in the Diplomatic Quarter in Peiping. This right was reaffirmed by Article 11 of the 1943 Treaty of Washington, by which the United States relinquished its extraterritorial rights in China.[160]

In January 1950 the Chinese Communist Military Authorities announced that 'certain countries in the past, taking advantage of the so-called right of stationing troops stipulated in the unequal treaties, occupied land in the City of Peking and built barracks'; the ownership of that land 'should be of course taken back by China as a result of the abrogation of the unequal treaties'.[161] On 7 January an order was issued to the US, French, and Dutch consuls to hand over the buildings in question without delay.[162]

The United States protested against the requisition of part of its consular compounds in the former barracks which it regarded as a violation of its rights under the 1943 Treaty.[163] Despite these protests the premises of the US Consulate General were seized by police and civilian officers on

---

[157] Feinberg, ibid., at 52; McKean, *Equality and Discrimination*, at 47; F. Capotorti, 'Minorities', in *Max Planck Encyclopedia of Public International Law*, viii, at 388.

[158] In this sense, G. Haraszti, *Some Fundamental Problems of the Law of Treaties* (Budapest, 1973), at 359; Giraud, 'Modification', at 57.

[159] Protocol of 7 Sept. 1901, W. H. Malloy, *Treaties, Conventions, International Acts, Protocols and Agreements between the US and other Powers* (Washington, 1910), ii, at 2010.

[160] Signed at Washington on 11 Jan. 1934, *AJIL* (1934), Supp., at 65.

[161] 'Peking Military Control Committee Requisitions Foreign Barracks in City', *New China News Agency* (19 Jan. 1950), in J. A. Cohen and H. Chiu, *People's China and International Law* (Princeton, NJ, 1974), ii, at 1054.

[162] Ibid. See also 22 Sept. *State Bull.* (1950), at 119–21.   [163] Ibid., at 120–2.

14 January.[164] On the same day the Department of State condemned the seizure as a 'flagrant violation of the US rights under the 1943 Treaty and of the most elementary standards of international usage and conduct'[165] and ordered the withdrawal of all US official personnel from Communist China.

The People's Republic of China did not consider that the requisition order ran counter to China's international obligations, because it regarded the 1943 Treaty as unequal:

it is already clearly stipulated in the Common Programme of the Chinese People's Political Consultative Conference that all imperialist prerogatives in China and *all unequal treaties are to be abolished* regardless of whether they are 'long-standing treaty rights' or were 'reaffirmed in 1943'. The Peking Military Control Committee has the obligation to carry out the Common Programme . . . *but has absolutely no obligation to execute these unequal treaties.* (emphasis added)[166]

'Unequal treaties' in general are considered by the PRC to be in violation of international law and subject to unilateral abrogation at any time.[167] The term 'unequal treaties' has more than one meaning.[168] Occasionally it refers to treaties concluded between States of unequal negotiating power.[169] Alternatively it is used in relation to agreements deemed to impose non-reciprocal obligations in violation of the principle of equality of States.[170]

With regard to the 1943 Treaty in particular, the available materials indicate that the PRC considered it to be unequal, probably because of its incompatibility with general customary law principles. It will be recalled that the PRC invoked the 1949 Common Programme as the basis of the abrogation of the 1943 Treaty. Under Article 55 of the Programme, the People's Republic of China would 'examine the treaties and agreements concluded between the Kuomintang and foreign Governments and . . . *in accordance with their contents,* recognize, abrogate, revise or reconclude them respectively' (emphasis added).[171] Pursuant to this provision, and depending on their compatibility with customary international law or

---

[164] Ibid., at 119, 121, 122–3.   [165] Press release of 14 Jan. 1950, ibid., at 119.

[166] Press Release of 19 Jan. 1950, *New China News Agency*, Cohen and Chiu, *People's China*, ii, at 1055.

[167] See 'A Comment on the Statement of the Communist Party of the USA' (editorial), *People's Daily*, 8 Mar. 1963, at 1, in H. Chiu, *The People's Republic of China and the Law of the Treaties* (Cambridge, 1972), at 63 n. 38.

[168] See G. L. Scott, *Chinese Treaties* (Dobb's Ferry, NY, 1975), at 85 *et seq.*, esp. 88 *et seq.*; Chiu, *People's Republic of China*, at 60 *et seq.*

[169] See Wang Yao-Tien, *International Trade and Agreements* (Peking, 1958), at 10, in Chiu, *People's Republic of China*, at 61–2. See also letter of 10 Mar. 1972 to the Chairman of the UN Special Committee on Decolonization concerning Hong-Kong and Macao, in Cohen and Chiu, *People's China*, i, at 384.

[170] Chou-Keng-sheng, 'The Principle of Peaceful Co-existence from the Viewpoint of International Law', in Cohen and Chiu, *People's China*, ii, at 131; Scott, *Chinese Treaties*, at 90, 92.

[171] Cohen and Chiu, *People's China*, i, at 1122.

'humanitarian principles',[172] some treaties were recognized by the PRC, while others, including the 1943 Treaty, were abrogated. In any event, irrespective of the substantive validity of China's claims, the United States protested against the *unilateral* termination of the 1943 Treaty.

4.8. TREATIES ON INTERNATIONAL WATERCOURSES

4.8.1. The Nile Waters Question

During the period of the British administration of Egypt and the Sudan, an agreement was signed in 1929 between Egypt and the UK Government governing the utilization of the Nile waters.[173] The revision of the 1929 Agreement following Sudan's independence is one example of treaty adaptation effected in order to take into account the interests of other riparians in the management and utilization of an international watercourse.[174]

The 1929 Agreement was based on the findings of the 1925 Nile Commission set up to examine how irrigation could be carried out 'with full consideration of the interests of Egypt and without detriment to her natural and historic rights'.[175] International law in force at the time of the establishment of the Nile Commission did not contain any specific rules governing the division of waters between riparian States. As a result, the Commission was assigned the task of devising a practical arrangement which would give priority to Egypt's irrigation needs in the area.

The final agreement subordinated the interests of the upper riparian territory, the Sudan, to the interests of the lower riparian State, Egypt. It provided that, save with the previous agreement of Egypt, no irrigation or power works or measures were to be constructed or taken on the Nile or its sources if they would entail any prejudice to the interests of Egypt, either by reducing the quantity of water arriving in Egypt, by modifying the time of its arrival, or by lowering its level. The Egyptian Government was free to construct in the Sudan any works on the river or its branches,

---

[172] The expression 'humanitarian principles' is normally used by the Chinese as equivalent to 'international customary law': ibid., at 77.

[173] Exchange of notes of 7 May 1929, *UNTS*, No. 17 (1929) (Cmd. 3348), 130 *Br. & For. State Papers* (1929-I), at 104.

[174] R. K Batstone, 'The Utilisation of the Nile Waters', 8 *ICLQ* (1959), at 523; D. P. O'Connell, *State Succession in Municipal Law and International Law*, ii (Cambridge, 1967), at 245; A. H. Garretson, 'The Nile Basin', in A. H. Garretson, R. Hayton, and C. Olmstead (eds.), *The Law of International Drainage Basins*, pt. II (New York, 1967), at 256; S. Hosni, 'The Nile Regime', 17 *Revue égyptienne de droit international* (1961), at 70; Y. Fisseha, 'State Succession and the Legal Status of International Rivers', in R. Zacklin and L. Caflisch (eds.), *The Legal Regime of International Rivers and Lakes* (M. Dordrecht, 1981), 177, esp., at 186 *et seq.*; C. A. Pompe, 'The Nile Waters Question', in *Symbolae Verzihl* (Dordrecht, 1958), at 275 *et seq.*   [175] Exchange of notes, 1929, at 107.

or to take any measures with a view to increasing the water supply for the benefit of Egypt, without the permission of the Sudanese Government and subject only to the agreement of the local authorities on measures safeguarding local interests. As a result, Egypt had a right of veto on development projects in the Sudan, without any corresponding restriction on her own freedom of development. In addition, it was provided that Egypt would have all the necessary facilities for the complete study and record of the hydrology of the Nile in the Sudan.

The 1929 Agreement contained no stipulation of duration and no denunciation or termination provisions. Although a report of the Nile Commission annexed to the agreement envisaged a possible future revision of the details of the irrigation arrangements, the general principles of the agreement, including the policy of safeguarding Egypt's rights in the waters of the Nile, was meant to 'be observed at all times and under any conditions that may arise'.[176]

Following Sudan's independence, the 1929 Agreement was attacked for being contrary to the principle of equality of States, because it subordinated Sudanese interests to those of Egypt. Sudan could 'no longer be regarded as a territory with a claim to development only after the interests of Egypt, present and potential, had been assured'.[177]

The Sudanese Government took the position that the 1929 Agreement was 'an unjust agreement because it limited the development of irrigation in the Sudan while leaving Egypt free to develop her irrigation as fast as she pleased'. As a result, Egypt 'had increased her established rights in the Waters of the Nile from 40 milliards in 1920 to 48 milliards at the present time'. Although Sudan did not 'dispute rights which had been established while her hands had been tied', she claimed that 'the time had now come to change the Nile Waters Agreement'.[178]

The dispute over the Nile waters became particularly acute in 1953, when Egypt announced its intention to construct a High Dam at Aswan without prior consultation with the Sudan. The Sudanese Government offered to agree to the construction of the dam on condition that the division of the water supply between the two countries should be determined before the commencement of the works.

After a prolonged dispute, during which threats were made to stop the flow of the Nile altogether, the Sudan denounced the 1929 Agreement in 1958.[179] In the meantime the United States and the United Kingdom, which had initially agreed to provide foreign exchange for the preliminary works

---

[176] Note of Lord Lloyd of 7 May 1929, mentioned in Batstone, 'utilisation', at 532.

[177] See Batstone, 'utilisation', at 539.

[178] *The Nile Waters Question* (Sudanese Ministry of Irrigation and Hydro Electric Power, 1955), cited in O'Connell, *State Succession*, ii, at 245.

[179] Rousseau, in *RGDIP* (1960), at 94.

on the Aswan Dam, withdrew their support of the project, because agreement between the riparian States had not been achieved.[180] The United States expressed itself in favour of a development of the Nile that would be of benefit to all riparian States,[181] and, in a discussion held in February 1957 at the House of Commons, the UK Government proposed that a conference of all riparians should be convened in order to ensure the 'best and most equitable use of the Nile waters'.

The 1929 Agreement was replaced in 1959 by a new agreement between Egypt and the Sudan based on the principle of equitable utilization of the Nile waters between the two States.[182] The 1959 Agreement substituted for the unilateral competence of Egypt a system of technical and financial co-operation that took into account Sudan's interests in the development of the Nile.

The agreement distinguished between rights with respect to the existing flow and rights with regard to the surplus resulting from the construction of river works. It provided that the waters used by each riparian State at the time of signature of the agreement constituted their established irrigation rights. The benefits resulting from future projects on the Nile would be equitably shared between the two countries.

The agreement safeguarded Sudan's right to construct on the Nile all works necessary for the effective utilization of its share in the waters. It also provided for technical co-operation between the parties through a permanent joint committee.

The Situation with Regard to Other Riparian States

Egypt's veto rights over development projects in the Nile pursuant to the 1929 Agreement applied not only to the Sudan but also to 'countries under British administration', which included Uganda, Kenya, and Tanganyika. Similar arrangements aimed at safeguarding British and Egyptian interests in the region were made with Ethiopia[183] and the Congo State.[184]

The other riparians were not invited to participate in the negotiations leading to the revision of the 1929 Agreement. The 1959 Agreement envisaged the possibility of discussions with other riparian States in the framework of wider co-operation within the region, but did not go as far as to institutionalize their participation in the management of the Nile. In particular, the parties agreed to take a unified view on any question relating to the Nile waters that would have to be discussed with other riparians,

---

[180] 3 *Whiteman's Digest* (1964), at 1008–9.   [181] Ibid., at 1009.

[182] Agreement of 8 Nov. 1959, 15 *Revue égyptienne de droit international* (1959), at 320.

[183] Anglo-Italian Protocol of 15 Apr. 1891, 83 *Br. & For. State Papers*, at 19; Treaty between Great Britain and Ethiopia of 15 May 1902, *UKTS*, No. 16 (1902).

[184] Agreement of 9 May 1906 between Great Britain and the Congo State, *UKTS*, No. 4 (1908).

including any claims for a share in the Nile waters. If discussions resulted in allocation to another riparian, the relevant quantity would be deducted equally from the shares of the two countries.

Some of the riparian States affirmed that their rights could not be affected by the 1959 Agreement and protested against their lack of participation in its conclusion. The position of Tanganyika, Kenya, and Uganda and their rights to negotiate for a share in the waters of the Nile at the appropriate time had been reserved by the UK Government.[185] After independence, Tanganyika announced that she no longer considered herself bound by the 1929 Agreement, which was, in her view, obsolescent.[186] Ethiopia also affirmed 'the full measure of her freedom of action' regarding any future discussion about the water flowing from her territory.[187]

4.8.2. The International Regime of the River Niger

The international regime of the River Niger was based on the 1885 General Act of Berlin.[188] The Act provided for complete freedom of trade for all nations in the basin of the Congo, immunity from all taxes and duties except for those constituting fair compensation for services rendered, and freedom of navigation for merchant ships of all nations on the Congo and Niger rivers.[189]

The Berlin Act, as revised by the General Protocol of Brussels of 1890,[190] was abrogated among some of its signatories[191] by the 1919 Treaty of Saint-Germain-en-Laye.[192] Under the 1919 Treaty, only its signatories and those member States of the League of Nations which would subsequently adhere to it would enjoy freedom of trade, customs immunity and freedom of navigation in the convention area.[193]

The issue of the continued validity of these treaties came to the fore in the 1960s when the riparian States gained their independence. The regime applicable to the Niger in particular was modified by two treaties adopted by the newly independent States at the Niamey Conferences of 1963 and 1964,[194] namely the 1963 Convention and Act Relating to Navigation and

---

[185] 552 *HC Deb.*, col. 2411, 18 May 1956; see also 6 *ICLQ* (1957), at 135–7.

[186] O'Connell, *State Succession*, at 247.

[187] A. Lester, 'State Succession to Treaties in the Commonwealth', 12 *ICLQ* (1963), at 501.

[188] 17 *Hertslet's Commercial Treaties* (1890), at 62.

[189] Articles I, III–IV, XII–XIV, XXVI–XXVII.

[190] 19 *Hertslet's Commercial Treaties*, at 304, annexed to the General Act of Brussels relative to the African slave trade, ibid., at 278.

[191] Namely Great Britain, Belgium, France, Italy, Japan, Portugal, and the United States (Article XIII).

[192] 93 *LNTS*, at 43; 160 *Br. & For. State Papers*, at 106; Cmnd. 3348.

[193] 29 *Hertslet's Commercial Treaties*, at 110.

[194] See T. O. Elias, 'The Berlin Treaty and the River Niger Commission, 57 *AJIL* (1963), at 873; T. Maluwa, 'Succession to Treaties and International Fluvial Law in Africa: The Niger

Economic Co-operation between the States of the Niger Basin and the 1964 Agreement concerning the Niger River Commission and the Navigation and Transport on the River Niger.[195]

The 1963 Agreements provided for freedom of navigation for all nations and banned all transit dues or tolls except for services rendered. They were based on the principle of co-operation between riparian States with a view to the rational exploitation of the resources of the Niger (Articles 1–7 of the Statute annexed to the 1963 Convention, Articles 3–4 of the 1963 Act).

The preambles to the 1963 Convention and Act indicate that the riparian States intended to replace the old treaties with agreements reflecting developments in the customary law on international watercourses.[196] While the old treaties were based on the principles of freedom of navigation and of equality of treatment, 'the principle of close co-operation of the riparian States had since been adopted in this field of international law with the purpose of using international rivers for the common good, including the rational use and non-depletion of their water resources'. This principle was an expression of 'the principle of co-operation and mutual assistance of all States with a view to exploiting the world's resources' which was 'today universally affirmed' (preamble).[197]

Although there was agreement that the treaty regime should be adapted to take account of the emergence of new customary principles, opinions differed as to whether the abrogation of the earlier conventional instruments was strictly necessary. During the negotiations preceding the conclusion of the 1963 Convention and Act, some States took the view that the old treaties had been rendered invalid from the date of independence of the riparian States by virtue of the *rebus sic stantibus* clause.[198] In the end, however, an express clause was included in the 1963 Act which provided that the Convention of Saint-Germain, as well as the Act of Berlin and the General Act and Declaration of Brussels, 'are and remain abrogated as far as they concern the River Niger'.

This provision was intended to produce legal effects *erga omnes*. However, since the Act was signed by the successors to only two of the original

Regime', 33 *NILR* (1986), at 334; M. Schreiber, 'Vers un nouveau régime international du fleuve Niger', 9 *AFDI* (1963), at 866; 'Accord relatif à la Commission du fleuve Niger et à la navigation et aux transports sur le fleuve Niger', 10 *AFDI* (1964), at 813.

[195] Schreiber, 'Nouveau régime', at 883; 'Accord relatif', at 815.

[196] See C.-A. Colliard, 'Évolution et aspects actuels du régime juridique des fleuves internationaux', 125 *RC* (1968-III), at 337 *et seq.*

[197] See also Maluwa, 'Succession', at 367–368.

[198] Elias, 'Berlin Treaty', at 880. As to whether 'dispositive' or 'localized' treaties, such as treaties providing rights of navigation on rivers, are affected by State succession, see Article 12 of the 1978 Vienna Convention on State Succession in Respect of Treaties, 17 *ILM* (1978), at 1488, and the ILC Commentary to Article 12, *YILC* (1974-I), pt. II, at 196 *et seq.*, esp. 197, 206; O'Connell, *State Succession*, ii, at 12 *et seq.*, 231 *et seq.*; Brownlie, *Principles*, at 669.

parties to the 1919 Treaty, namely the United Kingdom and France, it could not, being *res inter alios acta*, affect the rights of other States party to the 1919 Treaty. One of these parties, the United States, continued to regard the 1919 Treaty as one of its treaties in force even after the signature of the 1963 Act,[199] but never tried to enforce or exercise its conventional rights. The other parties to the 1919 Convention were not reported to have questioned the abrogatory effects of the 1963 Act.

As a result, it can be said that even if the abrogation clause contained in the 1963 Act did not bind non-signatories to the Act, it was probably the first step towards the *desuetude* of the original treaties based on the tacit consent of all interested parties.

4.9. THE SHATT-AL-ARAB BOUNDARY DISPUTE

According to the 1937 Treaty of Teheran, Iraq had sovereignty over the River Shatt-al-Arab that runs along its frontier with Iran.[200] The 1937 Treaty set the boundary line at the low-water mark of the Iranian side of the Shatt-al-Arab, except for a distance of about seven kilometres where the frontier ran at the 'thalweg' or median line of the river.

In April 1969 Iran declared that it no longer recognized the validity of the 1937 Treaty,[201] because *inter alia* it did not apply the thalweg principle to the whole river. Iran called the boundary provisions of the Treaty 'iniquitous',[202] because a river which is the common frontier of two countries cannot, 'on the basis of established rules and principles of international law', come under the jurisdiction and absolute sovereignty of only one of them.[203] A new treaty dividing the Shatt-al-Arab along the thalweg line, 'in accordance with established rules of international law and justice', should therefore be concluded.[204]

Iran argued that the 1937 Treaty should be revised on grounds of its incompatibility with general customary law, albeit *not new* custom.[205] According to Iran, the thalweg principle had '*always* [been] recognized as the frontier line where a large river is the common frontier of two countries', and formed part of customary law at the time when the negotiations

---

[199] *Treaties in Force* (US Dept. of State Publication, 1977), at 257.

[200] *LNTS*, vol. 90, No. 4423, p. 241.

[201] Statement by the Ministry of Foreign Affairs of Iran, 23 *Yearbook of the United Nations* (1969), at 245.

[202] Letter of 1 May 1969 from the permanent representative of Iran addressed to the President of the Security Council, S/9190, at 3.

[203] *GAOR*, 24th Session (1969), 1776th Meeting, 2 Oct. 1969, at 15; letter of 1 May 1969 to the President of the Security Council, S/9190, at 4; letter of 2 Sept. 1969, S/9425, at 2.

[204] Letter of 9 May 1969, S/9200, at 4.

[205] See K. H. Kaikobad, 'The Shatt-al-Arab River Boundary: A Legal Reappraisal', 56 *BYIL* (1985), 49 *et seq.* and the bibliography mentioned at 49 n. 2.

leading to the 1937 Treaty were initiated.[206] However, it is generally accepted that States are free to enter into agreements derogating from the general custom prevailing at the time of their conclusion, unless the general rules are *jus cogens*. Agreed derogations from ordinary custom cannot subsequently be challenged on grounds of their incompatibility with general rules.

Iraq rejected Iran's claim, because 'there is no binding general principle in International Law for the delimitation of riparian boundaries, except what the parties concerned agree to adopt. Either the thalweg or the median line may be adopted . . . or, alternatively, the whole river may be agreed to belong to one country.'[207] Although a new treaty applying the thalweg principle to the whole river was signed in Baghdad in 1975,[208] it seems that Iraq agreed to it in return for political concessions.[209]

4.10. THE ANTARCTIC TREATY REGIME

The Antarctic Treaty regime was signed on 1 December 1959 by twelve States which carried out exploration activities on the continent.[210] It froze all existing claims to sovereignty in Antarctica and prohibited the assertion of future claims. It provided that the continent should be used for peaceful purposes only, such as the promotion of scientific research.

Membership to the Antarctic Treaty is open to all States. Nevertheless, only the original signatories or States that demonstrated an interest in Antarctica by conducting substantial scientific research there are entitled to attend the Antarctic Treaty Consultative Meetings and decide on important treaty-related matters. The consultative parties have *inter alia* the power to adopt measures in furtherance of the principles and objectives of the Treaty, to modify the Treaty by unanimous agreement, and to ask for the review of its operation after the expiry of thirty years from its entry into force (Articles IX and XII).

In the early 1980s certain developing countries which were not party to the Antarctic Treaty regime asked for the revision of the 1959 Treaty to bring it into line with developments in customary law.[211] At the initiative of Malaysia, Antigua, and Barbuda, the question of Antarctica was included

[206] Letter of 1 May 1969 addressed to the President of the Security Council, S/9190, at 4; letter of 2 Sept. 1969, S/9425, at 2.

[207] Annex to letter of 11 July 1969, S/9323, at 16; also letter of 29 Apr. 1969, S/9185, at 1; *GAOR*, 24th Session (1969), 1776th Meeting, 2 Oct. 1969, at 27, para. 297.

[208] For the text see T. A. Ismael, *Iraq and Iran: Roots of Conflict* (Syracuse, 1982), 62–5.

[209] See statement by Mr Hammadi (Iraq), *GAOR*, 35th Session (1980), 22nd Meeting, 3 Oct. 1980, at 428.

[210] Antarctic Treaty of 1 Dec. 1959, 402 *UNTS* 71. The twelve signatories were Argentina, Australia, Belgium, Chile, the French Republic, Japan, New Zealand, the Union of South Africa, the USSR, the United Kingdom, and the USA.

[211] See F. Orrego Vicuña, *Antarctic Mineral Exploitation: The Emerging Legal Framework* (Cambridge, 1988).

in the agenda of the UN General Assembly and was discussed at the First Committee in 1983.[212] Discussions were resumed on 28 November 1984[213] on the basis of a report on Antarctica prepared by the Secretary-General.[214]

During the UN debate it was argued that the Antarctic Treaty should be revised to take account of the evolution of the international law. Two developments had allegedly occurred in state practice since the treaty was adopted: first, the principle of democratic decision-making had become one of the basic concepts of contemporary international law; and, secondly, the principle of the common heritage of mankind had been recognized by most States.

The principle of democratic decision-making was based on the principle of equality of States enshrined in the UN Charter.[215] It allegedly developed in State practice in parallel with the process of decolonization after the Second World War and gained general recognition in the 1960s and 1970s.[216]

According to the 'universally accepted concept' of common benefit and common heritage of mankind,[217] there was an obligation to share equitably the wealth and resources of areas beyond national jurisdiction that were of common interest to all States. These principles had allegedly become generally accepted as a result of the trend towards democratization of international affairs.[218] They had already been applied to the sea-bed[219] and outer space[220] and should also govern the exploration and exploitation of Antarctica.[221]

---

[212] 38 *GAOR* First Committee (42nd–46th Meetings), UN Doc. A/C.1/38/PV.42–6 (1983).

[213] 39 *GAOR* First Committee (50th–55th Meetings), UN Doc. A/C.1/39/PV.50–5 (1984); 40 *GAOR* First Committee (48th–55th Meetings), UN Doc. A/C.1/40/PV.48–55.

[214] *Question of Antarctica: Report of the Secretary-General*, 39 *GAOR* (Agenda item 66), UN Doc. A/39/583 (1984); for the views of States, see pt. II, vols. i–iii, of the Study.

[215] Cape Verde, 39 *GAOR*, 1st Committee 54th Meeting, at 47; Egypt, 38 *GAOR*, 1st Committee, 42nd Meeting, at 34; Sri Lanka, 40 *GAOR*, 1st Committee, 48th Meeting, at 48; Kenya, 54th Meeting, at 21; Pakistan, *Report of the Secretary-General*, pt. II, iii, at 33.

[216] See e.g. Malaysia, 38 *GAOR*, 1st Committee, 42nd Meeting, at 12; Zambia, *Report of the Secretary-General*, pt. II, iii, at 74, 137. Algeria, 40 *GAOR*, 1st Committee, 54th Meeting, at 13.

[217] Ghana, 38 *GAOR*, 1st Committee, 42nd Meeting, at 21; see also Sri Lanka, 38 *GAOR*, 1st Committee, 44th Meeting, at 14; Pakistan, at 10; Egypt, 42nd Meeting, at 33; Suriname, *Report of the Secretary-General*, pt. II, iii, at 74; Bangladesh, 39 *GAOR*, 1st Committee, 54th Meeting, at 52; Indonesia, 40 *GAOR*, 1st Committee, 52nd Meeting, at 47.

[218] See e.g. Malaysia, 38 *GAOR*, 1st Committee, 42nd Meeting, at 13; Egypt, at 34.

[219] See, GA Resolution 2574 of 1969 (the 'Moratorium Resolution'), 62 votes in favour, 28 against, 28 abstentions, 24 *GAOR* Supp. (No. 30) 11, UN Doc. A/7630; Resolution 2794 of 1970, 25 *GAOR* Supp. (No. 28) 24, UN Doc. A/8028, 108 votes to nil with 14 abstentions. See also Articles 136 *et seq.* of the 1982 Law of the Sea Convention, opened for signature 10 Dec. 1979, UN Doc. A/CONF. 62/122.

[220] Agreement governing the Activities of States on the Moon and Other Celestial Bodies, opened for signature 10 Dec. 1979, UN Doc. A/34/664; Treaty on Principles Governing the Activities of States in the Exploration and Use of Outer Space, including the Moon and Other Celestial Bodies, 27 Jan. 1967, 610 *UNTS* 205.

[221] Sri Lanka, 38 *GAOR*, 1st Committee, 44th Meeting, at 14; Malaysia, 42nd Meeting, at 20; Zambia, 39 *GAOR*, 1st Committee, 54th Meeting, at 42.

These principles were considered to have a bearing on the Antarctic Treaty regime as ordinary rules of customary law and not as rules of *jus cogens*.[222] Following their alleged general recognition by States, the aim of the initiative of the developing countries was to review the text of the Antarctic Treaty, which was considered to be still in force, in order 'to establish a truly universal framework for the promotion of international cooperation on an expanded basis taking into consideration the various legitimate interests involved'.[223]

In particular, the following modifications were regarded as necessary in order to adapt the Antarctic Treaty regime to the evolution of the law: first, the exclusive powers of the consultative parties under the Treaty should be abolished, and all decisions concerning Antarctica should be made by all Sates, irrespective of their level of technological development, and on the basis of the one-State-one-vote rule;[224] secondly, all States should be prevented from carrying out any exploration or exploitation activities in Antarctica; thirdly, the resources of the area should be shared by all States.[225] Of particular concern to developing countries was the prospect of exploitation of Antarctica's mineral resources by the Antarctic Treaty partners, because this activity was regarded as falling within the scope of the convention.[226]

It is by no means certain that the 1959 Treaty can be considered as incompatible with new customary law or that the common heritage principle is relevant to Antarctica. The parties to the Antarctic regime in fact argued that the Treaty was based on the principles of sovereign equality and co-operation between States[227] and that there was no international consensus for the application of the common heritage principle to Antarctica.[228] They also contended that the claims for revision were inadmissible, because they emanated from States not party to the Antarctic regime.[229]

---

[222] See e.g. Zambia, *Report of the Secretary-General*, pt. II, iii, at 74, 137.

[223] Tunisia, 38 *GAOR*, 1st Committee, 45th Meeting, at 3. See also Ghana, ibid., 42nd Meeting, at 21; Malaysia, ibid.

[224] Malaysia, 38 *GAOR*, 1st Committee, 42nd Meeting, at 17; study of the UN Secretary-General on Antarctica, pt. II, ii, at 110.

[225] See e.g. Zambia, *Report of the Secretary-General*, pt. II, iii, at 138; 39 *GAOR*, 1st Committee, 54th Meeting, at 42.

[226] See Recommendation XI-1 of 1981, 20 *ILC* (1981), at 1265, and the Convention of 2 June 1988, 27 *ILM* (1988), at 868, which regulates all prospecting, exploration, and development of mineral resources on the Antarctic continent, including the designation of appropriate areas.

[227] USA, 40 *GAOR*, 1st Committee, 51st Meeting, at 6; Hungary, ibid., at 27; Australia, 38 *GAOR*, 1st Committee, 42nd Meeting, at 23; West Germany, ibid., at 39; Bulgaria, 40 *GAOR*, 1st Committee, 49th Meeting, at 22; Denmark, 50th Meeting, at 36; Poland, 52nd Meeting, at 5; United Kingdom, 39 *GAOR*, 1st Committee, 52nd Meeting, at 33–5.

[228] Australia, 40 *GAOR* 1st Committee, 48th Meeting, at 22; Poland, 52nd Meeting, at 8; Belgium, 53nd Meeting, at 42; Chile, 38 *GAOR*, 1st Committee, 42nd Meeting, at 32; 39 *GAOR*, 1st Committee, 50th Meeting, at 57; France, 52nd Meeting, at 53–5.

[229] United Kingdom, 39 *GAOR*, 1st Committee, 52nd Meeting, at 33–5; Australia, 38 *GAOR* 1st Committee, 42nd Meeting, at 24.

However, the argument that treaties should be revised in the light of new custom was not dismissed. It was in fact considered that the Treaty itself contained revision mechanisms that enabled the parties to adjust it to the evolution of international law.[230]

4.11. REMOVAL OF INSTALLATIONS ON THE CONTINENTAL SHELF AND THE 1958 GENEVA CONVENTION

The United Kingdom is party to the 1958 Geneva Convention on the Continental Shelf,[231] which provides that any abandoned or disused installations on the continental shelf must be *entirely* removed (Article 5, para. 5). By contrast, the provisions of the 1982 Convention on the Law of the Sea (Article 60, para. 3)[232] envisage less then total removal in some cases:

Any installations or structures which are abandoned or disused shall be removed to ensure safety of navigation, taking into account any generally accepted international standards established in this regard by the competent international organisation. Such removal shall also have due regard to fishing, the protection of the marine environment and the rights and duties of other States. Appropriate publicity shall be given to the depth, position and dimensions of any installations or structures *not entirely removed.* (emphasis added)

The relationship between the provisions of the two conventions was discussed during the parliamentary debate on the Petroleum Bill introduced by the UK Government in 1986.[233] The bill envisaged less than total removal of abandoned or disused installations on the continental shelf.

Although at the time of the debate the 1982 Convention was not yet in force, the UK Government argued that the provisions of Article 60, para. 3, were part of new customary law. As a result, Article 5 of the 1958 Convention should be interpreted in the light of new custom as requiring total removal of installations only where necessary in order to prevent unjustifiable interference with other users of the sea.[234] On this basis, the proposed legislation was consistent with the United Kingdom's international obligations.[235]

---

[230] See e.g. statement by Brazil, a party to the Antarctic Treaty, 40 *GAOR*, 1st Committee, 49th Meeting, at 27: 'The Antarctic Treaty system is not static. We believe that in its capacity to anticipate events by adapting itself lies the foundation of the Treaty's durability. Brazil's support of the Antarctic Treaty is based on the notion that it must not remain indifferent to a rapidly evolving international reality.'

[231] Convention on the Continental Shelf, Geneva, 29 Apr. 1958, 499 *UNTS* 311.

[232] 1982 Law of the Sea Convention.

[233] See *United Kingdom Materials on International Law*, ed. G. Marston, 57 (1986), at 586; 58 (1987), at 604.

[234] 482, *HL Deb.*, col. 919; 3 Dec. 1986; 485 *HL Deb.*, col. 84: 23 Feb. 1987. See also reply of the Minister of State to Mr Rowlands MP, *HC Deb.*, Standing Committee B, Petroleum Bill, cols. 86–8: 9 Dec. 1986. [235] 483 *HL Deb.*, col. 1452: 29 Jan. 1987.

According to the UK Government, the 1982 Convention merely 'spelt out more clearly the obligations of signatory States in connection with the removal of platforms' and 'reflected international consensus that the purpose of the 1958 Convention can be achieved without the need for the entire removal of all installations'.[236]

However, it is not certain whether the text of the 1958 Convention providing that *any* abandoned installations must be entirely removed can be reconciled with the new custom allegedly contained in Article 60 of the 1982 Convention.[237] In fact, it can be argued that the 'new international consensus' reflected in the 1982 Treaty can be taken into account only to the extent that the modification of the 1958 Convention by new customary law is permissible.

The distinction between treaty interpretation and treaty modification is important, if it is accepted that new custom is only a ground of treaty termination or revision. On this basis a treaty incompatible with new custom remains in force and continues to be binding until it is terminated or revised by the parties. By contrast, if treaty interpretation in the light of new custom is possible, the new rules can immediately be incorporated into the treaty through the appropriate reading of the text.

[236] 486 *HL Deb.*, cols. 131–2; 24 Mar. 1987; see also vol. 485, cols. 448–9: 2 Mar. 1987; Lord Denning, ibid., col. 449.
[237] See Lord Kennet, 485 *HL Deb.*, col. 992: 10 Mar. 1987, and the reply of the Minister of Scottish Office, 486 *HL Deb.*, cols. 131–2: 24 Mar. 1987.

5

Decisions of International Tribunals

In the context of international adjudication, the claim may be made that a treaty rule is no longer applicable by reason of the evolution of customary law. Faced with this argument, tribunals will have to determine whether a treaty is still valid despite its incompatibility with more recent customary rules. Moreover, if the treaty is held to be valid, a tribunal may have to decide which of two rules on the same subject-matter, one conventional and the other customary, both of which are considered to be in force, will apply to the particular case. This chapter examines decisions of international tribunals dealing with these issues.

5.1. THE *FISHERIES JURISDICTION CASE* (*UNITED KINGDOM* v. *ICELAND*)

On 1 June 1958 Iceland declared a twelve-mile exclusive fishing zone. Following protests by the United Kingdom, an Exchange of Notes was signed in 1961 between the two countries,[1] by which the United Kingdom agreed to Iceland's claim, subject to a three-year phasing-out period. As to the area beyond twelve miles, it was agreed that the Icelandic Government would continue to work for the implementation of the Althing Resolution of 5 May 1959, by which Iceland sought to extend her fisheries jurisdiction to cover the whole of her continental shelf. Iceland would give to the UK Government six months' notice of any future extension and, in case of a dispute, the matter would, at the request of either party, be referred to the International Court of Justice.

In 1971 Iceland announced her intention to extend her fisheries jurisdiction to fifty miles. The United Kingdom protested and on 14 April 1972 initiated proceedings against Iceland before the International Court of Justice founding jurisdiction on the 1961 Agreement. The United Kingdom asked the Court to pronounce that the fifty-mile fishing zone was contrary to international law and, in any event, not opposable to the United Kingdom in view of the 1961 Agreement. In its decision of 2 February 1973[2] the Court held that it had jurisdiction to entertain the UK application and gave its judgment on the merits on 25 July 1974.[3]

---

[1] 397 *UNTS*, at 275.   [2] ICJ Reports (1973), at 3.
[3] ICJ Reports (1974), 3. A parallel case was brought by the Federal Republic of Germany, see *Jurisdiction of the Court, Judgment*, at 49; *Merits Judgment*, at 175. In this chapter reference is made to the *United Kingdom* v. *Iceland Case*.

5.1.1. The Decision on Jurisdiction[4]

Iceland did not participate in the proceedings. She claimed that the 1961 Exchange of Notes was no longer applicable and could not, therefore, serve as the basis of the Court's jurisdiction, because, *inter alia*, the general law on fisheries had changed since the Agreement was concluded: 'all the circumstances are completely changed from what they were when the Agreements were made, both as regards fisheries and fishery techniques, *as well as legal opinion on fisheries jurisdiction*. It is safe to say that it is unlikely that these Agreements would have been made, if we had then known how these matters would evolve...' (emphasis added).[5] As a result, 'in the opinion of the Icelandic Government, which is continuing to work for the implementation of the Althing Resolution in the light of increased knowledge and other developments that have occurred since that Exchange of Notes, the object and purpose of the provision for recourse to judicial settlement have been fully achieved'.[6]

The United Kingdom's understanding of Iceland's contention was that a new rule of *jus cogens* had emerged, which allowed a coastal state to extend its fisheries jurisdiction beyond twelve miles, and that the 1961 Agreement, being incompatible with it, was subject to unilateral termination.[7] However, Iceland never alleged that the twelve-mile rule had the character of *jus cogens*.

The Court held that Iceland's argument might be relevant to the jurisdictional issue 'on an hypothesis familiar in the law of certain States under the guise of failure of consideration'. It would then appear to be contended that 'the compromissory clause was the price paid by Iceland for the recognition at that time of the twelve-mile fishery limit by the other party' and that, 'if today the twelve-mile limit is generally recognized, there would be a failure of consideration relieving Iceland of its commitment because of the changed legal circumstances'. In effect, 'it was unlikely that the agreement would have been made if the Government of Iceland had known how these matters would evolve'.[8]

---

[4] R. B. Bilder, 'The Anglo-Icelandic Fisheries Dispute', 37 *Wisconsin Law Review* (1973), at 37; H. W. Briggs, 'Unilateral Denunciation of Treaties: The Vienna Convention and the International Court of Justice', 68 *AJIL* (1974), at 51; L. Favoreu, 'Les Affaires de la compétence en matière de pêcheries', 20 *AFDI* (1974), at 253; S. R. Katz, 'Issues Arising in the Icelandic Fisheries Case', 22 *ICLQ* (1973), 83; R. D. Kearney, 'Sources of Law and the International Law of Justice', in L. Gross (ed.), *The Future of the International Court of Justice* (New York, 1976), 610, at 681; P. H. Martin, 'L'Affaire de la compétence en Matière de pêcheries: Les Arrêts de la Cour Internationale de Justice du 2 février 1973', 78 *RGDIP* (1974), at 435; Tiewul, 'Fisheries Jurisdiction Case', at 455.

[5] Statement of 9 Nov. 1971 by the Prime Minister of Iceland at the Althing, *ICJ Pleadings* (*Fisheries Jurisdiction Case*), ii, at 89.

[6] Government of Iceland's Aide-Mémoire of 31 Aug. 1971, ibid., i, at 14.

[7] UK Memorial on Jurisdiction, *Pleadings* i, at 149 *et seq.*

[8] Ibid., at 16–17, para. 31.

On that basis the Court examined whether the 1961 Agreement should be considered as having been terminated on account of the application of the *rebus sic stantibus* rule. The conditions of the application of this rule were embodied in Article 62 of the Vienna Convention, which 'may in many respects be considered as a codification of existing customary law on the subject of the termination of a treaty relationship on account of change of circumstances'.[9]

The Court held that in principle 'changes in the law may under certain conditions constitute valid grounds for invoking a change of circumstances affecting the duration of a treaty'.[10] However, these conditions were not met in the present case for the following two reasons.

First, a change of circumstances may be a ground of treaty termination, only when the changed circumstances constituted an essential basis of the consent of *both* parties to be bound by the agreement. However,

in the present case, the object and purpose of the 1961 Exchange of Notes, and, therefore, the circumstances which constituted an essential basis of the consent of both parties to be bound by the agreement embodied therein, had a much wider scope. That object and purpose was not merely to decide upon the Icelandic claim to fisheries jurisdiction up to 12 miles but also to provide a means whereby the parties might resolve the question of validity of any further claims.[11]

Although it was possible that Iceland might find that some of the motives that induced it to enter into the 1961 Exchange of Notes had become less compelling or had disappeared altogether, this was not a ground justifying the repudiation of those parts of the agreement the object and purpose of which had remained unchanged:

in the case of a treaty which is in part executed and in part executory, in which one of the parties has already benefited from the executed provisions of the treaty, it would be particularly inadmissible to allow that party to put an end to obligations which were accepted under the treaty by way of *quid pro quo* for the provisions which the other party has already executed.[12]

Secondly, a change of circumstances could not be invoked as a ground for the termination of a treaty, unless it had radically transformed the extent of the obligations still to be performed under the treaty:

The change must have increased the burden of the obligations to be executed to the extent of rendering the performance something essentially different from that originally undertaken. In respect of the obligation with which the Court is here concerned, this condition is wholly unsatisfied ... The present dispute is exactly of the character anticipated in the compromissory clause of the Exchange of Notes.

---

[9] Ibid., at 18.   [10] Ibid., at 17, para. 32.   [11] Ibid.
[12] Ibid., at 18, para. 34; also individual opinion by Judge Fitzmaurice, at 32 *et seq.*

Not only has the jurisdictional obligation not been radically transformed in its extent; it has remained precisely what it was in 1961.[13]

In any event, the *rebus sic stantibus* rule would not operate so as to extinguish the treaty automatically or so as to allow Iceland to denounce it unilaterally. It would only confer on one party the right to call for the termination of the treaty and, if that call were disputed, to submit the dispute to some organ with power to determine whether the conditions for the application of the rule were met. In the present case, 'the procedural complement to the doctrine of changed circumstances is already provided for in the 1961 Exchange of Notes, which specifically calls upon the parties to have recourse to the Court in the event of a dispute relating to Iceland's extension of fisheries jurisdiction'.[14]

Consequently, the Court rejected Iceland's contention and held that the 1961 Agreement was still valid and applicable in the relations between the parties.

However, the judgment is important, because it accepts the principle that the evolution of general customary law may under certain conditions constitute a valid ground for the termination of a treaty. In the particular case, the Court looked at this issue in the light of the fundamental change of circumstances rule as embodied in Article 62 of the Vienna Convention. The circumstances of the case were considered to be inappropriate for the application of this rule. It would indeed be paradoxical to say that a treaty specifically providing for the settlement of disputes regarding the future state of general customary law on fisheries jurisdiction would never have been concluded if the parties had known that the customary law would change.

It is not clear whether the outcome of the case would have been different if the 1961 Exchange of Notes had not contained a jurisdictional clause but instead its object and purpose had been 'merely to decide upon the Icelandic claim to fisheries jurisdiction up to twelve miles'. According to the Court, changes in the general law regarding fisheries jurisdiction could be invoked as a ground for the termination of a treaty under Article 62 of the Vienna Convention only if they 'increased the burden of the obligations to be executed to the extent of rendering the performance something essentially different from that originally undertaken'.[15]

Strictly speaking, in the present case the obligations created by the 1961 Agreement had not been altered as a result of the general recognition of the twelve-mile fishery limit. Admittedly, in the light of the evolution of the law and with hindsight it could be considered that the contractual recognition of the twelve-mile fishery limit had lost its value as a *quid pro quo*, and Iceland's obligation to respect that limit now *appeared* to be more

---

[13] Ibid., at 21, para. 43.   [14] Ibid., para. 54.   [15] Ibid., para. 43.

burdensome. However, it is doubtful whether this would be sufficient grounds for the Court to hold that the *rebus sic stantibus* rule applied.

5.1.2. The Decision on the Merits

In statements made outside the ICJ proceedings, Iceland based her right to extend her fishery jurisdiction beyond twelve miles on legal developments that already were or at least would soon become generally recognized under international law:

a great development is taking place as regards the problem of coastal fisheries. It is generally admitted that the system of narrow fishery limits on the one hand and the so-called freedom of fishing ... on the other hand, was heavily weighted in favour of the countries that want to fish as close as possible to the coasts of other nations. This obsolete system is now being replaced by a new pragmatic approach. ... My Government is convinced that this new system already has the support of the international community and is preparing the extension of the Icelandic fishery limits in conformity with these views so as to cover the waters of the continental shelf of Iceland ... [Our action] is in conformity with the strong conviction that the progressive international law will replace the system which for far too long has been tolerated. Indeed, more than 20 nations have already proclaimed rules and regulations for their increased protection in this field.[16]

In order to determine the legality of the Icelandic extension under international law, the International Court of Justice discussed the relevance of the evolution of the law of the sea to the continued application of the provisions of the 1961 Exchange of Notes and the 1958 Geneva Convention. Both international agreements were incompatible with the notion of fishery zones beyond twelve miles.

The Court started its discussion of the applicable rules with the Geneva Convention on the High Seas of 1958.[17] After pointing out that the Convention was adopted 'as generally declaratory of established principles of international law', the Court referred to two of its provisions, namely Article 1, which defined the term 'high seas' as 'all parts of the sea that are not included in the territorial sea or in the internal waters of the State' and Article 2, which provided that the high seas shall be open to all States for navigational and fishing purposes.

The Court stated that, although both the 1958 and the 1960 Law of the

---

[16] Statement by Iceland's Minister of Foreign Affairs in the GA of the UN, 29 Sept. 1971, ibid., at 52. See also statement by Iceland's Minister of Fisheries, Meeting of the North East Atlantic Fisheries Commission, 15 Dec. 1971, ibid., at 56; statement by Ambassador Andersen before the Committee on the Peaceful Uses of the Sea-bed and Ocean Floor beyond the Limits of National Jurisdiction, 16 Mar 1971, ibid., at 57.

[17] ICJ Reports (1974), at 22, para. 50.

Sea Conferences failed to agree on rules governing the breadth of the territorial sea and the extent of the coastal State's fishery rights,[18]

two concepts had crystallized as customary law in recent years arising out of the general consensus revealed at the Conference. The first is the concept of the fishery zone, the area in which a State may claim exclusive fishery jurisdiction independently of its territorial sea; the extension of that fishery zone up to a 12-mile limit from the baselines appears now to be generally accepted. The second is the concept of preferential rights of fishing in adjacent waters in favour of the coastal State in a situation of special dependence on its coastal fisheries . . .[19]

On the basis of these pronouncements it was stated that the Court implicitly acknowledged that the new customary rules had modified the provisions of the 1958 Convention.[20] The 1958 Convention was based on the distinction between high seas and territorial waters and was incompatible with the novel concept of exclusive fishery zones, which did not fall within either category.[21] If the establishment of exclusive fishery zones up to twelve miles was now permissible under international law, the provisions of the Convention must have been modified accordingly or at least 'a gloss [must have] been put upon the literal interpretation of the Convention'.[22]

Judges Forster, Bengzon, Jiménez de Aréchaga, Singh, and Ruda clearly stated in their Joint Separate Opinion that the new customary rules had modified the 1958 Convention: 'It is true that a general practice has developed around that proposal (i.e. the 6-plus-6 formula which failed by one vote to be adopted at the 1960 Law of the Sea Conference) and has in fact amended the 1958 Convention *praeter legem*: an exclusive fishery zone beyond the territorial sea has become an established feature of contemporary international law.'[23]

Nevertheless, it is doubtful whether the Court's main judgment can be cited in support of the proposition that new customary law may automatically modify prior treaty rights. The 1958 Convention as such constituted no legal obstacle to the Icelandic extension, because it was not binding on Iceland as a matter of treaty law. As a result, the Court did not have to decide on the issue of treaty modification by new customary law and its pronouncements in this respect would be only *obiter dicta*.

Other passages from the Court's judgment reveal a much more cautious approach to the issue of treaty modification in the light of new customary

[18] Ibid., para. 51.   [19] Ibid., at 23, para. 52.

[20] Villiger, *Customary International Law*, at 214; cf. R. R. Churchill, 'The Fisheries Jurisdiction Cases: The Contribution of the International Court of Justice to the Debate on Coastal States' Fisheries Rights', 24 *ICLQ* (1975), 82, at 87.

[21] ICJ Reports (1974), at 24, para. 54.

[22] O'Connell, *International Law of the Sea*, i, at 532; Jennings, 'General Course', at 381.

[23] ICJ Reports (1974), at 47, para. 6.

law. The Court thus held that the concept of a twelve-mile fishery zone had been accepted with regard to Iceland in the substantive provisions of the 1961 Agreement and applied by the United Kingdom to its own coastal waters since 1964. Therefore, it was no longer a matter of dispute between the parties.[24] As to the concept of preferential rights, the Court considered that, in evaluating the Icelandic claim, it had to take into account not only the existing rules of international law but also the provisions of the 1961 Agreement, a treaty which was valid and in force.

Iceland's unilateral action constituted an infringement of the principle of reasonable regard to the interests of other States enshrined in Article 2 of the 1958 Convention and disregarded the rights of the United Kingdom under the 1961 Agreement.[25] As a result, Iceland's claim to fisheries jurisdiction beyond twelve miles was not opposable to the United Kingdom.

On the other hand, Iceland had the right to claim preferential rights with regard to the distribution of fishery resources in the adjacent waters. The United Kingdom also had established rights with respect to these fishery resources. As a result, the two Governments were under an obligation to negotiate an equitable solution having regard to the preferential rights of Iceland and the established rights of the United Kingdom.[26]

The obligation to negotiate an equitable solution flowed from the very nature of the respective rights of the parties. To direct them to negotiate would be a proper exercise of the judicial function in this case and would correspond to the provisions of the UN Charter concerning the peaceful settlement of disputes (Article 33).[27]

The Court thus accepted the need to reassess treaty rights and obligations in the light of the evolution of customary law. At the same time it considered that the necessary modifications to the treaty should be introduced through negotiations between the parties. In view of the absence of a negotiated settlement in the particular case, the 1961 Exchange of Notes remained in force and prevented Iceland from claiming a fishery limit beyond twelve miles in her relations with the United Kingdom.

5.2. THE UNITED KINGDOM–FRANCE CONTINENTAL SHELF ARBITRATION

In 1975 an Arbitral Tribunal was asked to delimit the continental shelf in the English Channel between the United Kingdom and France in accordance with the rules of international law applicable in the matter.[28]

---

[24] Ibid., para. 54.   [25] Ibid., para. 67.
[26] Ibid., paras. 68 *et seq.*   [27] Ibid., para. 75.
[28] Arbitration Agreement of 10 July 1975, *UKTS* No. 137 (1975), Cmnd. 6280.

The Tribunal's award[29] given on 30 June 1977[30] touched on the relationship between a treaty, the 1958 Geneva Convention on the Continental Shelf, and alleged new customary rules on the delimitation of continental shelves appertaining to adjacent or opposite States.[31]

Both the United Kingdom and France had ratified the 1958 Geneva Convention on the Continental Shelf,[32] which stipulated that 'in the absence of agreement and unless another boundary line is justified by special circumstances' the continental shelf boundary between two adjacent or opposite states shall be determined by a median line—that is, a line 'every point of which is equidistant from the nearest points of the baselines from which the breadth of the territorial sea is measured' (Article 6). France, however, contended that all the Geneva Conventions on the Law of the Sea, including the Continental Shelf Convention, had been rendered obsolete by 'the recent development of customary law, which was stimulated particularly by the work of the United Nations, the reactions of the Governments to this work, the discussions and negotiations at the Third Conference on the Law of the Sea, and the endorsement of this development in the practice of States with respect to economic zones and fishing zones of 200 miles'.[33]

The United Kingdom and France were among the States that had proclaimed 200-mile exclusive fishing or economic zones on the basis of the consensus formed at the Third UN Conference. These developments were 'clearly not compatible with the continuance in force of the Geneva Conventions on the Law of the Sea'.[34] As a result, the only applicable rules were the customary rules on this matter as reflected in the Draft Law of the Sea Convention. In particular, Articles 62 and 71 of the Revised Single Negotiating Text[35] provided that the delimitation of the 200-mile exclusive economic zone and of the continental shelf between adjacent or opposite States respectively 'shall be effected by agreement in accordance with

---

[29] See D. W. Bowett, 'The Arbitration between the United Kingdom and France concerning the Continental Shelf Boundary in the English Channel and South-Western Approaches', 49 *BYIL* (1978), at 1 *et seq.*; E. D. Brown, 'The Anglo-French Continental Shelf Case', 33 *YBWA* (1979), at 304 *et seq.*; 16 *San Diego Law Review* (1979), at 461 *et seq.*; D. A. Colson, 'The United Kingdom–France Continental Shelf Arbitration', 72 *AJIL* (1978), at 95 *et seq.*; D. M. McRae, 'Delimitation of the Continental Shelf between the United Kingdom and France: The Channel Arbitration', 15 *CYIL* (1977), at 173 *et seq.*; J.-P. Queneudec, 'L'Affaire de la délimitation du plateau continental entre la France et le Royaume Uni', 83 *RGDIP* (1979), at 53 *et seq.*; E. Zoller, 'L'Affaire de la délimitation du plateau continental entre la République Française et le Royaume Uni de Grande Bretagne et d'Irlande du Nord', 23 *AFDI* (1977), at 359 *et seq.*

[30] 18 *ILM* (1979), at 397; interpreted by the Tribunal in its subsequent decision of 14 Mar. 1978, ibid., at 462.   [31] Award of 10 July 1975, paras. 45 *et seq.*

[32] 499 UNTS 311; 52 *AJIL* (1958), at 858.

[33] Award of 10 July 1975, at 16; see also para. 45.   [34] Ibid.

[35] *Third United Nations Conference on the Law of the Sea (Official Records)*, v, at 176, 178 (Doc. A/CONF. 62/WP.8/Rev.1/PART II).

equitable principles, employing, where appropriate, the median or equidistance line, and taking account of all the relevant circumstances'.

The United Kingdom denied that new customary law had developed rules concerning the delimitation of exclusive economic zones. In any event, the course of conduct followed by France in her relations with the United Kingdom constituted 'a continuing recognition and acknowledgment that the 1958 Convention is a treaty in force between the two States'. Accordingly the 1958 Convention 'had not been abandoned by the Parties in their mutual relations nor rendered obsolete by subsequent developments in customary law'.[36]

The Tribunal held that, in cases like the present one, the application of the rules contained in the Draft UN text would not lead to a solution materially different from the one envisaged by the 1958 Convention.[37] In particular, Article 6 of the 1958 Convention gave expression to the general norm that, failing agreement, the boundary between States abutting on the same continental shelf should be determined on equitable principles, which might justify the use of the equidistance method in the particular case.[38]

In any event, the Tribunal addressed the French argument to the effect that the new customary rules had rendered the 1958 Convention obsolete. It acknowledged 'both the importance of the evolution of the law of the sea which is now in progress and the possibility that a development in customary law may, under certain conditions, evidence the assent of the States concerned to the modification, or even termination of previously existing treaty rights and obligations'.[39]

However, the information before the Court contained references by the French Republic and the United Kingdom to the Convention as an existing treaty in force, which were of a quite recent date. Consequently, in the particular case 'only the most conclusive indications of the intention of the parties to the 1958 Convention to regard it as terminated' would warrant treating it as obsolete and inapplicable, but such conclusive evidence was provided neither by the records of the Third UN Conference nor by the practice of States outside the Conference.[40]

On the other hand, the Tribunal held that the rules of customary law could be taken into account as 'a relevant and even essential means for interpreting and completing the provisions of Article 6' of the Geneva Convention and in particular for defining the precise conditions for the application of the equidistance–special circumstances rule.[41] Accordingly, the Tribunal concluded that proximity was only one of the criteria to be used when delimiting continental shelves appertaining to adjacent or opposite States, its significance depending on the geographical and other circumstances of the particular case.[42]

---

[36] Ibid., at 19. [37] Ibid., para. 96. [38] Ibid., para. 70. [39] Ibid., para. 47.
[40] Ibid. [41] Ibid., para 48. [42] Ibid., paras 75 and 80 *et seq.*

The following conclusions can be drawn from this award. First, new customary law does not automatically terminate or modify prior incompatible treaty rights or obligations. As long as the parties to a prior treaty have not terminated or modified it, either expressly or implicitly, the treaty remains in force and tribunals are obliged to treat it as part of the applicable law. Secondly, the parties' intent to terminate or modify a treaty must be specifically proven in each case and cannot be inferred simply from the fact that the parties are bound by new customary rules incompatible with the treaty provisions.

5.3. THE SPANISH FISHERMEN'S CASES BEFORE THE EUROPEAN COURT OF JUSTICE

The Facts

On 3 November 1976 the Member States of the European Community agreed to extend in concert their fishery limits in the North Atlantic and the North Sea to 200 miles from the coasts, as from 1 January 1977.[43] At the same time the EC started negotiations with third States whose vessels had traditionally fished in the newly proclaimed 200-mile zones.

One of those States, Spain, had treaty rights to fish between six and twelve miles from the coasts of seven EC Member States, namely Belgium, Denmark, France, Ireland, Italy, the Netherlands, and the United Kingdom, by virtue of the 1964 London Fisheries Convention[44] and the 1967 Franco-Spanish Fisheries Agreement concluded in implementation of the 1964 Convention.[45] A fisheries agreement between the EC and Spain was signed, and entered into force on 15 April 1980.[46] Even before the conclusion of the agreement, unauthorized fishing by Spanish vessels in the EC 200-mile zone was prohibited by a number of Community Regulations.

In 1978 Burgoa, the master of a Spanish fishing vessel, was caught fishing twenty miles off the coast of Ireland without a licence from the Irish authorities. He was prosecuted in an Irish Court for infringement of the 1978 Fisheries Amendment Act, which was adopted in implementation of the above-mentioned Community Regulations.

Burgoa argued that the Community fishery Regulations and the national legislation implementing them were incompatible with Article 234 of the Treaty of Rome, which safeguarded treaty rights acquired by third countries *vis-à-vis* Member States before the entry into force of the Treaty. The fishing rights granted by the 1964 Convention to third-country vessels within six to twelve miles from the coasts of Member States were an

---

[43] Council Resolution on Certain External Aspects of the Creation of a 200-Mile Fishing Zone in the Community with effect from 1 Jan. 1977, *QJ* (1981), C105/1.

[44] 581 *UNTS*, No. 8432, at 57.   [45] 712 *UNTS*, No. 10234, at 365.

[46] *OJ* (1980), L322/4.

example of prior treaty rights covered by Article 234. According to Burgoa, the 1964 Convention applied to the 12 to 200-mile belt, where he was caught fishing, because it was intended to safeguard the rights of third-country vessels within the whole area of coastal State fishery jurisdiction, as it would evolve through time.

The Irish Court asked the European Court of Justice to give a preliminary ruling under Article 177 of the Treaty of Rome *inter alia* on the compatibility of the Irish Fisheries Amendment Act with EC law.

This was the first of a number of cases[47] in which the European Court of Justice was confronted with the argument that international agreements on which the defendants based their rights had been superseded by subsequent developments in the general law on fisheries. The facts of the cases were similar. Spanish fishermen were prosecuted in French courts for fishing without a licence in the area between six and twelve miles from the French coasts in *Arbelaiz–Emazabel, Marticorena–Ortazo* and *Parada*, and between twelve and 200 miles in the other cases. In three cases, namely *Burgoa, Tome,* and *Arantzamendi–Osa*, the defendants were caught fishing *before* the 1980 EC–Spain Fisheries Agreement entered into force. In all cases, the European Court of Justice was requested to give preliminary rulings under Article 177 on the compatibility of the fisheries Regulations with EC law.

The Decisions

In addition to the 1964 London Convention and the 1967 Fisheries Agreement between France and Spain, the defendants also invoked the provisions of the 1958 Geneva Convention on the High Seas[48] as the source of their right to fish within the 200-mile Irish and French zones. The Community Regulations governing fishing by Spanish vessels in the 200-mile EC fishing zone, as well as the national laws implementing them, were allegedly invalid to the extent that they were incompatible with these international agreements.

[47] Case 812/79, *A.-G.* v. *Burgoa, ECR* (1980), at 2787, noted at 6 *ELR* (1981), at 398 (White); 52 *BYIL* (1981), at 353 (Akehurst); 18 *Common Market Law Review* (1981), at 227 (Schermers); 76 *AJIL* (1982), at 396 (Leigh). Joined Cases 180 and 266/80, *Tome* v. *Procureur de la République, Procureur de la République* v. *Yurrita, ECR* (1981), at 2997, noted at 7 *ELR* (1982), at 415 (White); 53 *BYIL* (1982), at 325 (Akehurst); *AFDI* (1981), at 322 (Philip). Case 181/80, *Procureur Général* v. *Arbelaiz–Emazabel, ECR* [1981], at 2961; joined Cases 138 and 139/81, *Directeur des Affaires Maritimes du Littoral du Sud-Ouest* v. *Marticorena–Ortazo* and *Parada, ECR* [1982], at 3819, noted at 54 *BYIL* (1983), at 350 (Akehurst). Joined Cases 137 and 140/81, *Directeur des Affaires Maritimes du Littoral du Sud-Ouest* v. *Sagarzazu; Administrateur des Affaires Maritimes* v. *Sagasti, ECR* [1982], at 3847; joined Cases 13–28/82, *Arantzamendi–Osa* v. *Procureur de la République and Procureur Général ECR* [1982], at 3927; joined Cases 50–58/82, *Administrateur des Affaires Maritimes* v. *Dorca Marina et al. ECR* [1982], at 3949, noted at 54 *BYIL* (1983), at 353 (Akehurst). See also R. R. Churchill and N. G. Forster, 'European Community Law and Prior Treaty Obligations of Member States: The Spanish Fishermen's Cases', 36 *ICLQ* (1987), at 504; Plender, 'The Role of Consent', at 154.
[48] 559 *UNTS*, No. 8164, at 285.

The 1964 Convention and the 1967 Agreement granted Spanish vessels fishery rights between six and twelve miles from the French coasts. Article 7 of the Geneva Convention prevented coastal States from unilaterally adopting conservation measures 'in any area of the high seas adjacent to their territorial sea', *inter alia*, if they discriminated, in form or in fact, against foreign fishermen.

During the proceedings it was argued that the treaties on which the defendants relied were no longer in force on account of new developments in customary law leading to the general recognition of a State's exclusive fishing rights up to 200 miles from its coasts. This development was incompatible with the 1964 Convention, which set the outer limit of a State's fisheries jurisdiction at twelve miles from the coasts, as well as with the 1958 Geneva Convention, which regulated fishing on the basis of the traditional distinction between territorial waters and high seas.

In the *Burgoa Case* Advocate-General Capotorti thus argued that the customary rules in force should be regarded as having abrogated the rules of the London Fisheries Convention.[49] The purpose of the Convention was to define a regime of fisheries of a permanent character, whereas the supervening customary rule revolutionized that regime by permitting States to exercise exclusive fishing rights to 200 miles from the coastline. It would be impossible to 'interpret' the provisions of the London Convention so as to reconcile them with the new rules. In the light of such a radical change in general international law, the sounder view would be to consider that the relevant treaty provisions had been terminated.[50]

The same conclusion should be reached with regard to the 1958 Geneva Convention:

recent developments in general international maritime law have caused the earlier incompatible provisions, both general and particular, to be abrogated. Article 7 of the Geneva Convention which dealt with the question of conservation of biological resources on the basis of the traditional division between territorial waters and the high seas, *can no longer be regarded as being in force* now that that division has been rendered extremely uncertain by recognition of the exclusive economic zone. (emphasis added)[51]

Similar views were expressed by the Attorney General of Ireland,[52] the French Government[53] and the Council of the European Community.[54] In

---

[49] *Burgoa*, at 2818.   [50] Ibid.   [51] *Arbelaiz–Emazabel*, at 2988.

[52] *Burgoa*, at 2795: 'The 1964 Convention has been effectively overtaken by events and has been deprived of its effect by the general extension of fishing limits to 200 miles.'

[53] *Tome and Yurrita*, at 3009: the Geneva Convention 'has been outstripped by the development of an international custom enabling coastal States to declare an exclusive fishing zone extending 200 miles from their coasts.'

[54] Ibid., at 3011: 'since 1975 a new customary rule of international law has developed, enabling coastal States to reserve for themselves all fishing rights in a zone adjacent to their territorial waters extending as far as 200 miles. The Council is of the opinion that the Geneva Convention may not be regarded as applying to the zone covered by the new custom.'

the *Burgoa Case* the Commission of the EC also alleged that the evolution of the general law had affected the continued validity of the 1964 Convention: 'the London Convention, which is based on the principle of twelve mile zones, is obsolete since there has been a fundamental change of circumstances brought about by the general recognition of 200-mile fishery zones.'[55]

The Court held that the defendants could no longer rely on the fisheries agreements concluded between Spain and EC Member States before the general recognition of the right of coastal States to 200-mile exclusive economic zones. The new relations established in the meantime between the EC and Spain, including the interim fisheries regime set up by Community Regulations pending the conclusion of the 1980 EC–Spain Fisheries Agreement, were 'superimposed on' or 'substituted for' the prior regime, '*in order to take account of the general development of international law in the field of fishing on the high seas*'.[56]

The legal situation with regard to Spain's fishing rights in the EC 200-mile zones was clearer in those cases where the defendants were caught fishing *after* the new EC–Spain Fisheries Agreement entered into force.[57] In the remaining cases, where the defendants were caught fishing before the entry into force of the 1980 Agreement,[58] the prior fisheries agreements had certainly not been terminated or suspended formally when the alleged offences took place. On the other hand, when the Community Regulations on fisheries were adopted, negotiations with Spain were well under way. Moreover, Spain co-operated with the EC over the implementation of the Community licensing system for fishing in the 200-mile zone, so that it could be considered to have tacitly consented to the modification of the old regime.[59]

In any event, the Court did not endorse the argument that the emergence of new customary law had abrogated the provisions of prior incompatible fisheries treaties. It noted instead the development of the general law on fisheries to conclude that it was against this background that the EC and Spain had modified their relations, initially by means of informal arrangements and later by concluding a new fisheries agreement. It was these

---

[55] *Burgoa Case*, at 2798. See also *Tome and Yurrita*, at 3011: 'the expression "area of the high seas adjacent to its territorial sea" contained in Article 7 of the Geneva Convention . . . is a transitional concept applied in the period between adoption of the Geneva Convention and the establishment of the new rules resulting from the proceedings of the Conference on the Law of the Sea and has now disappeared from positive customary law.'

[56] *Burgoa*, at 2807, para. 24; *Tome and Yurrita*, at 3016, para. 18; *Arantzamendi–Osa*, at 3937, para. 10; *Sagarzazu–Sagasti*, at 3862, para. 8; *Arbelaiz–Emazabel*, at 2982, para. 30; *Marticorena–Ortazo*, at 3934, para. 8.

[57] For doubts regarding the validity of the abrogation *vis-à-vis* the other parties to the 1958 and the 1964 Conventions, see Churchill and Foster, 'European Community Law', at 511 et seq.   [58] Namely in *Burgoa, Tome*, and partly in *Arantzamendi–Osa*.

[59] See Churchill, 'Fisheries Jurisdiction Cases', at 517; Meseguer, 'Accord', esp. at 530 et seq.

arrangements that had superseded the previous treaty regime and not the development of new customary rules alone.

Under this approach, new customary law does not automatically terminate prior treaty obligations but can be a ground for their adaptation. The treaty regime is modified by the parties in order to reflect supervening developments in general customary law.

5.4. THE *LA BRETAGNE* ARBITRATION

In the 1970s Canada established a twelve-mile territorial sea, from which fishing vessels of other countries were gradually excluded by means of phasing-out agreements. One of these agreements was concluded with France in 1972.[60] France renounced all prior fishing rights she enjoyed in Canadian waters. Exceptionally, in view of the special situation of Saint-Pierre and Miquelon, Article 4(*b*) of the agreement provided that a maximum of ten French trawlers registered in Saint-Pierre and Miquelon could continue to fish in the Canadian fishing zone within the Gulf of St Lawrence on an equal footing with Canadian trawlers. Canadian fishery regulations would apply without discrimination to these French fishing vessels (Article 6).

In 1985 Canada refused to give the French freezer-trawler *La Bretagne* permission to fillet its catch in the Gulf of St Lawrence.[61] France protested and the matter was submitted to international arbitration.[62] The Tribunal, which gave its award on 17 July 1986,[63] was asked to decide, in accordance with international law, whether the French trawlers covered by Article 4(*b*) of the 1972 Agreement were allowed to fillet their catch in the Gulf of St Lawrence.

France argued that Article 4(*b*) of the 1972 Agreement gave Canada the power to regulate only specific activities directly related to fishing, and these did not include filleting. According to Canada, in view of the evolution of law of the sea since 1972, it had been generally recognized that the coastal State was entitled to regulate *all* matters relating to the exploration and exploitation of its natural resources within its exclusive economic zone,

[60] Agreement of 27 Mar. 1972, *UN Legislative Series, National Legislation and Treaties relating to the Law of the Sea* (1974) ST/LEG/SER.B/16, at 570.

[61] See J.-M. Arbour, 'L'Affair du chalutier-usine "La Bretagne" ou les droits de l'état côtier dans sa zone économique exclusive', 24 *CYIL* (1986), at 61; C.-A. Colliard, 'Le Différend Franco-Canadien sur le "filetage" dans le Golfe du Saint-Laurent', 92 *RGDIP* (1988), at 273; H. Dipla, 'L'Affaire concernant le filetage à l'intérieur du Golfe du Saint-Laurent entre le Canada et la France', 32 *AFDI* (1986), at 239.

[62] By a *compromis* of 23 Oct. 1985, 90 *RGDIP* (1986), see decision, at p. 716.

[63] Ibid., at 713.

subject to any express treaty provisions to the contrary.[64] As a result, filleting fell within the scope of Canada's regulatory powers.[65]

The Tribunal held that the expression 'fishery regulations' in Article 6 of the 1972 Agreement should be interpreted in accordance with its original and ordinary meaning, which related only to the capture of fish and not to filleting.[66] However, in view of the alleged developments in the law regarding the rights of the coastal State in its exclusive economic zone, it was thought to be necessary to examine whether an adjustment of the ordinary meaning of Article 6 was required. This was no longer a question of the interpretation of the 1972 Agreement, but a question of its 'application over time',[67] which could result in the modification of the treaty provisions in the light of new customary law.

The Tribunal acknowledged that customary law had developed since 1972 on the basis of the Third UN Conference on the Law of the Sea and State practice within and outside the Conference. As a result, it was now generally accepted that the coastal State enjoyed sovereign rights within its exclusive economic zone for the purpose of exploring and exploiting, conserving and managing, its natural resources.[68] Both France and Canada had established 200-mile exclusive economic or fishing zones.

The Tribunal concluded that the readjustment of the 1972 Agreement in the light of the new customary rules was, in principle, possible. The 1972 Agreement contained no stipulation of duration, and its preamble reflected the parties' desire to 'adapt to the *present* circumstances their mutual relations in fishery matters' (emphasis added).[69] The subsequent conduct of the parties in the application of the licensing regime provided by the 1972 Agreement confirmed that the parties had not intended to freeze the situation prevailing in 1972, in particular with regard to Canada's rights within its fishery zone, but to 'place their agreement in the perspective of the development of the new law of the sea'.[70]

However, the Tribunal noted that the 1982 Convention was not yet in force and its provisions could be relevant only to the extent that they had become part of general customary law binding on the parties.[71] In any event, under both the 1982 Treaty and new general customary law, activities only indirectly related to fishing, such as filleting, were not regarded as part of the coastal State's sovereign rights in its exclusive economic zone. Under new general customary law in particular, the coastal State had the right to take measures relating to the management of the natural resources of its exclusive economic zone only if these measures had a conservation objective.[72] For these reasons, it could not be concluded that the evolution

[64] See Arbour, 'L'Affaire', at 79 *et seq.*   [65] Ibid., at 731, 745–6.
[66] *La Bretagne* Arbitration, paras. 32 *et seq.*   [67] See ibid., para. 58, p. 752.
[68] Ibid. at 746, para. 49.   [69] Ibid., at 747, para. 51.   [70] Ibid.
[71] Ibid., at 748, para. 51.   [72] Ibid., para. 50.

of the international law of the sea and the adoption of the new 1982 Convention 'had fundamentally modified the balance of rights and obligations'[73] under the 1972 Agreement.

Although the Tribunal only briefly addressed the issue of treaty modification in the light of new customary law, the following conclusions can be drawn from its pronouncements. First, developments in general customary law may in certain circumstances affect the application of prior treaty rights and obligations. In particular, this will be the case when it can be shown that the evolution of the general law has substantially altered the contractual balance of rights and obligations. Secondly, the parties to a treaty may exclude the application of supervening customary law by creating a special treaty regime of a permanent character. Thirdly, in cases where the requirements for the application of this rule are met, a tribunal may be prepared to read new customary law into the treaty text in the context of the determination of the applicable law, if this was the intention of the parties.

5.5. THE NAMIBIA ADVISORY OPINION

In the Namibia Advisory Opinion[74] the International Court of Justice had to decide on the validity of a Security Council Resolution adopted with the abstention of two permanent members.

According to Article 27, para. 3, of the UN Charter, decisions of the Security Council on non-procedural matters 'shall be made by an affirmative vote of nine members *including the concurrent votes of the permanent members*'. In practice, however, the Security Council had on various occasions treated a resolution adopted with the abstention of one or more permanent members as valid.

In his oral statement before the Court the representative of the UN Secretary-General Mr Stavropoulos argued that a rule of 'customary law of the United Nations' had evolved which enabled the Security Council to adopt non-procedural resolutions despite the abstention of permanent members.[75] This customary rule amounted to an authoritative interpretation or an amendment of Article 27, para. 3, of the UN Charter.[76]

The Court upheld the practice of the Security Council as a legitimate *interpretation* of the Charter: 'the proceedings of the Security Council extending over a long period supply abundant evidence that presidential rulings and the positions taken by members of the Council, in particular its permanent members, have consistently and uniformly interpreted the

---

[73] *La Bretagne* Arbitration, para. 50.   [74] ICJ Reports (1971), at 16 *et seq.*
[75] ICJ Reports (1970-II), at 39–40.   [76] Ibid.

practice of voluntary abstention by a permanent member as not constituting a bar to the adoption of resolutions.'[77]

Even assuming that the practice of the Security Council regarding Article 27 amounted to an amendment of the Charter, as some authorities believe,[78] it is, in any event, not an example of treaty termination or revision in the light of new customary law, but a case of treaty modification by the subsequent practice of the parties.[79] This *de facto* revision takes place when the parties to a treaty apply one or several of its provisions in such a way that their original meaning is altered. The treaty is, as a result, modified by means of a tacit agreement between the parties.[80] This process is not motivated by the emergence of a new rule of general customary law, but is treaty-oriented—that is, it takes place in the course of the application of the treaty with a view to the modification of its provisions.

5.6. THE GUINEA-BISSAU/SENEGAL MARITIME BOUNDARY ARBITRATION

On 12 March 1985 Senegal and Guinea-Bissau asked an international tribunal to decide, in accordance with the rules of international law, whether a 1960 Exchange of Letters between France and Portugal determining the maritime boundary of Senegal and Guinea-Bissau was still applicable in the relations between the parties. In case of a negative answer, the Tribunal was requested to draw the boundary line. The Tribunal gave its award in Geneva on 31 July 1989.[81]

Guinea-Bissau argued that she was no longer bound by the 1960 Agreement, which had been concluded at a time when she had not yet gained her independence.[82] In any event, the 1960 Agreement was concluded under the regime of the 1958 Geneva Convention and had to be verified or revised in the light of the contemporary rules on maritime delimitation contained in the new Law of the Sea Convention.[83]

Although the 1982 Law of the Sea Convention was not yet in force, its provisions on maritime delimitation could be relevant to the extent that they were part of customary law.[84] Guinea-Bissau thus argued that the 1960

---

[77] ICJ Reports (1971), at 22, para. 22. See also Separate Opinions of Judge Padilla Nervo, at 117, and Judge Dillard, at 153–4; Sinclair, *The Vienna Convention*, at 137.

[78] See the dissenting opinion of Judge Bustamante in the *Expenses Case*, ICJ Reports (1962), at 291; D. W. Greig, *International Law* (2nd edn. London, 1976), 490, 709; L. Gross, 'Voting in the Security Council: Abstention in the Post-1965 Amendment Phase and its Impact on Article 25 of the Charter', 62 *AJIL* (1968), 315, esp. at 327 *et seq.*; Tunkin, *Theory of International Law*, at 339–40; *Droit international public* (Paris, 1965), at 94–5.

[79] See Ch. 2.

[80] See Article 38 of the 1966 ILC Draft on the Law of Treaties, *YILC* (1966-II), at 236.

[81] Award of 31 July 1989, 94 *RGDIP* (1990), at 204 (in French); 83 *ILR* (1990), at 1 (in English). [82] Ibid., paras. 63 *et seq.*

[83] Ibid., para. 79. [84] See dissenting opinion of Arbitrator Bedjaoui, para. 80.

Agreement was void because of its incompatibility with new customary law[85] and that its readjustment to the new rules, in particular the verification of the equitable character of the boundary line, could be effected in the context of its application by the Tribunal.

The Tribunal dealt very briefly with this issue. After observing that the 1982 Law of the Sea Convention was not yet in force, the Tribunal examined the pertinence of Guinea-Bissau's argument under customary law. It noted in this respect that the 1960 Exchange of Letters was an agreement establishing the maritime boundary between the two countries. Agreements of this kind were by their nature final and, under customary law or general principles of law, there was no obligation to verify or revise them.[86] Accordingly, the Tribunal did not have to decide whether new customary law could affect the continued application of other kinds of treaties.

The finality of treaties determining boundaries is not unknown in treaty law. Article 62, para. 2, of the Vienna Convention provides in this respect that a fundamental change of circumstances cannot be invoked as a ground for terminating or withdrawing from, *inter alia*, a treaty establishing a boundary.

Interpretation in the Light of New Customary Law

The Tribunal held that a treaty should in principle be interpreted in the light of the law in force at the time of its conclusion.[87] However, it was prepared to take account of the evolution of the law of the sea in the particular case, provided that this would not be inconsistent with its function 'to interpret treaties and not to revise them'.[88]

The 1960 Agreement drew the boundary line dividing the two countries' territorial seas, contiguous zones, and continental shelves. The Tribunal was prepared to take into account the evolution of the general law regarding the meaning of the terms 'the territorial sea', 'the contiguous zone', and the 'continental shelf', because these concepts existed at the time of the conclusion of the 1960 Agreement. The Tribunal noted that the parties themselves specified in this respect that the object of their agreement was to define the maritime boundary 'taking into account the Geneva Conventions of April 29, 1958'.[89]

With regard to the continental shelf, in particular, the Tribunal noted that the definition of this term in 1960 contained the dynamic element of 'exploitability', which was bound to change with the evolution of technology. This was an additional reason for concluding that the 1960 Agreement should be interpreted as delimiting the whole extent of the continental shelf as defined at the time of the award.[90]

---

[85] Award of 31 July 1989, see p. 215.   [86] Ibid., at 265.
[87] Ibid., at 269, para. 85.   [88] Ibid., at 270, para. 68.
[89] Ibid.   [90] Ibid., at 271.

By contrast, the Tribunal refused to interpret the 1960 Agreement as applying also to maritime areas, such as the exclusive economic zone or the exclusive fisheries zone, which were not part of international law at the time when it was concluded. This 'interpretation' would in reality involve a modification of the text of the 1960 Agreement.[91]

5.7. THE IRAN–US CLAIMS TRIBUNAL

The Iran–US Claims Tribunal[92] was set up in 1981 by the Governments of Iran and the United States for the purpose of deciding claims of their nationals arising out of debts, contracts, expropriations, or other measures affecting property rights.[93]

A Treaty of Amity concluded between Iran and the United States in 1955[94] provided that 'just compensation' should be paid in the event of a lawful taking of property. Such compensation 'shall be in an effectively realizable form and shall represent the full equivalent of the property taken' and 'adequate provision shall have been made at or prior to the time of taking for the determination and payment thereof' (Article IV, para. 2).

US companies that filed compensation claims for the expropriation of their property by the Iranian Government relied on the 1955 Treaty. Iran, however, argued that the 'prompt, adequate and effective compensation' standard provided by Article IV had been superseded by developments in general international law, which imposed on the expropriating State less stringent compensation requirements.

In a number of cases the Tribunal did not find it necessary to rule on the continued validity of the 1955 Treaty, because there were no meaningful differences between the Treaty provisions regarding the definition of a 'taking' or the compensation obligations and the customary law requirements.[95] In the cases examined below, however, the Tribunal dealt with the effect of the customary rules on the 1955 Treaty.

---

[91] Ibid.

[92] For a selective bibliography on the Iran–US Claims Tribunal, see N. G. Ziadé, 2 *ICSID Review* (1987), at 534; see also D. W. Bowett, 'State Contracts with Aliens: Contemporary Developments on Compensation for Termination or Breach', 59 *BYIL* (1988), at 49; C. N. Brower, 'Current Developments in the Law of Expropriation and Compensation: A Preliminary Survey of Awards of the Iran–US Claims Tribunal', 21 *The International Lawyer* (1987), at 639; B. M. Clagett, 'Just Compensation in International Law', in R. B. Lillich (ed.), *The Valuation of Nationalized Property in International Law*, v (University Press of Virginia, Charlottesville, 1986), at 31.

[93] For the text of the Claims Settlement Declaration, see 1 *Iran–US CTR*, at 9.

[94] Treaty of Amity, Economic Relations and Consular Rights Between the United States of America and Iran, signed 15 Aug. 1955, 284 *UNTS* 93, 8 *UST* 899.

[95] *American International Group* v. *Iran*, 19 Dec. 1983, 4 *Iran–US CTR* 96, at 109; *Sea–Land Service Inc.* v. *Iran*, 20 June 1984, 6 *Iran–US CTR* 149, at 168; *Sedco* v. *NIOC and Iran*, 24 Oct. 1985, 9 *Iran–US CTR* 248, at 272–3.

5.7.1. *INA Corporation* v. *Iran*

The US Corporation, INA, filed a compensation claim for the expropriation of its shareholding in Shargh, an Iranian insurance company.

The Tribunal held[96] that in the present case it did not matter whether the 1955 Treaty or modern customary law applied, because both prescribed the same compensation standard — that is, 'adequate compensation' equal to the fair market value of the investment made.[97]

In any case, the Tribunal assumed that the Treaty, which had been invoked by INA, remained binding, because Iran did not contest its validity[98] and held that its provisions had priority over customary law: 'for the purpose of this case we are in the presence of a *lex specialis*, in the form of the Treaty of Amity, which *in principle* prevails over general rules' (emphasis added).[99]

The Dissenting Opinion of Judge Ameli

Judge Ameli criticized the Tribunal's dictum that the 1955 Treaty applied as *lex specialis*.[100] Judge Ameli stated that the 1955 Treaty was no longer binding,[101] and that, even if it were, 'the rules of treaty interpretation require that the relevant provisions on compensation should be *modified* to the extent required by international law at the time of interpretation' (emphasis added).[102] The parties to the 1955 Treaty provided for 'prompt, adequate and effective' compensation, because this was the customary law standard prevailing at the time of the conclusion of the Treaty. Their intention was, however, that the treaty standard for compensation should reflect the evolution of customary law.[103] Since modern customary law simply required 'appropriate' compensation,[104] it should be considered that the treaty standard had been modified accordingly.

This argument makes the effect of new customary law on a treaty conditional upon the intention of the parties as inferred from the treaty text. In the present case, the intention of the parties, as interpreted by Judge Ameli,[105] was to incorporate into the treaty text the customary law standard, as it may evolve from time to time.

5.7.2. *Sedco Inc.* v. *NIOC and Iran* (final Award)

Sedco filed a compensation claim for the expropriation of its Iranian subsidiary, Sediran. Following an earlier award on jurisdiction,[106] this Award[107]

---

[96] Award of 12 August 1985, 8 *Iran–US CTR* at 373.   [97] Ibid., at 378–9.
[98] Ibid., at 379.   [99] Ibid.   [100] Ibid., at 403.   [101] Ibid., at 431 *et seq.*
[102] Ibid., at 407; also at 450.   [103] Ibid., at 440.   [104] Ibid., at 407 *et seq.*
[105] For a different interpretation of Article IV, see Separate Opinion of Judge Brower in *Sedco Inc.* v. *NIOC*.
[106] See above, n. 95.   [107] Award of 27 March 1986, 10 *Iran–US CTR*, at 180.

had to determine the compensation due to Sedco for the expropriation of its shares in Sediran.

Iran argued that the full compensation standard provided by the 1955 Treaty was not applicable for two reasons. First, the Treaty was no longer binding.[108] Secondly, in any case, it embodied nothing but the prevailing principles and rules of international law, and its standard was intended to follow the evolution of international law, including the UN Resolutions providing that compensation should be calculated on the basis of the net book value of the company taken.[109]

The Tribunal ruled that Article IV, para. 2, of the Treaty was applicable to the present case,[110] but examined the state of the general law in view of the argument that Article IV simply incorporated custom as it may exist from time to time.[111] However, in the particular case the final result would be the same, because the full compensation standard provided by Article IV was also the customary rule.[112]

In his *Separate Opinion*, Judge Brower criticized the Tribunal for giving merit to Iran's 'forceful and imaginative argument' that Article IV, para. 2, was intended to reflect changes in customary law.[113] In his view, the intention of the parties to the 1955 Treaty must have been to apply in their relations specific compensation requirements, and, in particular, the 'prompt, adequate and effective' standard, irrespective of any future changes in customary law. Otherwise, the parties would have no reason for concluding their agreement.

5.7.3. *Sola Tiles Inc.* v. *Iran*

In another expropriation case,[114] the claimant, Sola Tiles, did not rely on the provisions of the 1955 Treaty but based its compensation claim on general principles of law and, in particular, the *dictum* of the Permanent Court of International Justice in the *Chorzów Factory Case*[115] to the effect that the level of compensation for expropriation should be based on 'the value of the undertaking at the moment of dispossession plus interest to the date of judgment'.

However, the Tribunal stated that the Treaty could not be ignored, because 'it must in some way form part of the legal background against which the Tribunal decides the case'.[116] In any case, it did not discuss the relationship between the Treaty and customary law any further, because

---

[108] Ibid., at 272.   [109] Ibid., at 183.
[110] Award of 27 March 1986, at 184, citing *Phelps Dodge* v. *Iran*, 19 Mar. 1986, 10 *Iran–US CTR* 121, at 132.
[111] Ibid.   [112] Ibid., at 187, 189.   [113] Ibid., at 195.
[114] Award of 22 April 1987, 14 *Iran–US CTR* at 223.
[115] *PCIJ* (1928), Ser. A, No. 17.   [116] Award of 22 April 1987, at 234.

it concluded, in line with earlier awards, that the same compensation standard would apply.

5.7.4. *Amoco* v. *Iran et al.*

The Tribunal examined[117] the legality of the expropriation of Amoco's 50 per cent shareholding in Khemco by Iran under the 1955 Treaty and under customary law. Iran argued that the Treaty had ceased to be operative in November 1979 at the latest, by reason of its breach by the United States and the general change of circumstances.[118]

The Tribunal concluded that the Treaty was in force at the time when the relevant facts of the case occurred.[119] As a *lex specialis* in the relations between the parties, the Treaty superseded customary law. However, customary law could be used 'to fill in possible *lacunae* of the Treaty, to ascertain the meaning of undefined terms in its text or, more generally, to aid interpretation and implementation of its provisions'.[120]

As a result, the Tribunal took account of customary law when determining the amount of compensation due to Amoco. Article IV provided that compensation should be the 'full equivalent of the property taken', but did not specify how it should be calculated.[121] In accordance with customary law, the Tribunal decided that the going-concern value of the property taken should be used as the basis of the calculation.[122]

In his *Concurring opinion*, Judge Brower criticised the Tribunal's holding that the Treaty required interpretation against the background of customary international law.[123] In his view, the term 'full equivalent of the property taken' should be given its plain meaning, that is 'going-concern' value of the property, including expected future profits, because to do otherwise would ignore the intention of the parties.[124]

5.7.5. *Phillips* v. *NIOC and Iran*

Phillips filed a compensation claim for the expropriation of its contractual rights under a petroleum exploration agreement with the National Iranian Oil Company.[125]

Iran argued that the provisions of the 1955 Treaty had been superseded by customary law, which no longer required full compensation, especially

---

[117] Award of 14 July 1987, 15 *Iran–US CTR* at 189.   [118] Ibid., at 214.

[119] Ibid., at 219; see also *Mobil Oil Iran Inc. et al.* v. *Iran*, 14 July 1987, 16 *Iran–US CTR*. 3, para. 74, at 25, and *Starret Housing Corporation* v. *Iran*, 14 Aug. 1987, 16 *Iran–US CTR* 112, at 195.   [120] Award of 14 July 1987, at 222, para. 112.

[121] Ibid., at 252, para. 209. See also 224, para. 117.

[122] Ibid., at 270.   [123] Ibid., at 298–9.

[124] Case No. 39, Chamber Two, Award no. 425–39–2, 29 June 1989.

[125] Ibid., para. 107.

in cases of large-scale nationalizations involving a State's natural resources.[126] The parties intended to incorporate into the treaty customary law as it developed through time, and, in any event, there was a general international law principle of 'dynamic' interpretation of treaties in the light of new customary law.

For the purpose of determining the amount of compensation, the Tribunal relied exclusively on Article IV of the 1955 Treaty as the applicable law for the following reasons.

First, in line with previous awards the Tribunal held that the 1955 Treaty of Amity was in force at the time when the claims arose and, therefore, 'is the relevant source of law on which the Tribunal is justified in drawing in reaching its decision'.[127] Secondly, the Tribunal concluded that the intention of the parties to the Treaty was 'clearly and completely [to] describe the requirements for takings and compensation'[128] in Article IV, so that it would not be modified by subsequent customary law. Thirdly, having concluded that the treaty compensation standard was intended to govern the relations between the parties irrespective of developments in customary law, the Tribunal refused to accept that the principle of 'dynamic interpretation' of treaties could override the specific intention of the parties: 'concerning the argument that treaties generally should be interpreted in the light of customary international law as it may evolve, the Tribunal has already found in the INA award that the treaty of Amity as a *lex specialis* prevails in principle over general rules. This is certainly the case for the Treaty's compensation provisions the purpose of which would otherwise be difficult to ascertain.'[129]

It will be recalled that in the Sedco Award the Tribunal had implied that the intention of the parties to the 1955 Treaty was to apply in their *inter se* relations the customary rules on compensation that would prevail at the time of the application of the Treaty. The Phillips Award adopted a different interpretation of Article IV of the Treaty which was in line with the opinion of Judge Brower in the Sedco and Amoco Awards.

General Remarks

The awards of the Iran–US Claims Tribunal examined here illustrate the limited scope of intervention that international tribunals have in the process of treaty readjustment to new customary rules.

First, a valid treaty will be regarded as binding, if no action has been taken by the parties in order to terminate or modify it (*Sedco Inc.* v. *NIOC*, *Amoco*).

Secondly, until the treaty provisions that are incompatible with new custom are terminated or modified in accordance with the appropriate

---

[126] Ibid., para. 103.   [127] Ibid., para. 107.   [128] Ibid.   [129] See *Sedco Inc.* v. *NIOC*.

procedure, international tribunals must consider them as 'a relevant source of law on which they would be justified in drawing in reaching their conclusions'.[133] In cases of this kind, the treaty will in principle apply as *lex specialis*, even if the customary rules are of more recent origin (*INA Corp. v. Iran, Amoco*).

Thirdly, modification of a treaty by a tribunal will only be possible if it can be established that this was the intention of the parties (*Sedco Inc. v. NIOC*). Otherwise, customary law can only be used to interpret unclear or incomplete treaty provisions (*Amoco*).

5.8. CONCLUSION

A number of judgments examined in this chapter support the proposition that new customary law may be a ground for the modification or termination of prior treaties. In the *Spanish Fishermen's Cases* the European Court of Justice implied that the revision of the fisheries regime governing the relations between Spain and the EC had taken place on account of the evolution of international law in the field of fishing on the high seas. In the *La Bretagne* Arbitration the Tribunal held that the evolution of the general law may require the adaptation of prior treaty provisions if it has substantially altered the balance of treaty rights and obligations, and provided that the parties did not intend to exclude the application of new custom. In the *Fisheries Jurisdiction Case* (Merits) the International Court of Justice directed the parties to take account of the evolution of the law of the sea in their fishery relations by negotiating an equitable solution. Finally, in the *Fisheries Jurisdiction Case* (Jurisdiction of the Court), the Court considered that a change in the general law may be a fundamental change under the conditions set out in Article 62 of the Vienna Convention.

Although these judgments agree on the principle that new customary law may be a ground of treaty termination, it is difficult to develop from them a consistent theory regarding the precise circumstances in which this rule applies. The relevant passages are sometimes too brief and inconclusive or the conditions they mention vary from case to case, because the issue is approached from a different angle.

In any case, in the context of international adjudication, a claim that a treaty is incompatible with more recent customary rules may be of limited practical value. Tribunals are reluctant to accept that new customary law automatically terminates or modifies prior treaty provisions, unless it can be shown that this is what the parties intended (Sedco Award). Even if the parties to a treaty are bound by the new customary rules, additional evidence of their intent to modify or terminate the treaty rights and obligations will be required (United Kingdom v. France Continental Shelf Arbitration).

As a result, a tribunal may declare that new customary law is a ground for the termination or revision of a treaty but cannot regard as void treaty provisions that have not been terminated or modified by the parties, either expressly or tacitly.

If a treaty provision is held to be still in force, it will prevail over customary law *qua lex specialis*. In cases where tribunals had to choose between a treaty rule and a more recent customary rule in the context of the determination of the applicable law, they gave priority to the treaty rule, without even trying to establish whether it was in fact more special either by virtue of its subject-matter or by virtue of the number of States bound by it.

Tribunals may have given absolute priority to treaties out of practical consideration, such as the clarity of the written word and the difficulty of determining the precise degree of generality of a customary rule. The principle of *pacta sunt servanda* and the concern to ensure treaty stability may also have influenced this attitude.

The Emergence of New Customary Law and Treaty Interpretation

Courts may take account of new customary law in the context of treaty interpretation—for instance, the case where a treaty contains technical terms whose meaning was intended to evolve with time. In the Guinea-Bissau/Senegal Arbitration the Tribunal held that the terms 'territorial sea', 'contiguous zone', and 'continental shelf' included in the 1960 Delimitation Agreement should be interpreted in accordance with their customary law meaning at the time of the award, because this would be consistent with the intention of the parties.

Courts also take account of new customary law in order to clarify or complete treaty provisions. In the United Kingdom v. France Continental Shelf Arbitration the Tribunal took account of developments in the law of the sea when applying Article 6 of the Geneva Convention on the Continental Shelf. In the Amoco Award the Iran–US Claims Tribunal decided on the appropriate method for the determination of the full value of the property taken on the basis of the rules of customary law.

In this context, courts are anxious to ensure that the application of new customary law will not modify prior treaty provisions. In the Guinea-Bissau/Senegal Arbitration the Tribunal refused to interpret the 1960 Agreement that delimited the parties' territorial seas, contiguous zones, and continental shelves as also delimiting the parties' exclusive economic or fisheries zones, because this would be inconsistent with the intention of the parties as reflected in the treaty text.[130]

---

[130] See also the Advocate-General of the European Court of Justice in the *Burgoa* case regarding the defendant's argument that the 1964 Convention should be 'interpreted' as applying to the 12 to 200-mile belt from the coasts.

This attitude is dictated by what courts regard as their usual function, which is to interpret treaties and not to revise them. If the application of a new customary rule alters the meaning of the treaty text, this is no longer a matter of treaty interpretation but of treaty modification. In these circumstances, a tribunal can at most indicate how the treaty should be revised in order to conform to new customary law.

6

Some Criticisms

6.1. THE VIENNA CONVENTION ON THE LAW OF TREATIES: THE SIGNIFICANCE OF AN OMISSION

The Vienna Convention does not mention supervening custom as a ground of termination of prior incompatible treaties. The 1964 ILC Draft on the Law of Treaties contained a provision on treaty *modification* 'by the subsequent emergence of a new rule of customary law relating to matters dealt with in the treaty and binding upon all the parties' (Article 68, para. *c*). This provision was subsequently deleted from the Draft.

It may be asked whether, as a result, the concept of treaty modification or termination on account of new custom was implicitly rejected. As explained below, in our view, the Commission did not clearly pronounce itself either in favour or against this concept, but decided not to retain Article 68, para. *c*, in the belief that, as drafted, it dealt inadequately with a complex issue which, in any case, fell outside the scope of the codification.

6.1.1. Article 68 of the 1964 ILC Draft

Origins

Sir Humphrey Waldock's Third Report on the Law of Treaties contained the following provision intended to deal with issues of intertemporal law:

Article 56—The intertemporal law
1. A treaty is to be interpreted in the light of the law in force at the time when the treaty was drawn up.
2. Subject to paragraph 1, the application of a treaty shall be governed by the rules of international law in force at the time when the treaty is applied.[1]

The second paragraph of Article 56 was regarded as a limited exception of the general principle of treaty interpretation contained in the first paragraph. It was meant to apply, for instance, to cases of conflict between rules of international law, such as a treaty rule and a subsequent rule of *jus cogens*.[2]

In the ensuing discussion at the ILC,[3] it was pointed out that the conflict between rules of international law prevailing at a given time was not strictly speaking a question of intertemporal law but raised issues of modification

---

[1] *YILC* (1964-II), at 8.   [2] Ibid., at 9.   [3] See *YILC* (1964-I), at 33 *et seq.*

of one rule by another.[4] 'Intertemporal law', by contrast, specified which of several rules prevailing at different moments in time should apply to a particular case.[5]

As a result, Article 56 was deleted and a new provision on treaty interpretation in the light of new customary law appeared in Waldock's Report:

Article 73—Effect of a later customary rule or of a later agreement on interpretation of a treaty

The interpretation at any time of the terms of a treaty ... shall take account of:
(a) the emergence of any later rule of customary international law affecting the subject-matter of the treaty and binding upon all the parties ...[6]

Although Article 73 seemed to deal only with treaty interpretation in the light of supervening custom, it was also intended to cover cases of conflict between a customary rule and a prior conventional rule:

when a later rule of customary law emerges or a later agreement is concluded, the question may arise as to how far they ought to be regarded as intended to supersede the treaty in the relations between the parties ... If the treaty was intended to create a special regime between the particular parties, they might not intend it to be displaced by the emergence of a new general regime created by treaty or custom. Accordingly, it seemed prudent to state only the broad principle and not attempt to define its results. Otherwise, it would seem necessary to elaborate the provisions of the Article considerably by reference to the possible differences in the intentions of the parties.[7]

During the discussion on Article 73[8] several members of the Commission pointed out that, in the case of a conflict between conventional and customary rules, what was really involved was not interpretation but modification, 'the limitation of the scope of a particular rule in the light of new rules'.[9] In the light of these comments, Sir Humphrey Waldock replaced Article 73 with a new provision entitled 'modification of a treaty by a subsequent treaty, by subsequent practice or by customary law',[10] which was unanimously adopted by the ILC[11] in its 1964 Draft.

Deletion from the Draft

Article 68 provided that: 'The operation of a treaty may also be modified ... (c) By the subsequent emergence of a new rule of customary law relating to matters dealt with in the treaty and binding upon all the parties.'[12]

---

[4] See e.g. Verdross, at 33, paras. 6–7; Reuter, at 35; Bartos, at 36; Tunkin, at 38, para. 43.
[5] See the discussions at 55 *AIDI* (1973), esp. m. Sørensen, 'Le Problème dit du droit intertemporel dans l'ordre international', 1, at 10 *et seq.*, 86; see also Karl, *Vertrag*, at 107.
[6] *YILC* (1964-II), at 53.   [7] Ibid., at 61, para. 32.
[8] For the discussion, see *YILC* (1964-I), at 275 *et seq.*
[9] Verdross, at 296, para. 35; see also de Luna, para. 36; Yasseen, at 279, para. 57.
[10] Article 69A, ibid., at 309.   [11] Ibid., at 318.   [12] *YILC* (1964-II), at 198.

When this provision was presented to governments for their observations, it generally received favourable comments. It was thus stated that Article 68, para. *c*, flowed naturally from the character of custom as an autonomous source, as a result of which new custom could modify or void all conventional rights, terminate them, or replace them with other rights and obligations;[13] it ensured that treaties automatically reflected changes in the general principles of international law, a necessity accepted by jurists and by world public opinion;[14] it enunciated a well-established rule of international law based on the maxim *lex posterior derogat legi priori*;[15] treaty modification by the establishment of new custom binding upon all the parties was a logical solution,[16] in keeping with 'the long-recognized principle that treaties are to be applied in the context of international law and in accordance with the evolution of that law'.[17]

At the same time some governments expressed doubts about the desirability of including Article 68, para. *c*, in the Vienna Convention. Treaty modification by new custom fell outside the scope of the codification. In view of the differences of opinion about what constituted customary law, it was, therefore, suggested to leave the principle incorporated in Article 68, para. *c*, to be applied under general international law, instead of including it as a specific provision in a convention on treaty law.[18]

Only two governments objected to the principle of treaty modification by customary law. These were Greece, because she found it difficult to accept that *opinio juris* resulting in the formation of customary law contrary to the provisions of the treaty could be established,[19] and the United Kingdom, because Article 68, para. *c*, disregarded the principle that treaties should not be modified without the consent of the parties.[20]

Sir Humphrey Waldock agreed with the United Kingdom that there might be cases where the solution proposed by Article 68 would disregard the will of the parties.[21] For instance, the very object of a bilateral treaty or of a treaty between a small group of States might be to set up a special legal regime derogating from existing custom. To say that the emergence of new customary law binding on the parties as a general rule was *necessarily* to modify the particular relations they set up between them might defeat their intention. The implications of the rule in the different cases where

[13] The Netherlands, 20 *GAOR* (1966), 6th Committee, 847th Meeting, at 46, para. 12.

[14] Romania, ibid., 848th Meeting, at 54, para. 9.

[15] Thailand, ibid., 850th Meeting, at 67, para. 13.

[16] Spain, *UN Conference on the Law of Treaties*, First Session, 37th Meeting of the Committee of the Whole (1968), at 74.

[17] The United States, *YILC* (1966-II), at 358. Also in favour, Portugal, at 335; Israel, at 300; Turkey, at 342; Yugoslavia, at 364.

[18] The United States, at 358; 20 *GAOR* (1966), 6th Committee, 842nd Meeting, at 16, para. 14. Kenya, ibid., 850th Meeting, at 70, para. 39.

[19] Ibid., 845th Meeting, at 38, para. 41.   [20] *YILC* (1966-II), at 345.

[21] Ibid., at 90, para. 13.

the problem might arise should be determined in a precise manner or else this provision should be deleted from the Draft.[22]

In the ensuing discussion,[23] certain members of the Commission thought that Article 68, para. c, should be retained in the Draft.[24] However, the majority of the Commission favoured its deletion[25] for the following reasons. The solution proposed by the Draft, i.e. that the mere emergence of supervening custom would *automatically* modify a treaty containing different rules, was not satisfactory. Unless the new customary rule was a rule of *jus cogens*, there was nothing preventing the parties from providing *ex ante* that the treaty rules would in any case prevail *qua lex specialis* or from reaffirming their agreement subsequent to the emergence of new custom.[26] In cases where the parties to a treaty contributed to the formation of a new customary rule of international law without any intention to derogate from their prior agreement, it was not clear whether custom should always take precedence over the treaty, since derogations from the new custom were allowed.[27]

It was, therefore, agreed that Article 68, para. c, as drafted failed adequately to cover all aspects of the problem, which was controversial and too complex for the Commission to deal with satisfactorily in the Draft.[28] The Commission 'had scratched the surface of the subject without really coming to grips with it'.[29] In any event, treaty modification by supervening custom fell outside the scope of the codification, because it formed part of the general topic of the relationship between different sources of international law.[30]

Consequently, the Article was referred to the Drafting Committee, which deleted paragraph (c).[31]

6.1.2. Article 42 of the Vienna Convention

It may be asked whether the notion of new custom as a ground of termination of prior incompatible treaties is excluded by Article 42 of the Vienna Convention. This Article provides that the termination of a treaty, its denunciation or the withdrawal of a party and the suspension of its operation 'may take place only as a result of the application of the provisions

---

[22] *YILC* (1966-II), at 91, para. 13.   [23] *YILC* (1966-I), at 2, at 163 *et seq.*
[24] Castren, at 164, para. 5; El-Erian, at 166, paras. 43, 46.
[25] Jiménez de Aréchaga, at 164, para. 10; Ago, para. 11; Rosenne, para. 12; Tunkin, 165, para. 20; Briggs, para 25.   [26] Ago, at 167, para. 50; Amado, para. 51.
[27] The Chairman, at 166, paras 40–41; Ago, at 167, para. 50; Tsuruoka, at 166, para. 32.
[28] The Chairman, at 166, paras. 40–1; Rosenne, at 168, paras. 59, 67; de Luna, at 165, para. 24. See also Reuter, *YILC* (1964-I), at *35,* para. 10.
[29] Sir H. Waldock, at 169, para. 67; also commentary to Article 38 of the 1966 Draft, *YILC* (1964-II), at 236, para. 3.
[30] Sir H. Waldock (1966-II), at 236, para. 3; Rosenne (1966-I), at 168, para. 59.
[31] *YILC* (1964-I part II), at 220.

of the treaty or of the present Convention'. It was indeed the intention of the Commission, 'as a safeguard for the stability of treaties, to underline in a general provision at the beginning of this part that the validity and continuance in force of a treaty is the normal state of things which may be set aside only on the grounds and under the conditions provided for in the present articles'.[32]

Nevertheless, it is doubtful whether Article 42 can prevent the application of grounds of treaty termination not included in the Convention but recognized under customary law. The Convention itself affirms in its preamble that 'the rules of customary international law will continue to govern questions not regulated by the provisions of the present Convention'. As already explained, it was the opinion of the ILC that the relationship between conventional and customary rules fell outside the scope of the Vienna Convention. As a result, general customary law and not the provisions of the Convention should determine whether new custom may be a ground of treaty termination.[33]

Conclusion

The ILC rejected Article 68, para. *c*, because it provided that supervening custom would *automatically* modify a prior incompatible treaty. On the other hand, it did not decide whether supervening custom could be invoked as a ground of treaty termination by one of the parties.

The Commision was uncertain about the state of the law and decided not to legislate on the effect of supervening custom on a prior incompatible treaty, especially since it considered that, in any event, the relationship between conventional and customary rules fell outside the scope of the codification of the law of treaties.

Two criticisms of the notion of treaty termination or modification by supervening custom raised during the discussion of Article 68, para. *c*, will be discussed next. The first criticism relates to a problem that is not specific to treaty termination by new custom but arises in all cases where new custom derogates from prior rules, either conventional or customary: if one of the requirements for the creation of custom is the belief of States that their practice is required by law, new custom cannot be in conflict with an existing custom or treaty. The second criticism is as follows. If new custom does not have the character of *jus cogens*, it allows derogations by agreement. Consequently, in cases where supervening custom is in conflict with a prior treaty, the treaty, being *lex specialis*, should continue to apply between the States party to it.

---

[32] See Commentary to the Final Draft, *YILC* (1966-II), at 236. For criticisms of the Commission's approach, see Sinclair, The Vienna Convention, at 163–5; Capotorti, 'L' Extinction', at 519. See also 52 AIDI (1967-I), esp. at 108 *et seq.*, 388 *et seq.*, 258 *et seq.*

[33] See S. Rosenne, 52 *AIDI* (1967-I), at 89; W. Jenks, ibid., at 281; Capotorti, 'L'Extinction'.

6.2. *OPINIO JURIS*

State practice, even if frequently repeated, does not generate customary law unless it is accompanied by *opinio juris*. Acts of States forming the basis of custom must thus be 'accepted as law',[34] 'they must be such, or be carried out in such a way, as to be evidence of a belief that this practice is rendered obligatory by the existence of a rule of law requiring it'.[35] Conduct motivated by considerations of morality or courtesy, such as many international acts in the field of ceremonial and protocol, does not generate legally binding rules, even if it is generally and consistently followed.

This definition of *opinio juris* contains a paradox: in order for States to change existing customary law, they must believe that the new rules they are about to create are *already* the law.[36] The same paradox arises with regard to supervening custom in conflict with a prior treaty: State behaviour incompatible with the treaty text would appear to create new law by a series of breaches of the existing law, but in theory States acting *contra legem* would be supposed to believe that their conduct is required by law.

In order to solve this problem, it is sometimes said that, at least during the initial period of the formation of new custom, States must be considered to act in legal error.[37] According to a different view, *opinio juris* need not be present at all stages of the custom-generating process. At the earlier stages of the formation of a customary rule, States act without *opinio juris*, but only out of a sense of comity or morality. As practice gradually accumulates, States form the belief that their acts are in conformity with an emerging rule of customary law. In the end, after a large number of States have accepted the new rule, State practice comes to be regarded as generally obligatory.[38] It is, however, difficult to reconcile this explanation of the law-creating process with the basic idea behind the notion of *opinio juris*, namely that acts carried out of comity cannot acquire the character of a legal obligation through mere repetition.

Other authors adopt a different definition of *opinio juris*. It is thus said that the States whose conduct forms the basis of the custom must believe that they apply a norm, but not necessarily a legal norm; they must simply 'consider themselves bound by any norm whatsoever'.[39] Or State conduct must be motivated by

---

[34] Article 38 of the ICJ Statute.   [35] *North Sea Continental Shelf Cases*, at 44.

[36] See e.g. H. Kelsen, 'Théorie du droit international coutumier', *Revue internationale de la théorie du droit*, 1 (1939), 253, at 263 *et seq*: Thirlway, *International Customary Law*, at 47.

[37] Cheng, 'United Nations Resolutions on Outer Space', at 259, n. 107; J. L. Kunz, 'The Nature of Customary International Law', 47 *AJIL* (1953), 662, at 667. *Contra*, D'Amato, *The Concept of Custom*, at 66–7.

[38] See A. Verdross, 'Entstehungsweise und Geltungsgrund des Universellen Völkerrechtlichen Gewohnheitsrechts', 29 *ZaöRV* (1969), at 640, 645 *et seq*; Sørensen, *Sources*, at 106.

[39] H. Kelsen, *General Theory of Law and State* (Cambridge, Mass., 1945), at 114; *Principles,* at 440.

some sentiment of obligation—not necessarily and not primarily of a legal nature and not necessarily accompanied by an apprehension of sanction in case of non-compliance ... In that sense a course of action constantly pursued and believed to be dictated by duties of neighbourliness, reasonableness and accommodation, may, in the interest of international stability and good faith assume the complexion of binding international custom.[40]

In our view, the definition of *opinio juris* as a State's *belief* that its actions are in accordance with existing law sets a requirement impossible to fulfil. If the function of *opinio juris* is to distinguish a legally binding rule from acts carried out of comity or a sense of morality, to identify which acts out of many have legal consequences, it is sufficient that the law-creating character of state practice becomes adequately manifest. States must, therefore, assert, but not necessarily believe, that their behaviour is the law, or they must make it clear that they wish to change the law.

This definition of *opinio juris* is consistent with the manner in which new customary norms come into effect. The first instances of state practice are necessarily breaches of the existing rules and become law only after the deviating norm has been generally accepted. This law-making process is gradual and conditional upon the positive reaction or acquiescence of other States.[41] The first States engaging in the practice must, therefore, pretend that the deviating norm is already the law, or they must manifest their intention to change the law by articulating 'an objective claim of international legality' giving other States notice that their acceptance or rejection of the deviating norm will have legal implications.[42]

6.3. THE TREATY AS *LEX SPECIALIS*

It is said that the possibility of treaty termination by supervening custom not having the character of *jus cogens* is incompatible with the *lex specialis* principle. According to this principle, a treaty is special law that should continue to apply in the relations between the parties notwithstanding the development of conflicting general custom. To consider otherwise would disregard the will of the parties.

A treaty rule is considered to be special either because it binds a limited number of States, as opposed to a rule binding *erga omnes (lex specialis ratione personae)*, or because it introduces in the relations between the parties an exception from the general regulation of the subject-matter.

There are three main arguments against this criticism: first, the *lex specialis*

[40] Lauterpacht, *International Law*, i, at 63–4.
[41] Higgins, 'Development of International Law', at 120.
[42] See D'Amato, *The Concept of Custom*, at 74–5; Akehurst, 'Custom', at 36–7; Thirlway, *International Customary Law*, at 53–4.

is only a reasonable rule of thumb for the solution of conflicts between rules of international law and not an axiomatic truth; secondly, the application of the *lex specialis* principle should be limited to those cases where the treaty rule is truly special—that is, an intended derogation from the general rule; thirdly, the acceptance of custom as a ground of treaty termination does not exclude the possibility that the prior treaty can continue to apply in cases where this is in accordance with the will of the parties.

6.3.1. Legal Nature of the *lex specialis*

As explained above,[43] the *lex specialis* is one criterion used for the solution of conflicts between rules of international law, another being the *lex posterior*, according to which the more recent expression of the will of States supersedes the earlier one. Both principles are not considered to be rules of positive international law,[44] but only maxims of interpretation, i.e. 'means of giving effect to the presumed intention of the law-giver'[45] or principles of legal logic. The *lex specialis*, for example, is merely 'a presumption that the authority laying down a general rule intended to leave room for the application of more specific rules which already existed or which might be created in the future' and can be rebutted by evidence to the contrary.[46] Since these principles merely 'express in the form of quasi-rules conclusions reached by means of the logical technique of treaty interpretation',[47] 'none of these can be regarded as of absolute validity but ... they must be weighed and reconciled in the light of the circumstances of the particular case'.[48]

If the special character of a rule is determined on the basis of its more specific subject-matter, the *lex specialis* principle seems to state the obvious, namely that when the parties intended to establish a special regime, this should prevail over general rules. An additional word of caution is necessary, namely that the treaty rule is truly special only when it is established that the parties wanted it to be a derogation not only from the customary law prevailing at the time of its conclusion, but also from any new general customary rules which might evolve from time to time. By contrast, the indiscriminate application of the *lex specialis* principle is difficult to justify in cases where the special character of the treaty rule is determined on the basis of the limited number of States bound by it. In

---

[43] Ch. 2.

[44] Schwarzenberger, *International Law*, i, at 472; 'in view of the self-eliminating character of these maxims and counter-maxims, it is hardly arguable that any of them epitomises a rule of customary international law'; see also C. W. Jenks, 'The Conflict of Law-Making Treaties', 30 *BYIL* (1953), 401, 436 *et seq.* Cf. Karl, *Vertrag*, at 67.

[45] Akehurst, 'Hierarchy', at 273 n. 3; H. Aufricht, 'Supersession of Treaties in International Law', 37 *Cornell Law Quarterly* (1951–2), 655, at 698.

[46] Akehurst, 'Hierarchy', at 273.

[47] Schwarzenberger, *International Law*, i, at 472.   [48] Jenks, 'Conflict', at 436.

these cases there is no reason to imply that the treaty rule was necessarily intended to be a permanent derogation from general customary law.[49]

6.3.2. The Relationship between *lex posterior* and *lex specialis*

The tension between the *lex posterior* and the *lex specialis* becomes apparent in cases where the more recent rule is also the more general. In these cases it is difficult to decide which of the two principles should apply: while the more recent rule is the latest expression of the will of States, the special rule is best suited to the particular circumstances.

The origins of the *lex posterior* and the *lex specialis* are found in the writings of Grotius. Grotius proposed rules of interpretation ('conjectures') for the solution of conflicts between parts of the same document that arise from chance, out of some unexpected turn of affairs.[50] Grotius distinguished these 'conflicts arising from circumstances' from 'antinomies'—that is, real contradictions.[51] While an 'antinomy' would arise when words on different parts of a document were directly opposed in meaning, in the case of a 'conflict arising from circumstances' words, although not directly opposed in meaning, would come into conflict as a result of some unexpected turn of affairs.[52]

In cases where an 'antinomy' arose, a later agreement between the contracting parties would annul earlier agreements, 'since no one could at the same time have had contradictory desires. Such is in truth the nature of acts dependent on the will that they can be relinquished through a new act of volition'.[53] This is a description of what modern authors would call the *lex posterior* principle, and if Grotius relied on it exclusively for the solution of 'antinomies', he also relied on the *lex specialis* principle for the solution of 'conflicts arising from circumstances': 'among agreements which are equal in respect of the qualities mentioned, that should be given preference which is most specific and approaches more nearly to the subject in hand; for special provisions are ordinarily more effective than those that are general.'[54]

Grotius was followed by Pufendorf[55] and Vattel[56] and the same criteria for the solution of conflicts have since been used in the relevant literature.

---

[49] See Karl, *Vertrag*, at 89–90.

[50] Grotius, *De jure belli ac pacis,* ii (1925), bk. II, ch., XVI, sects. XXVIII *et seq.*

[51] Ibid., sects. IV, XXVIII.

[52] This distinction was followed by Pufendorf, *De jure naturae et gentium,* (*trans.* C. H. Oldfather and W. A. Oldfather), ii (Oxford, 1934), bk. V, ch. XII, 820, and Vattel, *The Law of Nations* (London, 1811), bk. II, ch. XVII, §311.

[53] Grotius, *De jure belli ac pacis,* sect. IV. Similarly, Pufendorf, *De jure naturae et gentium,* at 798.   [54] Grotius, *De jure belli ac pacis,* at p. 428.

[55] Pufendorf, *De jure naturae et gentium,* at 822.

[56] Vattel, *Law of Nations,* at §§315–16.

It is thus suggested that a prior treaty rule will remain unaffected by supervening custom only if it can be interpreted as an exception from the application of the general law. If this is not possible, the treaty rule should be terminated or modified in the light of news custom.[57]

In our view, this is an appropriate delimitation of the scope of application of the *lex specialis* principle. A prior treaty is truly special only if it was intended to be a derogation from the general rules. In this case the will of the parties should prevail and supervening custom should not bring about the termination of the treaty. By contrast, a treaty binding a limited number of States is not *lex specialis* in the above-mentioned sense and should not necessarily prevail over supervening custom binding *erga omnes*.

6.3.3. The Role of the Will of the Parties

According to the thesis presented in this book, supervening custom can terminate or modify prior incompatible treaties as a result of the exercise by one party of a right to that effect. The unilateral exercise of this right will not be necessary if it is clear that the parties intended to keep the treaty in force as special law applicable in their *inter se* relations. This is possible because by definition new custom is not *jus cogens*, and derogations by agreement are allowed.

The parties may, for instance, provide in the treaty itself that, in the event of development of conflicting custom, the treaty will nevertheless remain in force as originally drafted. Or, following the emergence of new conflicting custom, they may decide to continue applying the treaty in their *inter se* relations in a manner indicating their intent to retain it as special law. In both cases the will of the parties will prevail and the treaty will remain in force as a derogation from general custom.

---

[57] See e.g. Karl, *Vertrag*, at 58–9, 66.

7

Conclusions: Supervening Custom as a Ground of Treaty Termination or Revision

In this book we have examined a number of incidents where a treaty became incompatible with supervening customary law. In our view, the manner in which they were resolved supports the proposition that one party has the right to call for the termination or revision of a treaty on account of the development of new custom.

State practice offers a number of examples where one or several of the parties clearly and forcefully argued for treaty termination or revision on account of its incompatibility with supervening custom. In some cases the consensus was rapidly formed that the treaty relationship should be re-assessed in the light of the evolution of the law. In the end the treaty was expressly abrogated, revised, or replaced by a new treaty;[1] or it was brought to an end or modified by subsequent practice of the parties.[2] In other cases the process of treaty adaptation to supervening custom was longer and at times more controversial, but the same result was finally achieved.[3]

A pattern of behaviour evidencing the belief that a ground of treaty termination or revision exists emerges from these incidents. It takes the form of claims for change followed by express acceptance or acquiescence of the other parties. Even in cases where these claims were not successful, they were not dismissed in principle but on factual grounds—for instance, because it was not generally agreed that the treaty was incompatible with new custom.[4]

Indications for the existence of this rule can also be found in the case law of international tribunals.[5] A number of judgments (*Spanish Fishermen's Cases*, *La Bretagne* Arbitration, *Fisheries Jurisdiction Case*) suggest that new customary law may be a ground for the termination or revision of a prior treaty, in the sense that it confers upon one party the right to call for its abrogation or the alteration of its provisions.[6] The relevant passages from the judgments do not always clearly specify the conditions for the existence of a ground of treaty termination or revision in these circumstances. However, it can at least be said that tribunals are reluctant

---

[1] See e.g. the regime of the River Niger, the abolition of the Capitulations, fisheries in the North Atlantic.

[2] See e.g. the extradition regime in the East Indies, probably the minorities treaties.

[3] See e.g. the Nile waters question, the Treaty on the Panama Canal, Spain's fishing rights in EC waters.   [4] See e.g. the Antarctic Treaty regime.

[5] See Ch. 5.   [6] See conclusions of Ch. 5.

to accept that supervening custom automatically abrogates or modifies prior incompatible treaties, unless this is what the treaty partners intended.[7] The parties' consent to be bound by the new customary law is not in this respect sufficient, because it does not prove their intent to terminate or revise a prior treaty.

Treaty adjustment as a result of the exercise of a ground of treaty termination or revision is distinct from *desuetude* or modification by subsequent practice. However, there are cases where following developments in general customary law, the parties to a treaty do not expressly terminate it or revise it, but either let it lapse or modify it *de facto* in recognition of the need to take the new general rules into account. In this case, *desuetude* or *de facto* revision are substitutes for express termination or revision.

7.1. CONDITIONS OF APPLICATION

New customary law may be invoked as a ground for the termination or revision of a prior treaty if: (i) it is incompatible with the treaty provisions; (ii) it is different from the customary law in force at the time of the conclusion of the treaty; and (iii) it is binding upon all parties to the treaty, unless (iv) the parties intended that the treaty should continue applying as special law.

(i) The new customary rule must be *incompatible with the conventional rule*, in the sense that the two rules cannot be applied simultaneously. For instance, a treaty providing that the parties have the right to exercise exclusive fisheries jurisdiction up to a distance of twelve miles from their coasts is incompatible with a new general custom recognizing wider zones because under the treaty fishing beyond twelve miles is free for all as part of the freedoms of the high seas.

There may be cases where supervening custom is inconsistent with the assumptions on the basis of which particular treaty provisions were drafted. Consider for instance a treaty granting foreign fishing vessels access within three miles from a State's coasts, because three miles is the extent of territorial waters at the time the agreement is made. Supervening general custom that recognizes wider zones of exclusive fisheries jurisdiction changes the basic principles in view of which the fishing rights were granted. In cases where the assumptions on which certain provisions were drafted form part of the treaty text, changes must be introduced into the treaty to make them compatible with new custom. These changes will necessitate the reassessment of the whole treaty relationship, including the provisions relating to fishing rights which, strictly speaking, are not incompatible with new customary law.

---

[7] See Sedco Award, UK v. France Continental Shelf Arbitration.

(ii) The customary law prevailing at the time when the treaty was made must have *subsequently changed*. If the treaty provisions were an agreed derogation from general custom, there are no new elements requiring that the contractual situation should be reassessed.

The change in customary law does not have to be 'fundamental'—that is, of a kind that radically transforms the extent of the obligations still to be performed under the treaty. In this respect, new customary law as a ground of treaty termination or revision can be distinguished from treaty termination or revision as a result of a fundamental change of circumstances.

(iii) The new custom must be *binding on all parties to the treaty*. If one party has persistently objected to the creation of new customary law and is not bound by it as a matter of general international law, all its relations with other States, including any prior treaty rights and obligations, should not be affected by the development of supervening custom.

(iv) A State does not have the right to ask for the termination or revision of a treaty on account of supervening custom, if the treaty excludes this possibility. It may indeed have been the intention of the parties that the treaty or some of its provisions should apply in their *inter se* relations as *special law* even if different customary rules subsequently develop. Consider, for instance, the special regime applicable to the Minquiers and Ecrehous by virtue of the 1839 Treaty between France and Great Britain, which continued to apply alongside the new general fisheries limit introduced by the 1964 London Fisheries Convention; or the special provisions of the 1972 Fisheries Agreement between France and Canada in respect of Saint-Pierre and Miquelon that were not affected by the extension of Canada's fisheries jurisdiction.[8]

The intention of the parties to create a special regime may be expressly provided in the treaty or result from the interpretation of time clauses or other provisions. It is not sufficient that the treaty binds a limited number of States. State practice shows the untenability of bilateral treaties of treaties with limited membership in the face of subsequent custom binding *erga omnes*.

Special Customary Law as a Ground of Treaty Termination or Revision

In most of the incidents we have examined treaties were terminated or revised on account of the development of new *general* custom, that is custom of general application, binding *erga omnes* with the exception of persistent objectors.

New custom may also be *special* —that is, binding upon a limited number of States and applicable in their *inter se* relations only. Special custom may

---

[8] See Ch. 3; see also *La Bretagne* Arbitration discussed in Ch. 5.

be formed in the initial stages of the development of new general custom and apply until the new norm is generally accepted; or, following the development of new general custom, the old norm may continue to apply as special custom in the relations between persistent objectors.

There have been cases where emerging custom was invoked as a ground of treaty termination or revision.[9] In cases where special custom binds all parties to a prior incompatible treaty, it must indeed be accepted that it should produce the same effect on the treaty as general custom.

Special custom as a ground of treaty termination or revision must be distinguished from new rules of general application that complete or clarify principles enunciated in a prior treaty. These rules are special by virtue of their subject-matter, but do not constitute special custom, because they are binding *erga omnes*. Moreover, they are not incompatible with the treaty but complement its provisions and can be taken into account when interpreting the treaty.

Duration of Treaties

Treaties are of varying duration. Some are concluded for a stated term, at the end of which they expire unless specifically renewed or extended. Others fix no period for their duration and do not provide for denunciation or withdrawal (permanent treaties). Treaties intended to remain in force for a very long period of time, although not strictly speaking permanent, are lasting enough to raise similar issues of adaptation to new custom. Finally, treaties may contain a denunciation provision sometimes exercisable after an initial period. It is possible that even treaties of short duration provide for denunciation in the currency of their term.

It seems that supervening custom may operate as a ground of termination or revision irrespective of the duration of a treaty. Treaties that were terminated or revised in the light of supervening custom were mostly of unlimited or long duration.[10] However, even short-term treaties were challenged on account of supervening custom.[11] As a result, although some treaties of short duration were intended to remain in force in the currency of their term under all circumstances, it is not certain that a general presumption against their termination or revision exists.

Locus standi

It is not clear in what circumstances non-parties have *locus standi* to demand the termination or revision of a treaty on account of new custom. Attempts by non-members to bring about the revision of the Antarctic

---

[9] See fisheries dispute between UK and Denmark, fishing rights in Canadian waters.

[10] See e.g. the Treaty on the Panama Canal, the Capitulations, the Nile Agreement, as well as a number of fisheries agreements examined in Ch. 3.

[11] See fisheries disputes between Russia and Japan, UK and Denmark.

Treaty were strongly resisted by the parties. However, non-members may be in a better position to challenge a treaty that directly affects their legal situation.[12]

7.2. SUPERVENING CUSTOM AS A FUNDAMENTAL CHANGE OF CIRCUMSTANCES

Customary law forms part of the general circumstances in view of which treaties are concluded. If it changes, it can be said that an assumption on the basis of which the agreement was made has been altered. Had the parties known how the law would evolve, they would probably not have concluded the same treaty. It is stated, therefore, that legal changes may in certain conditions constitute valid grounds for the application of the *rebus sic stantibus* rule as enunciated in Article 62 of the Vienna Convention on the Law of Treaties.[13]

We have already examined the applicability of the fundamental change of circumstances rule in cases where new custom develops.[14] It was concluded that, although the wording of Article 62 of the Vienna Convention does not exclude this possibility, it was not probably envisaged that this Article would apply in cases where the changed circumstances are legal.

In any event, a fundamental change of circumstances may bring a treaty to an end only if it increases 'the burden of the obligations to be executed to the extent of rendering the performance something essentially different from that originally undertaken'.[15] It is doubtful whether this requirement will be met in many cases where supervening custom is incompatible with a prior treaty.

Consider, for instance, the relationship between the principle of the territoriality of laws and the obligation imposed on the host State by the Capitulations treaties to accept the application of foreign laws to nationals of other States residing in its territory; or the relationship between the concept of non-interference in a State's internal affairs as understood in contemporary international law and the obligation imposed on Panama to grant in perpetuity the use, occupation, and control of the Canal as well as all sovereign rights, power, and authority to the United States. In both cases, strictly speaking, the development of new custom did not have an impact on the extent of the obligations to be performed under the treaty.

The same applies with regard to the fisheries treaties we have examined in this book. It will be recalled that one type of fisheries agreement specified, either expressly or by reference to prevailing customary law, the extent

---

[12] See the impact of new custom on the Vienna Regulations.
[13] See *Fisheries Jurisdiction Case*, ICJ Reports (1973), analysed in Ch. 5.
[14] See Ch. 2.   [15] *Fisheries Jurisdiction Case* (1973).

of the coastal State's exclusive fisheries jurisdiction—for instance, three miles—and granted foreign vessels the right to fish in that area. By implication the area beyond three miles was high seas, where fishing was free for all under general customary law.

New custom recognizing fisheries zones of 200 miles does not radically transform the extent of the treaty obligations for the following reasons. First, the obligation of the coastal State to limit the exercise of exclusive fisheries jurisdiction within three miles from its coasts may appear unduly restrictive when compared to new custom. However, its performance has not become more onerous. Secondly, the obligation to respect fishing rights of foreign vessels within three miles is not affected by the new custom. Thirdly, fishing rights beyond three miles which under the treaty were by implication part of the high seas are no longer guaranteed under the new custom, because this area is now part of the coastal State's exclusive fisheries zone. However, these rights will be lost only if the State can enforce the 200-mile limit *vis-à-vis* the other party despite the existence of the three-mile limit agreed in the treaty. This brings us back to the first point.

In our view, these situations are more appropriately described as cases of conflict between successive legal norms, unless the change of the general law affects the implementation of a treaty in a manner that brings the *rebus sic stantibus* rule into play. In the fisheries cases we have examined, supervening custom was indeed invoked as a ground of termination or revision on account of its incompatibility with the treaty, and the extent to which the contractual balance had been affected was not raised. In other cases a distinction was specifically made between termination or revision as a result of a change in the law and termination or revision as a result of the application of the *rebus sic stantibus* rule.[16]

7.3. EFFECT OF SUPERVENING CUSTOM ON THE TREATY RELATIONSHIP

Supervening custom as a ground of termination or revision confers upon one party the right to call for the adjustment of a prior incompatible treaty, and, in cases where this right is disputed, to submit the issue to an organ with power to determine whether the conditions for its exercise are met. Revision would be more appropriate in cases where the treaty is still adjustable to the new situation. If the changes in the law are so far-reaching that adjustment is no longer possible or even conceivable, termination may be the only option open to the party invoking supervening custom.

Supervening custom does not, therefore, automatically terminate or

---

[16] See abolition of the Capitulations in Turkey.

modify a prior incompatible treaty and does not entitle one party unilaterally to effect the required changes. Two consequences follow. First, since the development of new custom does not coincide with the abrogation of the treaty, the parties have the opportunity to decide whether the treaty should nevertheless continue to apply in their *inter se* relations as special law. This is possible, because by definition the new custom is not *jus cogens* and derogation by agreement of the parties is permissible. Secondly, in cases where one party claims that the treaty has become incompatible with supervening custom, the others can express their views on whether this claim is well founded and submit the dispute to third-party settlement, if necessary.

In some of the incidents examined in this book a treaty was unilaterally denounced on account of its incompatibility with new custom.[17] However, these attempts to unilateral termination were either symbolic acts accompanied by an invitation to negotiate the revision of the treaty or their validity was contested by other parties. It seems, therefore, that State practice repudiates unilateral action as the means for adapting obsolete treaties to new custom.

7.3.1. Enforcement of Claims to Treaty Termination or Revision

Following the development of customary law the parties to a prior treaty may all agree that it is incompatible with the new custom and needs to be revised accordingly. Or the need to review the treaty in the light of new custom may be asserted by some and denied by others. As in every international dispute, the parties must also in this case seek to settle their disagreement by peaceful means, including negotiations and third-party settlement, such as mediation, conciliation, arbitration, judicial settlement, or recourse to the UN or regional agencies.[18]

The enforcement of claims to treaty termination or revision against the will of other parties has its limitations because of the nature of the international legal system. International law lacks, as a rule, compulsory and binding settlement procedures independent of the consent of the disputing parties. The Vienna Convention on the Law of Treaty provides for compulsory conciliation for the settlement of disputes, but these provisions do not apply to treaty termination or revision on account of supervening custom, because it is not one of the grounds of treaty termination mentioned by the Convention.

The parties to a dispute concerning the existence of a right of termination or revision may use political means of settlement such as Article 14

---

[17] See e.g. fisheries in the North Atlantic, fisheries dispute between Morocco and Spain, abolition of Capitulations in Turkey.

[18] Articles 2, para. 3, and 33 of the UN Charter.

of the UN Charter providing that the General Assembly may recommend measures for the peaceful adjustment of 'any situation, regardless of origin, which it deems likely to impair the general welfare or friendly relations among nations'. In cases where the continuance of a dispute 'is likely to endanger the maintenance of international peace and security', the Security Council may recommend appropriate methods of adjustment or the actual terms of settlement. Neither the General Assembly nor the Security Council can compel the parties to terminate or revise a treaty on account of its incompatibility with new custom or otherwise settle their dispute.

Judicial settlement—that is, any procedure for the settlement of disputes by a binding decision and on the basis of the rules of international law, including international adjudication and arbitration[19]—is also based on the consent of the parties. The consent of the parties may be given *ad hoc*, in the form of a special agreement submitting the dispute to an international tribunal (*compromis*). It may also be given in advance, by means of clauses establishing jurisdiction for disputes arising out of the application of the treaty. With regard to the International Court of Justice in particular, a State may accept in advance 'as compulsory *ipso facto* and without special agreement, in relation to any other State accepting the same obligation', the jurisdiction of the Court in respect of whole categories of disputes.[20]

According to these general rules, third-party settlement will not always be available to a party claiming that a treaty should be terminated or revised on account of supervening custom. On this basis it must be asked whether unilateral termination, although initially unacceptable as a means for adapting treaties to new custom, may be used as a last resort solution in cases where other means of settlement are unavailable or meaningless—for instance, because the other parties refuse to negotiate in good faith or to give their consent to third-party settlement. State practice indicates that unilateral denunciation may be acceptable in these circumstances[21] as a form of legal sanction or counter-measure due to a breach of the rules of good faith. In these cases a competent tribunal could be asked to determine whether unilateral denunciation may be or has been properly exercised.

7.3.2. The Right to Demand the Revision of the Treaty

Revision will in some cases be the most appropriate way of adapting treaties to supervening custom. The procedure to be followed in these cases is the same as applies in cases of termination. One party may ask for the

---

[19] For the International Court of Justice in particular, see Articles 36–7 of the ICJ Statute.
[20] Article 36, para. 2, of the ICJ Statute.
[21] See abolition of the Capitulations in Egypt, fisheries dispute between UK and Denmark.

revision of the treaty and have recourse to a settlement procedure where available, if its claim is disputed. It cannot, on the other hand, unilaterally introduce the required amendments into the treaty, because no State can be bound by a new or revised treaty without its consent.[22] Strictly speaking, the parties in these circumstances are not required to revise the treaty but to negotiate in good faith with a view to revising it.

Although there is no general duty to negotiate in good faith with a view to revising treaties, the concept of revision is not unknown in international law—for instance, in cases where the circumstances on the basis of which the treaty was concluded have fundamentally changed. Article 62 of the Vienna Convention does not expressly provide for this possibility. However, when the Article was discussed, several members of the International Law Commission stated that, in their view, the *rebus sic stantibus* rule gave a party the right to demand the revision of a treaty and imposed on the other parties the obligation to negotiate in good faith.[23]

Good faith[24] negotiations in general imply a duty 'to seek, by preliminary negotiations, terms for an agreement' and 'to accept in good faith all communications and contracts which could, by a broad comparison of interests and by reciprocal good will, provide States with the best conditions for concluding agreements'.[25] States must 'conduct themselves so that the negotiations are meaningful';[26] they must act 'with a genuine intention to achieve a positive result'.[27]

In response to claims for revision on account of supervening custom, the parties must therefore negotiate in good faith with a view to adjusting the treaty to the new customary rules.[28] The obligation to negotiate does not imply an obligation to reach an agreement.[29] However, a breach of the rules of good faith may have the following consequences. First, a tribunal

---

[22] In this sense McNair, *Law of Treaties*, at 534.

[23] Tsuruoka, *YILC* (1963-I), at 138, para. 18; Lachs, at 140, para. 46; Tunkin, at 145, para. 24; at 155, para. 55; Bartos, at 148, para. 60; Gros, at 153–4; Ago, at 154; para. 46; Verdross, at 155, para. 51; Sir H. Waldock, at 157; ILC Commentary to the final Draft, *YILC* (1966-II), at 275. See also Algeria's comment to the 1963 Draft, 18 *GAOR*, 6th Committee, 789th Meeting, para. 31; Switzerland, *Vienna Conference Official Records* (1968), A/CONF. 39/11, at 368, para. 26; Australia, ibid., at 372, para. 22.

[24] On good faith, see Rosenne, *Developments in the Law of Treaties*, at 135 *et seq.*; E. Zoller, *La Bonne Foi en droit international public* (Paris, 1977).

[25] Lake Lanoux Arbitration (*France* v. *Spain*), *ILR* (1957), 101, at 128, 129–30.

[26] *North Sea Continental Shelf Cases*, ICJ Reports (1969), 4, at 47; see also *Fisheries Jurisdiction Case*, ICJ Reports (1974), 3, at 31–3.

[27] *Gulf of Maine Case*, ICJ Reports (1984), at 292, para. 87.

[28] Cf. *North Sea Continental Shelf Cases*, at 47, 53, holding that the parties had the obligation to negotiate a delimitation agreement on the basis of equitable principles, taking all circumstances into account and in such a way as to leave as much as possible to each party the parts of the continental shelf that constituted a natural prolongation of its land territory.

[29] See e.g. Lake Lanoux Arbitration, at 130; *Railway Traffic between Lithuania and Poland, PCIJ*, Ser. A/B, No. 42 (1931), at 116; *Opinion on the Status of South West Africa*, ICJ Reports (1950), at 128, 139; see also Zoller, *La Bonne foi*, at 59.

with power to consider the dispute may direct the parties to conduct negotiations or to repeat them, if this appears to be meaningful in the circumstances of the case.[30] Secondly, 'sanctions can be applied in the event, for example of an unjustified breaking off of the discussions, abnormal delays, disregard of the agreed procedures, systematic refusals to take into consideration adverse proposals or interests, and more generally, in case of violation of the rules of good faith'.[31] Unilateral termination of the treaty may be a form of sanction provided that it can be considered as a proportional measure in the circumstances of the case. Thirdly, under the law of State responsibility a party to the treaty may seek damages for injury caused as a result of the breach of the rules of good faith by another party.[32] For instance, substantial material loss may be caused by a recalcitrant State's insistence on exercising fishing rights acquired under the old legal regime and by its refusal to contemplate revision.

7.3.3. Multilateral Treaties and Supervening Custom

In the case of multilateral treaties it is possible that supervening custom operates as a ground of treaty termination or revision only between some of the parties. One party may thus withdraw from the treaty, in which case it is released from its obligations, but the treaty remains in force and operates between the remaining parties.[33] Or in cases where one party calls for revision, the treaty may be modified or replaced by a new treaty applicable in the relations between some of the parties only.

It is a general principle of treaty law that an amended treaty or a new treaty on the same subject-matter will bind only those signatories of the original treaty that become party to the amended or new treaty.[34] In cases where membership of the two treaties is not identical, two parallel sets of rules will be created binding different sets of parties, the original treaty continuing to operate in the relations between States parties to both treaties and States parties to the original treaty only. In these circumstances, there may be scope for the denunciation of the original treaty by a party invoking supervening custom, if, as explained above, there is a breach of the rules of good faith by the other parties.

In the incidents we have examined in this book there were cases where States withdrew from a multilateral treaty and the treaty continued to apply between the remaining parties until they also agreed to its termination

---

[30] *North Sea Continental Shelf Cases*, at 48; *Fisheries Jurisdiction Case* (1974), at 33.

[31] *Lake Lanoux Arbitration*, at 128.

[32] See Draft Articles on State responsibility, pt. I, Article I, *YILC* (1973-II), at 165; Articles 16–17, pt. II, *YILC* (1976-II), at 69. See also Article 20 dealing with the breach of an international obligation requiring the adoption of a particular course of conduct, *YILC* (1977-II), at 5.   [33] Cf. Article 70, para. 2, of the Vienna Convention.

[34] Cf. Articles 30, 40–1 of the Vienna Convention.

or revision.[35] Multilateral treaties may also be revised in the light of super-vening custom between only some of the parties.[36]

There may be cases where, as a result of State succession, a treaty cre-ating an international regime[37] may bind States other than its original sig-natories. In these cases all successor States should be invited to any bilateral negotiations aiming at the revision of the original treaty, if their legal situation would thereby be affected.[38] States that did not become party to the amended or new treaty may subsequently act in a manner establishing their intent to renounce their rights and obligations under the original treaty.[39]

7.3.4. The Role of International Tribunals

The effect of supervening custom on a prior incompatible treaty has more than one aspect that could be of interest to parties to judicial proceedings. An international tribunal may, for instance, be asked to determine whether a treaty should be terminated or revised on account of supervening cus-tom.[40] Or it may need to decide whether a treaty is still in force following the development of new custom, when this is required by the *compromis*,[41] when its jurisdiction is based on the treaty,[42] or for other reasons.[43] In cases where the treaty is considered to have remained in force a tribunal may have to determine which of two incompatible obligations—one deriving from the treaty and the other from the new custom—should apply to the matter at issue.

In other cases one party may seek compensation for damages caused by the failure of other parties to behave in good faith in response to a request for termination or revision. Or a tribunal may have to decide whether a party that refuses to comply with its treaty obligations on account of new custom has committed a breach of the treaty.[44]

If a tribunal holds that the treaty should be terminated or revised on account of supervening custom, this does not always prevent the applica-tion of the conventional rule to the matter at issue. Unless it is established that a ground of termination has operated to bring the treaty to an end, the tribunal cannot terminate the treaty but must consider it as a valid

---

[35] See fisheries in the North Atlantic, US participation in international fisheries organizations.
[36] See Spain's fishing rights in EC waters.
[37] Such as the regimes applicable to the waters of the Nile or to the River Niger.
[38] See revision of the Nile regime.   [39] See revision of the Niger regime.
[40] See Guinea-Bissau/Senegal Maritime Boundary Arbitration.
[41] See *La Bretagne* Arbitration.
[42] See *Fisheries Jurisdiction Case* (Judgment on Jurisdiction).
[43] See *Spanish Fishermen's Cases*, where the European Court of Justice had to pronounce on the compatibility of treaty obligations of EC Member States with subsequent EC Regu-lations based on new custom.
[44] See S. Rosenne, *Breach of Treaty* (Cambridge, 1985).

source of rights and obligations.[45] Equally the tribunal cannot itself revise the treaty, but may at most indicate the terms of a revised agreement it considers appropriate in the light of the new customary rules. The decisions examined in this book confirm that international tribunals are not likely to tolerate unilateral attempts to modify a treaty under the guise of 'interpretation' and are not prepared to 'interpret' a treaty in the light of new customary law unless there are ambiguities or gaps in the treaty text.[46]

7.4. FINAL REMARKS

7.4.1. Termination of a Contractual Source of Obligation

On the basis of the above, new custom does not automatically abrogate a prior treaty but may bring it to an end following a joint act of the parties or a series of steps taken by one party in exercise of a right conferred by international law. By contrast, new custom is regarded as having automatically replaced prior customary rules on the same subject-matter without proof of separate intention or specific acts of the States concerned.

These different legal procedures reflect the different ways in which treaty and customary law are expressions of a State's consent to the creation of binding rules. Customary law is the result of a general consensus to create rules binding upon all States. By contrast, a treaty is a meeting of wills of individual States that creates rights and obligations between them only.

When new custom is formed, the general State practice establishing it undermines support for the continued application of old custom. In these circumstances old custom can be regarded as having been abandoned, because it no longer reflects the will of States.

By contrast, new custom does not necessarily prove a specific intent to abrogate prior incompatible treaties, because the *opinio juris* required for its formation only reflects a will to change the general law. For this reason the meeting of wills expressed in the treaty cannot be regarded as having automatically been superseded by new custom, but needs to be reassessed in the light of the evolution of the law following a procedure based on the parties' initiative.

7.4.2. The Rationale for Supervening Custom as a Ground of Treaty Termination or Revision

We have argued in this book that the legal basis of supervening custom as a ground of treaty termination or revision is State practice expressed in the

---

[45] See Morelli, *AIDI* (1967-I), at 293; contra, Rosenne, Breach of Treaty, at 113 and n. 60.
[46] See Guinea-Bissau/Senegal Maritime Boundary Arbitration.

form of claims made by some States and accepted by others as a matter of legal obligation. A different question, however, is why new custom should have this effect on prior incompatible treaties.

In our view, this is explained by the relationship between treaty and custom. In the process of international law creation, custom has logical priority over treaties in the sense that it forms the legal background against which contractual rights and obligations are created. This is true both with regard to bilateral and multilateral treaties, including conventions codifying pre-existing custom. When the general law changes, the basis of the normative unit which custom and treaty form is altered, and the contractual relations deriving from the prior legal regime need to be reassessed accordingly.

In this context, the following consequences for treaty-making may be postulated. First, the possibility that custom may evolve outside the treaty may need to be taken into consideration when the treaty is drafted. Treaties concluded for an indefinite duration are not sheltered from change. Even arrangements made 'in perpetuity' are open to challenge, unless it can be specifically shown that the parties intended to create a permanent derogation from custom. Such intention can, for instance, be inferred from a provision to the effect that, irrespective of the development of new custom, the treaty shall continue to apply in the relations between the parties as originally drafted. Secondly, 'perpetuity' clauses seem to be in any case out of vogue. State practice is already moving away from agreements in perpetuity towards more flexible arrangements, such as treaties concluded for a short term, or treaties with mechanisms of periodic review ensuring that any changes needed on account of the evolution of the law are effected smoothly and with the least possible damage to the treaty relationship.

Bibliography

AGO, R., 'Droit des traités à la lumière de la Convention de Vienne', *RC* 134 (1971-III), 297.

AKEHURST, M., 'Custom as a Source of International Law', *BYIL* 47 (1974–5), 1.

—— 'The Hierarchy of the Sources of International Law', *BYIL* 47 (1974–5), 273.

ALEXIDZE, L. A., 'Legal Nature of *jus cogens* in Contemporary International Law', *RC* 172 (1981-III), 219.

APOLLIS, G., 'La Réglementation des activités halieutiques dans l'Acte d'adhésion de l'Espagne et du Portugal au Traité C.E.E.', *AFDI* 31 (1985), 837.

ARANZIO-RUIZ, G., 'The Normative Role of the General Assembly and the Declaration of Principles of Friendly Relations', *RC* 137 (1972-III), 419.

ARBOUR, J.-M., 'L'Affaire du chalutier-usine "La Bretagne" ou les droits de l'état côtier dans sa zone économique exclusive', *CYIL* 24 (1986), 61.

ATTARD, D. J., *The Exclusive Economic Zone in International Law* (Oxford, 1987).

AUFRICHT, H., 'Supersession of Treaties in International Law', *Cornell Law Quarterly*, 37 (1951–2), 655.

BASTID, S., *Les Traités dans la vie internationale* (Paris, 1985).

BATSTONE, R. K., 'The Utilisation of the Nile Waters', *ICLQ* 8 (1959), 523.

BAXTER, R. R., 'Multilateral Treaties as Evidence of Customary International Law', *BYIL* 41 (1965–6), 275.

—— 'Treaties and Custom', *RC* 129 (1970-I), 25.

—— and CAROLL, R. D., *The Panama Canal* (Dobb's Ferry, NY, 1965).

BERBER, F., *Lehrbuch des Völkerrechts*, i (Munich, 1975).

BERNHARDT, R., 'Interpretation and Implied (Tacit) Modification of Treaties', *ZaöRV* 27 (1967), 491.

—— 'Customary International Law', in *Max Planck Encyclopaedia of Public International Law*, vii (1984), 61.

BILDER, R. B., 'The Anglo-Icelandic Fisheries Dispute', *Wisconsin Law Review*, 3 (1973), 37.

BOS, M., 'Recognized Manifestations of International Law', *GYIL* 20 (1977), 9.

—— 'The Hierarchy among the Recognized Manifestations of International Law', in *Estudios de Derecho Internacional Homenaje al Profesor Miaja de la Muela*, i (Madrid, 1979), 363.

BOWETT, D. W., 'The Arbitration between the United Kingdom and France concerning the Continental Shelf Boundary in the English Channel and South-Western Approaches', *BYIL* 49 (1978), 1.

—— 'State Contracts with Aliens: Contemporary Developments on Compensation for Termination or Breach', *BYIL* 59 (1988), 49.

BOYER, A., 'La Notion d'eaux territoriales et la convention de Londres du 9 Mars 1964', *RGDIP* 69 (1965), 1051.

BRIERLY, J. L., *The Law of Nations*, ed. H. Waldock (6th edn., Oxford, 1963).

BRIGGS, H. W., 'Procedures for Establishing the Invalidity or Termination of Treaties under the International Law Commission's 1966 Draft Articles on the Law of Treaties', *AJIL* 61 (1967), 976.

—— 'Unilateral Denunciation of Treaties: The Vienna Convention and the International Court of Justice', *AJIL* 68 (1974), 51.

BRINTON, J. Y., *The Mixed Courts of Egypt* (New Haven, Conn., 1930).

BROWER, C. N., 'Current Developments in the Law of Expropriation and Compensation: A Preliminary Survey of Awards of the Iran–US Claims Tribunal', *International Lawyer*, 21 (1987), 639.

BROWN, E. D., 'The Anglo-French Continental Shelf Case', *YBWA* 33 (1979), 304; *San Diego Law Review*, 16 (1979), 461.

BROWNLIE, I., *Principles of Public International Law* (4th edn., Oxford, 1990).

CAPOTORTI, F., 'L'Extinction et la suspension des traités', *RC* 134 (1971-III), 427.

—— 'Minorities', in *Max Planck Encyclopedia of Public International Law*, viii (1985), 385.

CARROZ, J. E., 'Institutional Aspects of Fishery Management under the New Regime of the Oceans', *San Diego Law Review*, 21 (1984), 513.

CASSESE, A., *International Law in a Divided World* (Oxford, 1986).

CASTBERG, F., 'La Méthodologie du droit international public', *RC* 43 (1933-I), 309.

CHARNEY, J. I., 'The Persistent Objector Rule and the Development of Customary International Law', *BYIL* 56 (1985), 1.

CHENG, B., 'United Nations Resolutions on Outer Space: Instant International Customary Law?', in B. Cheng (ed.) *International Law: Teaching and Practice* (London, 1982), 237.

CHIU, H., *The People's Republic of China and the Law of the Treaties* (Cambridge, Mass., 1972).

CHURCHILL, R. R., 'The Fisheries Jurisdiction Cases: The Contribution of the International Court of Justice to the Debate on Coastal States' Fisheries Rights', *ICLQ* 24 (1975), 82.

—— and FOSTER, N. G., 'European Community Law and Prior Treaty Obligations of Member States: The Spanish Fishermen's Cases', *ICLQ* 36 (1987), 504.

—— and LOWE, A. V., *The Law of the Sea* (2nd edn., Manchester, 1988).

CLAGETT, B. M., 'Just Compensation in International Law', in R. B. Lillich (ed.), *The Valuation of Nationalized Property in International Law*, v (Charlottesville, Va., 1986), 31.

CLAUDE, I., *National Minorities: An international problem* (New York, 1955).

COHEN, J. A., and CHIU, H., *People's China and International Law* (Princeton, NJ, 1974), i–ii.

COHEN, J. G., 'La Coutume locale', *AFDI* 7 (1961), 119.

COLLIARD, C. A., 'Évolution et aspects actuels du régime juridique des fleuves internationaux', *RC* 125 (1968-III), 337.

—— 'Le Différend Franco-Canadien sur le "filetage" dans le Golfe du Saint-Laurent', *RGDIP* 92 (1988), 273.

COLSON, D. A., 'The United Kingdom–France Continental Shelf Arbitration', *AJIL* 72 (1978), 95.

COT, J. P., 'La Conduite subséquente des parties à un traité', *RGDIP* 70 (1966), 632.

D'AMATO, A. A., 'Treaties: A Source of General Rules of International Law', *Harvard International Law Journal*, 3 (1962), 1.

D'AMATO, A. A., 'The Concept of Special Custom in International Law', *AJIL* 63 (1969), 211.

—— 'Manifest Intent and the Generation by Treaty of Customary Rules of International Law', *AJIL* 64 (1970), 892.

—— 'The Authoritativeness of Custom in International Law', *Rivista de diritto internazional* (1970), 491.

—— *The Concept of Custom in International Law* (Ithaca, NY, 1971).

—— 'Trashing Customary International Law', *AJIL* 81 (1987), 101.

DELEAU, O., 'Les Positions françaises à la Conférence de Vienne sur le droit des traités', *AFDI* 15 (1969), 7.

DE VATTEL, E., *The Law of Nations*, trans. from the French (London, 1811).

DE VISSCHER, C., 'Coutume et traité en droit international public', *RGDIP* 59 (1955), 353.

—— *Theory and Reality in Public International Law* (Princeton, NJ, 1957).

—— 'Positivisme et jus cogens', *RGDIP* 75 (1971), 5.

—— 'Cours général de droit international public', *RC* 136 (1972-II), 1.

DIPLA, H., 'L'Affaire concernant le filetage à l'intérieur du Golfe du Saint-Laurent entre le Canada et la France', *AFDI* 32 (1986), 239.

DIXIT, R. K., 'Amendment or Modification of Treaties', *Indian Journal of International Law* 10 (1970), 37.

DUNN, F. S., *Peaceful Change* (New York, 1937).

DUPUY, R.-J., 'Codification et règlement des différends: Les Débats de Vienne sur les procédures de règlement', *AFDI* 15 (1969), 70.

—— 'Coutume sage et coutume sauvage', in *Mélanges offerts à Ch. Rousseau* (Paris, 1974), 75.

—— and VIGNES D. (eds.), *Traité du nouveau droit de la mer* (Paris, 1985).

ELIAS, T. O., 'The Berlin Treaty and the River Niger Commission', *AJIL* 57 (1963), 873.

—— *The Modern Law of Treaties* (Leiden, 1974).

—— 'The Doctrine of Intertemporal Law', *AJIL* 74 (1980), 285.

FALK, R. A., 'On the Quasi-Legislative Competence of the General Assembly', *AJIL* 60 (1966), 782.

FAUCHILLE, P., *Droit international public*, i, pt. 3 (Paris, 1926).

FAVOREU, L., 'Les Affaires de la compétence en matière de pêcheries', *AFDI* 20 (1974), 253.

FEINBERG, N., 'The Legal Validity of the Undertakings concerning Minorities and the clausula rebus sic stantibus', in *Studies in International Law* (Jerusalem, 1979), 17.

FISSEHA, Y., 'State Succession and the Legal Status of International Rivers', in R. Zacklin and L. Caflisch (eds.), *The Legal Regime of International Rivers and Lakes* (Dordrecht, 1981), 177.

FITZMAURICE, G., 'The Law and Procedure of the International Court of Justice, 1951–1954: General Principles and Sources of Law', *BYIL* 30 (1953), 1.

—— 'The Law and Procedure of the International Court of Justice 1951–1954: Treaty Interpretation and other Treaty Points', *BYIL* 33 (1957), 203.

—— 'Some Problems Regarding the Formal Sources of International Law', in *Symbolae Verzihl* (The Hague, 1958), 153.

FLEISHER, C. A., 'Norway's Policy on Fisheries', in *Developments in the Law of the Sea: 1958–1964* (British Institute of International and Comparative Law Special Publication, London, 1965), 92.

FOSTER, J. W., *The Practice of Diplomacy* (Boston and New York, 1906).

FRIEDMANN, W., *The Changing Structure of International Law* (London, 1964).

FROWEIN, J. A., *'Jus cogens'*, in *Max Planck Encyclopedia of Public International Law*, vii (1984), 327.

FULTON, T. W., *The Sovereignty of the Sea* (Edinburgh and London, 1911).

GAJA, G., *'Jus cogens* beyond the Vienna Convention', *RC* 172 (1981-III), 271.

GARRETSON, A. H., 'The Nile Basin', in A. H. Garretson, R. Hayton, and C. Olmstead (eds.), *The Law of International Drainage Basins*, pt. II (New York, 1967), 256.

GIRAUD, E., 'Modification et terminaison des traités collectifs', *AIDI* 49 (1961-I), 5.

GOMEZ ROBLEDO, A., 'Le *jus cogens* international: Sa genèse, sa nature, ses fonctions', *RC* 172 (1981-III), 9.

GONZALES CAMPOS, J. D., 'Las Relaciones entre España y la CEE en materia de pesca', in F. Leita and T. Scovazi, *Il regime della pesca nella Communità Economica Europea* (Studi e Documenti sul Diritto Internazionale del Mare, 4; Milan, 1979), 131.

GOTLIEB, A. E., 'The Canadian Contribution to the Concept of a Fishing Zone in International Law', *CYIL* 2 (1964), 55.

GREENWOOD, C., 'State Contracts in International Law: The Libyan Oil Arbitrations', *BYIL* 53 (1982), 27.

—— 'The Relationship between *Jus ad bellum* and *Jus in bello*', *Review of International Studies*, 9/4 (1983), 221.

GROSS, L., 'Voting in the Security Council: Abstention in the Post-1965 Amendment Phase and its Impact on Article 25 of the Charter', *AJIL* 62 (1968), 315.

GROTIUS, H., *De jure belli ac pacis libri tres*, trans. F. W. Kelsey, 3 vols. (Oxford, 1925).

GRZYBOWSKI, K., 'The US Fishery Conservation and Management Act 1976: A Plan for Diplomatic Action', *ICLQ* 28 (1979), 685.

GUGGENHEIM, P., 'Locales Gewohnheitsrecht', *ÖZöR* 11 (1961), 327.

—— *Traité de droit international public*, i (Geneva, 1967).

HACKWORTH, G. H., *Digest of International Law* (Washington, 1940–1943) 7 vols.

HARASZTI, G., *Some Fundamental Problems of the Law of Treaties* (Budapest, 1973).

—— 'Treaties and the Fundamental Change of Circumstances', *RC* 146 (1975-III), 1.

HEILBORN, P., 'Les Sources du droit international', *RC* 11 (1926-I), 1.

HEYKING, A., 'L'Exterritorialité et ses applications en Extrême-Orient', *RC* 7 (1925-II), 237.

HIGGINS, R., *The Development of International Law through the Political Organs of the United Nations* (Oxford, 1963).

—— 'The Development of International Law by the Political Organs of the United Nations', *Proceedings of the American Society of International Law* (1965), 116.

—— 'The United Nations and Law-Making: The Political Organs', *Proceedings of the American Society of International Law* (1970), 37.

HILL, C., 'The Doctrine of *rebus sic stantibus* in International Law', *The University of Missouri Studies*, 3 (1934), 2.

HOLZ, L., 'L'Extradition entre l'Inde française et l'Empire anglo-indien', *RGDIP* 18 (1910), 449.

HOSNI, S., 'The Nile Regime', *Revue égyptienne de droit international*, 17 (1961), 70.

JENKS, C. W., 'The Conflict of Law-Making Treaties', *BYIL* 30 (1953), 401.

—— *The Prospects of International Adjudication* (New York, 1964).

JENNINGS, R. Y., 'General Course on Principles of Public International Law', *RC* 121 (1967-II), 323.

—— 'What is International Law and how do we Tell it when we See it?', *Revue suisse du droit international*, 37 (1981), 59.

JESSUP, P. C., *The Law of Territorial Waters and Maritime Jurisdiction* (New York, 1927).

JIMÉNEZ DE ARÉCHAGA, E., 'General Course in Public International Law', *RC* 159 (1978-I), 1.

JOHNSON, D. H. N., 'The Effect of Resolutions of the General Assembly of the United Nations', *BYIL* 32 (1955), 97.

—— 'European Fishery Limits', in *Developments in the Law of the Sea: 1958–1964* (British Institute of International and Comparative Law Special Publication, No. 6; London, 1965), 48.

KAIKOBAD, K. H., 'The Shatt-al-Arab River Boundary: A Legal Reappraisal', *BYIL* 56 (1985), 49.

KARL, W., *Vertrag und Spätere Praxis im Völkerrecht* (Berlin, 1983).

KATZ, S. R., 'Issues Arising in the Icelandic Fisheries Case', *ICLQ* 22 (1973), 83.

KEARNEY, R. D., 'Sources of Law and the International Law of Justice', in L. Gross (ed.), *The Future of the International Court of Justice* (New York, 1976), 610.

—— and DALTON, R. E., 'The Treaty on Treaties', *AJIL* 64 (1970), 495.

KEETON, E. W., 'Exterritoriality in International and Comparative Law', *RC* 72 (1948-I), 287.

KELSEN, H., 'Theorie du droit international coutumier', *Revue internationale de la theorie du droit*, 1 (1939), 253.

—— *Principles of International Law* (2nd edn., New York, 1966).

KIRGIS, F. L., 'Custom on a Sliding Scale', *AJIL* 81 (1987), 146.

KUNZ, J. L., 'The Nature of Customary International Law', *AJIL* 47 (1953), 662.

—— 'The Present Status of the International Law for the Protection of Minorities', *AJIL* 48 (1954), 282.

KWIATKOWSKA, B., *The 200-Mile Exclusive Economic Zone in the New Law of the Sea* (Dordrecht, 1989).

LAUTERPACHT, H., 'Peaceful Change: The Legal Aspect', in C. A. W. Manning (ed.), *Peaceful Change: An International Problem* (London, 1937), 133.

—— *The Development of International Law by the International Court* (London, 1958).

—— *International Law: Collected Papers* (ed. E. Lauterpacht), i (Cambridge, 1970); iii (Cambridge, 1977).

LECA, J., *Les Techniques de révision des conventions internationales* (Paris, 1961).

LISSITZYN, O. J., 'Treaties and Changed Circumstances', *AJIL* 61 (1967), 895.

LOWE, A. V., 'Do General Rules of International Law Exist?', *Review of International Studies*, 9/3 (1983), 207.

McDOUGAL, M. S., and BURKE, W. T., *The Public Order of the Oceans* (New Haven, Conn., 1962; repr., 1987).

MACGIBBON, I. C., 'Customary International Law and Acquiescence', *BYIL* 33 (1957), 115.

McKEAN, W., *Equality and Discrimination under International Law* (Oxford, 1983).

McNAIR, A. D., *The Law of Treaties* (Oxford, 1961).

McRAE, D. M., 'Delimitation of the Continental Shelf between the United Kingdom and France: The Channel Arbitration', *CYIL* 15 (1977), 173.

McWHINNEY, E., 'The Time Dimension in International Law', in J. Makarczyk (ed.), *Essays in International Law in Honour of Judge Manfred Lachs* (Dordrecht, 1984), 181.

MALUWA, T., 'Succession to Treaties and International Fluvial Law in Africa: The Niger Regime', *NILR* 33 (1986), 334.

MAREK, K., 'Contribution à l'étude du *jus cogens* en droit international', in *Recueil d'études en droit international en hommage à Paul Guggenheim* (Geneva, 1968), 426.

MARTIN, P.-M., 'L'Affaire de la compétence en matière de pêcheries: Les Arrêts de la Cour Internationale de Justice du 2 février 1973', *RGDIP* 78 (1974), 435.

MESEGUER, J. L., 'La politica pesquera de la CEE ante el derecho internacional: Relaciones hispano-comunitarias', *Revista de las instituciones europeas* (Madrid, 1977), 701.

—— J. L., 'Accord de pêche entre l'Espagne et la CEE', *Revue du Marché Commun*, 23 (1980), 527.

—— 'Le Régime juridique de l'exploitation des stocks conjoints de poissons au delà de 200 miles', *AFDI* 28 (1982), 885.

—— 'La cooperación internacional para la ordenación del atun en el Oceano Atlantico', in *The Law and the Sea: Essays in Memory of J. Carroz* (Rome, 1987), 121.

MILES, E. L., 'The Evolution of Fisheries Policy and Regional Commissions in the North Pacific under the Impact of Extended Coastal State Jurisdiction', in *The Law and the Sea: Essays in Memory of J. Carroz* (Rome, 1987), 139.

—— and BURKE, W. T., 'Pressures on the United Nations Convention on the Law of the Sea of 1982 Arising from New Fisheries Conflicts: The Problem of Straddling Stocks', *ODILJ* 20 (1989), 343.

MINER, D. C., *The Fight for the Panama Route* (New York, 1966).

MODEEN, T., *The International Protection of National Minorities in Europe* (Abo, 1969).

MONACO, R., 'Cours général de droit international public', *RC* 125 (1968-III), 93.

—— 'Observations sur la hiérarchie des sources du droit international', in *Festschrift für H. Mosler* (Berlin, 1983), 599.

MORIN, J.-Y., 'La Zone de pêche exclusive du Canada', *CYIL* 2 (1964), 77.

NGUYEN QUOC DINH, 'Evolution de la jurisprudence de la Cour Internationale de la Haye relative au problème de la hiérarchie des normes conventionelles', in *Mélanges offerts à Marcel Waline*, i (Paris, 1974), 215.

NGUYEN QUOC DINH, DAILLER, P., and PELLET, A., *Droit international public* (3rd edn., Paris, 1987).

O'CONNELL, D. P., *State Succession in Municipal Law and International Law* (Cambridge, 1967), i–ii.

—— *The International Law of the Sea* (ed. I. A. Shearer), i (Oxford, 1982); ii (Oxford, 1984).

OHIRA, Z., 'Fishery Problems between Soviet Russia and Japan', *Japanese Annual of International Law*, 2 (1958), 1.

O'MALLEY WADE, S., 'A Proposal to Include Tunas in US Fishery Jurisdiction', *ODILJ* 16 (1986), 255.

OPPENHEIM, L., *International Law*, i (London, 1905; 8th edn.) ed. H. Lauterpacht (London, 1955).

ORREGO VICUÑA, F., *Antarctic Mineral Exploitation: The Emerging Legal Framework* (Cambridge, 1988).

PADELFORD, N. J., *The Panama Canal in Peace and War* (New York, 1942).

PARRY, C., *The Sources and Evidences of International Law* (Manchester, 1965).

—— 'The Law of Treaties', in M. Sørensen (ed.), *Manual of Public International Law* (London, 1968), 175.

PINTO, M. R., 'Prescription en droit international', *RC* 87 (1955-I), 390.

PLENDER, R., 'The Role of Consent in the Termination of Treaties', *BYIL* 57 (1986), 133.

POCH DE CAVIADES, A., 'De la clause *rebus sic stantibus* à la clause de révision dans les conventions internationales', *RC* 118 (1966-II), 109.

POMPE, C. A., 'The Nile Waters Question', in *Symbolae Verzihl* (Dordrecht, 1958), 275.

PUFENDORF, S., *De jure naturae et gentium libri octo*, trans. C. H. Oldfather and W. A. Oldfather, 2 vols. (Oxford, 1934).

QUENEUDEC, J.-P., 'L'Affaire de la délimitation du plateau continental entre la France et le Royaume Uni', *RGDIP* 83 (1979), 53.

RECHID, A., 'La Condition des étrangers dans la République de Turquie', *RC* 46 (1933-IV), 169.

REUTER, P., 'Principes de droit international public', *RC* 103 (1961-II), 425.

—— *La Convention de Vienne du 23 mai 1969 sur le droit des traités* (Paris, 1970).

—— *Introduction au droit des traités* (Paris, 1985).

ROSENNE, S., *The Law of Treaties: A Guide to the Legislative History of the Vienna Convention* (Leiden, 1970).

—— 'The Settlement of Treaty Disputes under the Vienna Convention of 1969', *ZaöRV* 31 (1971), 1.

—— *Breach of Treaty* (Cambridge, 1985).

—— *Developments in the Law of Treaties: 1945–1986* (Cambridge, 1989).

ROSENSTOCK, R., 'The Declaration on Principles of International Law concerning Friendly Relations', *AJIL* 65 (1971), 713.

ROUSSEAU, C., *Principes généraux de droit international public* (Paris, 1944).

—— *Droit international public*, i (Paris, 1970); ii (Paris, 1974).

ROZAKIS, C. L., *The Concept of jus cogens in the Law of Treaties* (Amsterdam, 1976).

SATOW, E., *Guide to Diplomatic Practice* (London, 1907; 4th edn., 1957; 5th edn., 1979).

SCELLE, G., *Théorie juridique de la révision des traités* (Paris, 1936).

SCHACHTER, O., 'The Relation of Law, Politics and Action in the United Nations', *RC* 109 (1963-II), 169.

SCHERMERS, H. G., note on *A.-G.* v. *Burgoa, Common Market Law Review*, 18 (1981), 227.

SCHEUNER, U., 'Conflict of Treaty Provisions with a Peremptory Norm of General International Law and its Consequences', *ZaöRV* 27 (1967), 520.

SCHREIBER, M., 'Vers un nouveau régime international du fleuve Niger', *AFDI* 9 (1963), 866.

—— 'Accord relatif à la Commission de fleuve Niger et à la navigation et aux transports sur le fleuve Niger', *AFDI* 10 (1964), 813.

SCHWARZENBERGER, G., *International Law as Applied by International Courts and Tribunals I* (London, 1957).

—— 'International "jus cogens" ', *Texas Law Review*, 43 (1965), 455.

—— *International Law and Order* (London, 1971).

—— '*Clausula rebus sic stantibus*', in *Max Planck Encyclopedia of Public International Law*, vii (1984), 22.

SCOTT, G. L., *Chinese Treaties* (New York, 1975).

SCOTT, J. H., *The Law Affecting Foreigners in Egypt as a Result of the Capitulations* (Edinburgh, 1907).

SÉFÉRIADES, S., 'Aperçus sur la coutume juridique internationale', *RGDIP* 43 (1936), 129.

SINCLAIR, I., *The Vienna Convention on the Law of Treaties* (Manchester, 1984).

SKUBISZEWSKI, K., 'Resolutions of the General Assembly of the United Nations', *AIDI* 61 (1985-I), 29.

SLOAN, B., 'General Assembly Resolutions Revisited', *BYIL* 58 (1987), 39.

SØRENSEN, M., *Les Sources du droit international* (Copenhagen, 1946).

—— 'Principes de droit international public', *RC* 101 (1960-III), 1.

—— 'Le Problème dit du droit intertemporel dans l'ordre international', *AIDI* 55 (1973), 1.

STEIN, T. L., 'The Approach of the Different Drummer: The Principle of the Persistent Objector in International Law', *Harvard Journal of International Law*, 26 (1985), 457.

STRUPP, K., 'Les Règles générales du droit de la paix', *RC* 47 (1934-I), 258.

SZÉKELY, A., 'Implementing the New Law of the Sea: The Mexican Experience', in B. J. Rothschild (ed.), *Global Fisheries: Perspectives for the 1980s* (New York, 1983), 51.

SZTUCKI, J., *Jus cogens and the Vienna Convention on the Law of Treaties* (New York, 1974).

TAMMES, A. J. P., 'Interaction of the Sources of International Law', *NILR* 10 (1963), 225.

THIRLWAY, H. W. A., *International Customary Law and Codification* (Leiden, 1972).

TIEWUL, S. A., 'The Fisheries Jurisdiction Case and the Ghost of *rebus sic stantibus*', *New York University Journal of International Law and Politics*, 6 (1973), 455.

TRUYOL Y SERRA, A., 'L'Expansion de la société internationale aux XIXe et Xe siècles', *RC* 116 (1965-III), 95.

TUNKIN, G. I., 'Co-existence and International Law', *RC* 95 (1958-III), 1.

—— 'Remarks on the Juridical Nature of Customary Norms of International Law', *Californian Law Review*, 49 (1961), 419.

—— *Droit international public* (Paris, 1965).

—— *Theory of International Law*, trans. W. E. Butler (London, 1974).

—— 'International Law in the International System', *RC* 147 (1975-IV), 1.

VALLÉE, Ch., 'Sur quelques poursuites engagées contre les pêcheurs espagnols ayant pratiqué la pêche dans les eaux territoriales ou dans la zone économique de la France', *RGDIP* 83 (1979), 220.

VAN HOOF, G. J. H., *Rethinking the Sources of International Law* (1983).

VERDROSS, A., and SIMMA, B., *Universelles Völkerrecht* (Berlin, 1984).

VERZIJL, J. H. W., *International Law in Historical Perspective*, i (Leiden, 1968).

VILLIGER, M. E., *Customary International Law and Treaties* (Dordrecht, 1985).

VIRALLY, M., 'La Valeur juridique des recommendations des organisations internationales', *AFDI* 2 (1956), 66.

—— 'Réflexions sur le *jus cogens*', *AFDI* 12 (1966), 5.

—— 'The Sources of International Law', in M. Sørensen (ed.), *Manual of Public International Law* (London, 1968), 116.

—— 'A propos de la "lex ferenda" ', in *Mélanges offerts à P. Reuter* (Paris, 1981), 519.

—— 'Cours général de droit international public: Panorama du droit international contemporain', *RC* 183 (1983-V), 9.

WALDOCK, H., 'General Course on Public International Law', *RC* 106 (1962-II), 1.

WEIL, P., 'Vers une normativité relative en droit international?', *RGDIP* 86 (1982), 5; Eng. Trans.: 'Towards Relative Normativity in International Law', *AJIL* 77 (1983), 413.

WHITEMAN, M., *Digest of International Law* (Washington, 1963–1973), 15 vols.

WOLFKE, K., *Custom in Present International Law* (Wrokław, 1964).

—— '*Jus cogens* in International Law', *PYIL* 6 (1974), 145.

WRIGHT, Q., 'Article 19 of the League Covenant and the Doctrine *rebus sic stantibus*', *Proceedings of the American Society of International Law* (1936), 55.

YAOTONG TCHEN, Y., *De la disparition de la jurisdiction consulaire dans certains pays de l'Orient* (Paris, 1931).

ZOLLER, E., *La Bonnne Foi en droit international public* (Paris, 1977).

—— 'L'Affaire de la délimitation du plateau continental entre la République Française et le Royaume Uni de Grande Bretagne et d'Irlande du Nord', *AFDI* 23 (1977), 359.

Index